PERSONALITY HACKER

Harness the power of your personality type
to transform your work, relationships and life

Joel Mark Witt and Antonia Dodge

Published in the United States by:
Ulysses Press
P.O. Box 3440
Berkeley, CA 94703
www.ulyssespress.com

ISBN: 978-1-61243-766-8
Library of Congress Control Number 2017952129

Printed in Canada by Marquis Book Printing
10 9 8 7 6 5 4 3 2

Acquisitions: Bridget Thoreson
Managing editor: Claire Chun
Editor: Shayna Keyles
Proofreader: Bill Cassel
Front cover design: Justin Shirley
Interior design and production: Jake Flaherty
Artwork: cover, section/chapter pages © Bygermina/shutterstock.com;
    page 440 © Joel Mark Witt and Antonia Dodge

Contents

Appendix. 427

Acknowledgments 439

About the Authors 440

Preface

The real problem of humanity is the following: We have Paleolithic emotions, medieval institutions, and god-like technology.
— E. O. Wilson

Our Generation's Identity Crisis

Identity questions often take center stage in our society. People talk about gender identity, national identity, cultural identity, sexual identity, and even lost identity. Humanity seems to be in the midst of a collective identity crisis.

We don't really know who we are anymore. We face crippling insecurity. On a micro level, online comment wars break out over anything from politics to vaccinations to child-rearing. On a macro level, real international wars break out over religion, culture, or national pride. These conflicts are rooted in identity and the defensiveness of our egos.

We may be so defensive because we feel our identities are constantly under attack. When a person lacks a strong sense of who they are, it is easier for them to marginalize or undermine another's sense of self.

We are all searching for ourselves in an ocean of conflicting narratives.

How We Got into This Mess

We believe there are several reasons why humanity faces this identity crisis: Technology evolves too fast, there's a glut of information, and the world is increasingly globalized.

Technology Evolves Too Fast

Technologies are outpacing our ability to adapt. Just over ten years ago, Bill Baker wrote in *Destination Branding for Small Cities*, "We are living in the most over-communicated time period in history." At the time of his writing, the first iPhone—a piece of consumer technology that changed the game of connectedness and communication—had not yet been released.

According to Moore's Law, the capacity of technological hardware doubles every two years, rendering advancements in consumer tech both more powerful and more affordable. This is why the phone in your pocket is more powerful than the room-sized computers NASA relied upon to calculate the Apollo moon landings. And on those phones, we install an infinite array of apps that we use to engage with each other, while simultaneously complaining about how we lack true connection and intimacy.

This is not to say that consumer technology is at fault or that our modern world is somehow wrong. Technology and digital communication aren't the problems; it's that their evolution outpaces our own. We fear being ostracized and disliked. According to our Paleolithic emotions, being disliked by a large group is similar to getting kicked out of the tribe—a fate equal to death. Because of this, our mental wiring causes us to react to negative words from someone online as if our survival were in imminent danger. We have ancient imprints telling us to be careful, for if an entire group of people were to dislike us, we might die. Being hated by a group has negative survival implications, and there just hasn't been enough time to upgrade these DNA-level blueprints.

Technology gives us new opportunities, but also pressures us to keep pace in a fast-moving world.

Information Overload

We spend a lifetime attempting to know about everything but struggle to know ourselves. We have too much data coming at us, all too fast. We can't sort through and vet the rapid outpouring of information in a constantly connected world. The internet is great for organizing and distributing all the world's information, but it also creates in us a hunger for producing (and consuming) more and more.

People today know more about global politics, world events, and celebrity relationships than any previous generation knew. Yet somehow, we are often baffled about ourselves and the people we spend the most time around.

Globalization Leads to Fragmentation

The world is becoming more globalized, yet also more fragmented and chaotic. We as humans used to strongly identify with our immediate families, tribes, and even nation-states, but as national borders dissolve and humans connect globally, we are left without strong group identities and we lose our individual roles within those groups.

So, we gravitate to ideologies that bind us together. And we know that ideologies, rooted deeply in our egos, are often the source of escalated conflict. We then find ourselves tethered to our ideals rather than to other humans. We can see this with the rise of authoritarian leadership. Lacking individual identities, masses grasp at any cult of personality that can give them markers of strong identity. Even when the leadership is harsh and acts against the people's best interest, people tend to accept it because it helps them feel a sense of self.

Why We Need to Know Ourselves

Humans need to move past superficial markers of identity. It's time to reach out and experience a deep sense of self-knowing. People need to know themselves to love themselves, and they need to love themselves to love others. We, the authors, believe that a strong sense of identity will help you learn to do those things, as well as achieve a greater sense of personal security and reduced anxiety.

Acceptance of Self and Others

When you have a strong sense of identity, you can make space for and accept others. We believe that by understanding and honoring your own individuality, you will become empowered to claim your life's passion, purpose, and mission.

A strong identity is built on feeling secure. Security comes from a modest self-evaluation, without inflating or diminishing your own talents. It is knowing you'll be okay with whatever life throws at you. When we all show up as our secure selves, we will create a more peaceful world that makes space for others.

This often means agreeing to disagree. There will be disagreements as we create a world that honors individual expression and supports everyone becoming the person they were meant to be. But disagreements and peace can coincide when individuals are confident in who they are. We nurture confidence when we take advantage of the tools designed to understand ourselves better.

Personal Security

A strong sense of identity inoculates you from being "hacked" by others who know you better than you know yourself. There is a growing amount of evidence that the 2016 United States presidential election was swayed by foreign governments and private research firms. These actors used a combination of misinformation campaigns, personality insights, and psychographic data to "hack" into people's behaviors, preferences, and motivations to influence the election's outcome.

We are racing toward a new frontier of psychological possibilities, including psychological exploitation. Will you be prepared for the coming mental divide? There will be people who understand how their minds work, which will give them the control and power over themselves. They will have a strong sense of who they are, giving them greater influence over their own decisions. And there will be people who don't learn about their personalities, don't claim their identities, and could become sitting ducks for exploitation.

If you don't know who you are and what motivates you, control is out of your hands. You are at the mercy of people who know how your mind works better than you do. Do you want to be vulnerable or would you like to get to know yourself, your learning styles, and your motivational core?

Reduced Anxiety

Nearly all people grapple with the same series of questions: "What is my purpose, my meaning?" "What should I spend my life doing?" "Who should I spend it with?" When the answers to these questions don't make themselves known, we can become anxious, afraid we're running out of time, or uncertain of our own futures.

When you spend time and effort getting to know yourself, you 1) spot opportunities when they are right for you, 2) avoid wasting time on the wrong things, and 3) trust that things will happen when the timing is right, without heaping blame on yourself or otherwise getting into self-destructive cycles.

Introduction

Who are you really? How do you describe yourself?

How do you discover your true inner self and forge a path forward?

We're a technological species, so let's stick with what we're good at. If we can develop consumer technologies that make our daily tasks effortless and medical technologies that will keep us alive past the age of 100, then why can't we look at social technologies that can empower us through the chaos of our lives?

Social and personal technologies have been in development for thousands of years. They are our religions, belief systems, meditation practices, and politics. We organize ourselves and our information into what Timothy Leary would call "reality tunnels": These are our preferred ways of experiencing the world, and we try to stay in alignment with those tunnels.

It's possible, in a world that overwhelms the ancient programming of our nervous systems, to find and develop technologies that can help us hack into the systems of our very identity to become the change the world desperately needs. No other technologies are slowing down anytime soon. We need to play some catchup.

This book introduces you to one of the personal and social technologies we've found to have the most power in our lives: personality typology.

Of course, no model or system will ever completely explain your identity. You are much too complex for that. Just as standing on a map doesn't transport you to a given location, learning about an element of your personality doesn't suddenly deconstruct you to being only that thing. And just as a finger can point you to the moon, you don't want to get too enamored with the finger. Focus instead on what it's pointing to.

Once you gain increased awareness of all the elements of yourself, you can use your understanding in a million different applications. But one application we do request of you (it's not a little thing): Please use the contents of this book to become the best version of yourself possible. The world needs us all to show up, be less consumed in our own egos, and infect the social ecosystem with the best ideas and memes possible. As a happy coincidence, doing this also means becoming a generally happier person with greater success rates in all areas of life.

One of the best tools we've found for discovery of the self is personality. Your personality isn't who you are, but it can be a map or guide to discover who you are. And it is our belief that personality can not only help you find yourself as you are, but can also be a guide to help you become who you want to be.

In this book, we address the Myers-Briggs typology system and its foundation, the eight cognitive functions defined by psychiatrist Carl Jung. Using these models, we can see that there are unique and powerful expressions of the self that live deep inside each of us. It's our life's work to uncover and grow that true self.

What You'll Gain from This Book

This book goes beyond general personality-type descriptions and dives into Carl Jung's cognitive functions, or what we've come to think of as the wiring of your mind. It takes personality theory to the next level and gives you a host of benefits, including:

- Insight into how your mind learns information and makes decisions

- Discovering the best decision-making criteria to increase both the strength of your judgments and your confidence in yourself

- Awareness of which activities will help you grow as a person and improve your life

- A diagnostic of your natural strengths and blind spots

- The ability to get into a flow state

- Knowledge of how to manage and improve your own energy cycles

- Creating mastery by reallocating time toward your natural preferences

- Finding your hidden talents and bringing them into the world

- Recognizing all parts of yourself, even the unfamiliar, and learning how to integrate them into your identity

- Giving yourself permission to be who you really are, and giving others permission to be themselves, as well

How This Book Is Organized

This book is divided into two basic sections: "System and Theory" and "The 16 Types."

Section 1: System and Theory

- Chapter 1 shows you how your personality isn't static, but is an entire system that produces *you* as the emergent (or result) of that system.

- Chapters 2 and 3 shows you the original psychological model that Carl Jung developed and Myers-Briggs built upon. We then show you how to decode your four-letter personality type to determine your mental wiring.

- Chapter 4 introduces the Car Model. We designed this simple tool to help you understand how your mind is wired, create a growth plan, and handle your blind spots.

- Chapter 5 details each of the cognitive functions.

Section 2: The 16 Types

- In Chapters 6 through 21, each of the 16 Myers-Briggs personality types will be discussed in depth and analyzed according to the Car Model.

- Chapter 22 discusses a model we developed called "FIRM" to help you work through the fixations of each of the types. Each personality type's fixation is determined by the part of themselves with which they most identify and with their unmet needs.

The book concludes with "The Path Forward." Here, we discuss the importance of understanding our own sovereignty, having control over ourselves, and undertaking personal growth. We also focus on three vital steps: awareness, permission, and development.

Getting the Most from This Book

This book is not designed to be a deep dive into all things Myers-Briggs, though it does cover the Myers-Briggs personality types in detail. Its purpose is to focus on growth and advice so you can become the best version of your personality type. It's a primer of sorts. A map legend. A beginner's field guide to help you navigate the sometimes treacherous landscape that is the world of Myers-Briggs, and in particular, the seemingly elusive and sometimes frustrating cognitive functions that were at the heart of Carl Jung's theory of type.

You may be tempted to flip to the chapter on your individual personality type, but to better understand those chapters, we recommend first reading the chapters about the Car Model and how the cognitive functions work on a basic level.

Additionally, the book has a self-reporting personality test to help you determine your type. All personality instruments have an error rate, so the results of this test aren't intended to be gospel truth. It is the first point of entry on your journey. Be open to other type possibilities as you read the book and look for the personality type that fits you like a glove. That's your best-fit type, no matter what the results of the test were.

There is redundancy in the chapters that detail the Myers-Briggs types. For types that share the same cognitive functions, similar language has been used to describe both the characteristics and the exercises recommended for growth (though there are subtle changes when appropriate). This was a stylistic choice to allow you, the reader, to focus on your type description with an uninterrupted flow, and without needing to constantly reference other parts of the book.

Throughout the book, you'll notice Learning Point Pauses that are designed to help you integrate the more challenging elements of the system. We have intentionally designed this to be in a workbook style to teach you a new language of sorts. We also have included "Reflection" questions to help you apply the information to your life and personal growth plan.

At the end of the book, you will find a template journal entry that allows you to fill out the "car model" for your personality type. This is key to taking all you learn and applying it to your life.

Our recommendation is that you read this book with a beginner's mindset. While we enjoy geeking out on typology information, that's not truly the intent of this book. We believe that getting the most out of this content requires a bit of radical honesty and humility about yourself.

Okay, enough setup. Let's get started!

Section One

SYSTEM AND THEORY

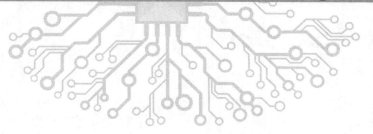

CHAPTER 1

System of Personality

Your personality is a type of technology that can be upgraded. But unlike the operating system on your computer or phone, there's no corporation creating the upgrade for you. You are responsible for your own upgrades. This book is an instruction manual on how to hack into your own system to design, build, and implement a self-directed software upgrade for your personality.

Personality is one of those things no one can adequately explain, yet we all have a sense of what it is. Your personality is more tied to your experience of reality than any other single influence, making it both familiar and inscrutable. When you look at a piece of technology, like your smartphone, you experience it as separate from yourself. When it comes to your personality, you are inside it and immersed in it. Like a fish trying to describe water, where do we even begin?

When asked to explain something both intrinsic and complex like this, humans tend to either grossly oversimplify it, make it appear as if it's out of our control, or call it static, unchangeable, and divinely ordained. How many times have you heard someone justify their behavior by stating, with a shrug, "That's just my personality"?

While we tend to avoid taking ownership of our personalities when they manifest in less-than-ideal ways, we are at the same time proud and overprotective of them. Most of us can't handle criticism of our behaviors, much less what we see as our identity. However, we seem to have no problem spotting the same types of walls and defensive strategies erected by others.

Inner work is hard—it's time consuming, uncomfortable, and requires us to take ego hits. If we have to change, it means we weren't okay in the first place. Seeing others as plastic and ourselves as static lets us off the hook. The work is on their shoulders, not ours.

But what if we could upgrade our strategies, thoughts, and feelings on a deep, core level—in those parts of us that we take for granted and assume were handed to us by divine origin? What if we could tinker with our deepest imprints, hack the programming that inhibits us, and upgrade defensive messages into happiness, empowerment, and a general feeling of contentment?

Let's choose a definition of personality for the sake of this book and stick with it (most of the time). We say "choose" because there are seemingly a million options.

Personality is:

1. The interface you use to engage with the world outside of yourself.

2. Your nervous system's preferred attunement and attention to specific types of information.

3. The instrument you use to measure the information your nervous system picks up.

Our interface with the world is how we show up when interacting with others and the environment. It's usually the most accessible part of how we experience ourselves because it allows a response from others and the environment, providing us with real-world feedback. The feedback provides a mirror, and we can mistake how we're perceived with the entirety of who we are. But that's not the full story.

Additionally, since your personality is your nervous system's gauge for what's interesting and what's not, it also acts as an instrument that chooses what your nervous system will pick up on and what it will ignore. The attunement part your personality is, to borrow a phrase from computer programming, the GIGO mechanism: Garbage In, Garbage Out. It determines the quality of information you'll be inputting and the quality of information you'll be outputting.

Ultimately, as our attention becomes more narrowed and focused on the things that naturally attract us and give us better experiences, we also calibrate how we evaluate what comes into our awareness. It's not just quality of information; it's our ability to determine how we define quality. "That's good, and that's bad" eventually becomes an entire value system, which influences our beliefs and judgments of how the world should work. We are pickier about the information we're willing to take in and self-directed toward things which interest us.

Information in this sense also includes aspects of you—your behavior, your beliefs, the mental scripts you have running, your imprints,[1] and the models you use to understand life. Each of these grows in sophistication to become separate technologies, but the root is in the information you pay attention to and determine as worthy: the accumulation of your experiences and how they struck you, which ones you decided to make part of you and which ones you decided to forget, your current values and interests, and a slew of things your DNA has added to the pile.

Our Favorite Personality Map

Over the years of producing the *Personality Hacker* podcast, we've become familiar with a lot of technologies for understanding ourselves. The ones we like the best provide maps for navigating the different parts within us. We use the word *map* intentionally.

"The map is not the territory," as it's been said, and we hold to that. Each system or model is simply a map of how things could be working, not an empirical representation of actual reality. Our mentor, the author and philosopher Robert Anton Wilson, once said, "A true map of New York would be utterly useless. Not only would you have to account for every detail of the city as it is, you'd have to account for every detail of how it had been since its inception. Every human, every rat, every element would have to be accounted for if it was 'actual' reality." And, of course, that would be more information than is usable.

---

1   "Imprints" are the positive or negative programs that the brain is genetically designed to accept during certain points in development.

That's why we create maps—they are intentionally oversimplified representations. And they are manageable chunks of information. For any terrain, multiple aspects can be represented on a map—road systems, attractions, topography, economics, political affiliations, climate—but rarely are they all displayed at once. We separate them out in order to master one piece of information at a time. We can build on accumulated knowledge, but it's much harder to take all of that information in simultaneously.

The same is the case with personality maps, which help us understand who we are and how we perceive reality. When people dismiss a map of personality typology for being incomplete or limiting, we always look at each other and say, "Of course it's not complete. No single map is. That's its point in existing."

Simply stated, maps are not reality. They are a representation of reality, just inaccurate enough to be useful. The goal is to familiarize ourselves with each personality map—or representation of the node in the system of who we are—and eventually see how all of these parts interrelate.

That said, some maps are better than others. Rand McNally puts out a better atlas than our daughter Piper's "pirate's treasure" maps, and the same applies with models of development. Of course, the quality of the map is entirely subjective. Our six-year-old nephew Jaxon prefers Piper's maps to Rand McNally's.

All maps should be held loosely. By definition, they're just inaccurate enough to be useful, and sometimes it's tough to determine that sweet spot. Ultimately, the maps you choose will match your experience and gut responses, and often it's the faith we have in certain "cartographers" that help us vet our choices. So these are the cartographers we will turn our attention to in this book: Carl Jung, Katharine Briggs, and Isabel Briggs Myers.

In 1921, psychiatrist Carl Jung published a book called *Psychological Types* in an attempt to reconcile some of the prevailing theories of personality at the time. He determined that there was a pattern in how people perceive information and how they evaluate that information. This research on how one's mind is wired to perceive and judge became the theory of cognitive processes, a.k.a. cognitive functions.

In the 1940s, Katharine Briggs and her daughter Isabel Briggs Myers (both Jung enthusiasts) developed an instrument (or test) to determine which cognitive functions an individual was predisposed to use. The original Myers-Briggs Type Indicator used the four-letter designations, called "dichotomies," as a "secret decoder ring" for identifying a person's cognitive functions. It's rarely used this way now, though increased online awareness of cognitive functions is turning that around.

Each year we teach a Profiler Training Course. The course is designed to teach our students how to cold-read others' personality types with a high degree of accuracy. One of the first exercises we ask them to do is identify the ways in which they are already profiling people and how they think other people use profiling. We can almost predict the results of the exercise each year. Students group people into gender, race, age, socio-economic status, style, the car they drive, etc. You can pick up some elements of a person from these things, of course, but how the individual is wired to think is found under the surface of these outward markers.

For example, the way someone is dressed may give some indication of who they are, but it's not a particularly sophisticated map. How we interpret what their style means is laden with so much narrative from our own biases. It can be really unreliable due to oversimplification and lack of fidelity.

A really good map helps account for our biases. It's based on pattern recognition from many sources, and it ensures that our subjective experience isn't as influential when evaluating who an individual is underneath.

CHAPTER 2

Myers-Briggs Dichotomies and Cognitive Functions

In 2010, we were presenting at a conference on personality types. Though it was a five-day affair, we had only ninety minutes to present the one glaring omission from the event: Jungian cognitive functions.

During the talk, a young man in the front row was furiously writing. Every few minutes his hand cramped, he shook it out, and he resumed writing as fast as he could. Afterward, he came up to us and said, "I'm Myers-Briggs-certified, and I have *never* heard any of the stuff you were teaching."

That was our first clue. Despite the entire Myers-Briggs system being built upon the concept of cognitive functions, for decades the functions stayed in the realm of esoteric knowledge. The internet has made huge efforts in bringing cognitive functions to the forefront, but it's been a slow process.

There's a barrier of entry to the deeper aspects of Myers-Briggs, and even in the online communities that love to talk about the functions, many have the attitude that if you can't figure out cognitive functions on your own, you don't deserve to know.

Some amazing books have been written on cognitive functions, Isabel Briggs-Myers' book *Gifts Differing* being the seminal work. Lenore Thomson's book, *Personality Type: An Owner's Manual,* is extraordinarily insightful, as are the books produced by Dario Nardi and Linda Berens, among others.

If you've ever read an article about how overvalued Myers-Briggs is, we guarantee it was written by a person who has never heard of how it relates to the cognitive functions. And we get it—the concept truly isn't easy to grasp. It contains a lot of seemingly repurposed phrases and plenty of jargon, and if the tip of the iceberg of a model has enough value (which, in this case, it almost does), there's really no need to plunge the icy depths in search of the rest.

However, to loosely quote Robert Anton Wilson, the best models are useful both when pared down to their essentials and when indefinitely expanded upon. While Myers-Briggs has usefulness at its most shallow levels, the rewards are commensurate with the work put into understanding it. The further down you go, the more beneficial the journey.

We want you to use this book as if it were your scuba equipment. You still have to plunge into the icy depths, but we're going to make it as easy on you as possible. The world may not need yet another Myers-Briggs book, but until the phrase "Myers-Briggs" becomes synonymous with cognitive functions, we have to try.

There have been many books written about Myers-Briggs, but arguably the most famous work on the topic is David Keirsey and Marilyn Bates' *Please Understand Me*, a *New York Times* bestseller that focuses on a theory called the four temperaments.

The four temperaments is a cool theory and a modernized version of the four humors, a personality type system that is so classic, it may have roots in ancient Egypt. The four temperaments are: Guardians (SJ), Artisans (SP), Idealists (NF), and Rationals (NT). You may already be familiar with them. However, we will not be discussing the four temperaments or the four humors in this book, as they do not relate directly to cognitive functions.

Myers-Briggs Dichotomies Explained

Remember when we said the four letters of your Myers-Briggs type can be used as a "decoder ring" to determine which cognitive functions you're using? That's because the functions came first, and the four-letter codes came later. But we're going to start with the dichotomies, because they're more recognizable than the cognitive functions, and are often the easiest access point.

There's something very important for you to remember as we go through these. You may get attached to some of the principles you learn about dichotomies in this chapter. But the concepts of dichotomies and cognitive functions build on each other, so we recommend seeing dichotomies as a starting point. Keep that in mind as you later learn about the cognitive functions.

What follows is just an overview of the dichotomies. Think of this as the 20,000-foot view needed to get an overview of the landscape. As we gain topographical precision of the map, some of these concepts will seem almost silly in their simplicity.

The four dichotomies are sets of opposing characteristics meant to describe certain aspects of a personality. They are:

- Introversion vs. Extraversion[2]

- Sensing vs. iNtuition[3]

- Thinking vs. Feeling

- Judging vs. Perceiving

If you're a Myers-Briggs enthusiast, you've seen a million descriptions of each of these characteristics. And even if you're not an enthusiast (and this is the first Myers-Briggs personality book you've ever picked up, God help

---

2   We've chosen to use the Jungian spelling of Extravert and extraversion with an "a," as opposed to the conventional spellings of Extrovert and extroversion.
3   In Myers-Briggs, Intuition is abbreviated as N, which is why we've chosen to write it as iNtuition in some places.

you[4]), you've at least heard about introversion and extraversion, both of which are popular concepts at the time of this writing.

Most descriptions of the dichotomies will include lists of behaviors to help you evaluate which side of the fence you fall on. And while we're also going to do that, it's important to know that your behaviors are influenced by a boatload of things: training from childhood, societal messaging, deep-rooted fears, etc. Behaviors are the emergent properties of the system of your personality, and the dichotomies are simply one node in that system.

For example, if you read a bulleted list of Introvert traits and one item is "reticence in conversation," but you're super chatty in social situations, don't automatically assume you're an Extravert. You could be an Introvert whose life circumstances make conversations easier for you.

Introversion vs Extraversion: Inner World vs. Outer World Reality

Most resources say this dichotomy is about energy management, and they're not wrong. But descriptions of how energy is managed can be oversimplified and misleading. Here's an example of oversimplification that we often read: "Introverts gain their energy by being alone, Extraverts by engaging with people." This doesn't seem to align with the chatty Introvert who loves to be around people, or an Extravert who can't seem to leave a party fast enough.

The actual difference between introversion and extraversion is this: For Introverts, the inner world (the world inside of themselves) is the "real world," the world that really matters. For Extraverts, the external world (the world outside of themselves) is the real world. It is this inner or outer reality from which a host of behaviors emerge.

This is why Introverts will pause slightly before they speak, as if they're making sure their words first resonate internally before they put them out into the world. Extraverts are the opposite—they'll often speak while they're thinking, because hearing it outside of themselves helps them determine the value or truth of their own statement.

---

4   Just kidding. You've made a fabulous decision.

Relationships with Other People

Not everything in the external world will resonate with the complex internal world of the Introvert. Introverts are put in the position of constantly reviewing information and reconciling it with what they know to be true internally. This can be quite taxing after a while, and time to themselves becomes a necessary reprieve.

The exception to this is when an Introvert makes space for another person in that inner world. This is most commonly seen when they mate or develop an extremely tight bond. The Introvert remaps their inner world to include the other person, who no longer seems at odds with the Introvert's internal world. Introverts in this situation have reported that they could actually spend all their time with that person, and they usually feel lonely when that person is away.

On the other hand, Extraverts feel most at home when they are interacting with their environment. As a general rule, they find variety stimulating, and the more people they come in contact with it, the more interesting it all is. Too much time to themselves leaves them bored and restless, and they need to interact with their environment to recharge. But this doesn't always require people. Simply going for a walk, getting out and about, or studying interesting things can be enough.

We all make space inside ourselves for special people. But for Extraverts who are charged and fueled by variety in their environment, spending too much time with a single person can begin to feel like being alone. Intending no insult to their loved one, they can become restless and want to get out into the world, with or without that person accompanying them.

Introverts, gun-shy from years of having to adjust themselves to fit the outside world, can become bashful and protective of their energy. Extraverts, realizing other people are full of new information and energy, can become extremely social to pursue that energy. But each person is unique, and how the two frames of mind show up can be counterintuitive.

For example, Introverts can become pontificators, people who take control of the conversation and just talk and talk and talk. Instead of adjusting to the outside world, they attempt to force the outside world to adjust to their inner world. In these situations, doing all the talking prevents a back-and-forth conversation that would quickly wear on the Introvert. An alternative example is the Extravert who is very aware of, and can fear, approval and disapproval from others. To an Extravert who is oriented to the outer world, disapproval can feel like an objective evaluation, and they may become shy despite wanting to be social.

There is an approximately 50/50 split in the population between Introverts and Extraverts, with some statistics indicating fractionally more Introverts.

Here's what to look for as you determine whether you are an Introvert or Extravert:

EXTRAVERT	INTROVERT
• Outer world is the "real world"	• Inner world is the "real world"
• Gets energy through engaging with environment	• Gets energy through alone time
• Less wary of new experiences	• Self-protective and more wary of new experiences
• Uses open vowels when speaking, projects voice, "broadcasts"	• Closed mouth, softer tonality, holds back
• Animated, energetic; "loud" gestures	• More subdued gestures
• Uses "we" language	• Uses "I" language
• Outwardly directed, more aware of environment	• Inwardly directed, less aware of environment
• "After thinker"— cannot understand life until they've lived it	• "Before thinker"— cannot live life until they've understood it

Reflection

Which world is the real world to you? The inner world or the outer world?

_____

_____

How much alone time do you crave and feel the need for each day?

_____

_____

Sensing vs. iNtuition: How We Perceive Reality

This next dichotomy in your four-letter code deals with how you perceive your world. Sensors prefer reliability of information, and iNtuitives prefer speed and depth of insight.

The first difference is that iNtuitives learn to trust pattern recognition to help them understand information quickly and perceive hidden connections between seemingly disparate things. They're comfortable theorizing and speculating on what could be, both here and now as well as into the future. Basically, they extrapolate implications from only a few data points.

Sensors, of course, have this same ability. But they don't trust it, so they don't hone it. Instead, they trust reliable information, things that can be verified in the real world. Therefore, they become masters of historical information—their own history, as well as other people's. Sensors also become fantastic at manipulating physical objects, have quicker reaction times, and tend to live in the moment. They don't understand a need to question reality when it's right there in front of them. Reality is reliable. Speculation isn't.

Second, Sensors and iNtuitives have different relationships with time. If real, reliable, solid information is what Sensors choose to focus on, then the past and present contexts are most important. Sensors can't rely on what hasn't happened yet, so the future is far less interesting. On the other hand, iNtuitives are comfortable with seeing what isn't there. The past doesn't really hold their interest as more than a reference point for future predictions.

Third, the Sensor/iNtuitive dichotomy alters values and basic interests. For Sensors, values surrounding things like family, tradition, enjoying the moment, being responsive and getting ahead of problems, etc., are all rooted in the known and knowable, and therefore can be trusted. For iNtuitives, values focus more on the abstract: meaning-making, narratives, imagination, possibilities, perspectives, and "what if" questions. Conversation will generally revolve around these things, with little interest in small talk.

Both Sensors and iNtuitives have an important role in our world. Sensors often hold down the fort, managing and stewarding infrastructures that keep us going as a society. iNtuitives are generally the trailblazers, coming up with new ways of looking at and doing things that end up producing new technologies and paradigms. It makes sense that fewer iNtuitives would be needed—too much innovation, and everything collapses. But without innovation, the world stagnates.

There is an approximately 75/25 split in the population between Sensors and iNtuitives, favoring Sensors.

Here's what to look for as you are determining whether you are a Sensor or iNtuitive:

SENSOR	INTUITIVE
• Likes verifiable/reliable information, comfortable with using five senses	• Likes speed of information and deep insight, comfortable with speculation
• Seeks contentment	• Often restless
• Craves enjoyment, faces life observantly	• Craves inspiration, faces life expectantly
• More observant than Ns regarding outside world, can be observant at the cost of imagination	• Sees how things could be as opposed to how things are
• Talent for recreating/living in the moment	• Can be imaginative at the cost of observation
• Tends to create an enjoyable present and let the future take care of itself	• Struggles to be "present," is future oriented
• More safety-oriented and risk averse, in an ideological way if not in a physical way (i.e., prefers tried-and-true belief systems)	• More initiative/ambition for getting to the next phase
	• Less risk-averse, more ideological; asks more "what if" questions
• More straightforward communication style	• More comfortable with failure for the sake of innovation
	• Uses more symbols and analogies

Reflection

What captures and arrests your attention more often: what could be, or what already exists?

_____

What is your threshold for abstract conversation?

_____

What is your threshold for small talk and who/what/where conversation?

_____

_____

————— ⬛ —————

Thinking vs. Feeling: How We Evaluate Information and Make Decisions

The third dichotomy in your four-letter code deals with how you make decisions and evaluate information. Thinkers use impersonal metrics to determine the value of an object, idea, or situation, while Feelers use personal, human-based considerations. Of course, all Thinkers *feel* and all Feelers *think*. Feelers can use analytical, cerebral processes to come to their conclusions just as Thinkers do. At the same time, Thinkers can use emotion-based considerations when deciding their values.

The most obvious way to observe a Thinker's emotions in their value system is seeing how frustrated, upset, or even downright irate they become when people ignore what they believe to be accurate, effective, true, or real. If their metrics aren't honored, it can take quite an emotional toll on the Thinker.

On the other hand, Feelers can ignore their own emotions in order to maintain what they believe is right. Social considerations usually rank high on their list of values, and it's not uncommon for a Feeler to put aside their emotions to keep harmony in an awkward situation.

It makes sense, however, that Thinkers would have data and metrics on their mind far more often, and would therefore be more comfortable and adept in careers, relationships, and other situations where data and resource management are favored. Feelers, by the same token, would have people and human interests on their radar, and so they will feel more at home with displays of emotion and interpersonal dynamics.

There is an approximately 55/45 split in the population between Feelers and Thinkers, favoring Feelers. When gender is taken into consideration, women highly skew toward Feeling, whereas men only moderately skew toward Thinking.

Here's what to look for as you are determining whether you are a Thinker or Feeler:

THINKER	FEELER
• Prefers impartial, impersonal data and metrics	• Prefers being personal and human-oriented
• Cool socially, more distant, and won't jump to connect; more interested in your info/data	• Friendly and warmer in tone, often enjoys connecting and seeking connection
• Won't nod while listening, unresponsive	• Often nods in encouragement when others are talking
• Can be tactless, values truth over tact	• Values tact over truth
• Can have stronger executive ability	• Makes a stronger politician and tends to have better social skills
• More likely to question other people's conclusions	• More interested in humans, including the speaker, when conversing
• Usually has a steady gaze and is more monotone when speaking	• Connects with personal stories
• Only emotions that "make sense" are valid in both self and others	• Tends to agree with others rather than be confrontational, unless a value is in conflict
• Ignores emotions in favor of data	• Sees all emotions as valid
• More businesslike than personal in conversation	• Ignores data in favor of emotional experience
	• More personal, less business-oriented

Reflection

When making decisions, are you more persuaded by the impact the decision will have on people (yourself included), or are you more persuaded by data, metrics, and analysis?

When making decisions, do you listen to your head or your heart?

_____

What angers you more: lack of thought or lack of empathy?

_____

_____

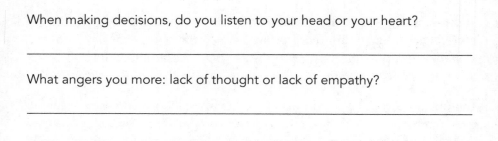

Judging vs. Perceiving: Do You Want Freedom or Organization?

The fourth and final dichotomy in your four-letter code deals with how you organize your world. Perceivers organize their inner world to allow outer-world freedom, and Judgers organize their outer world to allow inner-world freedom.

When Judgers think, they like to wander the garden of their minds. Ideas and thoughts come to them the same way fish swim around in a koi pond, and it requires calm and peace to really focus or even see them clearly. If Judgers are deep in thought and are disrupted, it's like disturbing the waters of that koi pond—the little ideas swim away, and the Judger may or may not be able to get them back.

This requires the Judger to have a measure of control over their external environment. They must be vigilant against potential disruptions. What starts out as a simple need to think grows into an all-encompassing need to have order in their environment. Judgers often report that they think better when their house is organized and they have no visual clutter. Therefore, it's easier to keep the house tidy most of the time. It's the same for their vehicle, work desk, private room, etc.

Perceivers are the exact opposite. Their thoughts and feelings are well-organized, and if you interrupt a Perceiver in the middle of a thought, their mind generally tags and files it for later. Recalling it is simply a matter of finding the right subject, category, or mental sticky note to retrieve it. However, some Perceivers are unaware of this phenomenon inside of themselves. They are unconsciously competent in having organized thoughts and feelings. On the other hand, Judgers are more aware of the lack of internal organization, most likely due to the frustration they experience at losing track of their thoughts when interrupted.

The ability to organize and track thoughts allows Perceivers to engage in their number-one favorite activity: improvisation. For Perceivers, having complete freedom to act in the outer world, keeping all their options available, is extremely satisfying. But Perceivers must be able to make decisions quickly if they wish to effectively improvise or capitalize on opportunities.

> A Perceiver's mind may be illustrated by a batter in a baseball game, anticipating the moment when the pitcher throws the ball. They need to respond extremely quickly, making the executive decision when exactly to swing the bat. Having immediate access to information like the effect of the wind, the curve of the ball, and the weight required behind the hit gives the batter far more precision to effectively hit the ball in a controlled direction.

The result can be observed in Perceivers while they are driving, dancing, and in conversation. While Judgers can be quick-witted, it is usually Perceivers who are the best improv comedians. However, it also means they aren't usually all that concerned about disruptions, and so household organization can get put on the back burner. It's a common Perceiver trait to throw clothes around negligently, ending up with a "floordrobe."

Another trait of Judgers is planning. Unless the Judger has taught themselves to be okay with improvisation and acting on the fly, they will usually be quite uncomfortable when thrown into a situation they didn't expect. Even a little bit of warning as to what's coming up next will help a Judger relax. The more a Judger gets to plan, the better they feel.

Perceivers can also benefit from planning, but they will often excel in situations that put pressure on them. They may unconsciously procrastinate on assignments and projects, having learned over time that they perform best in the eleventh hour. This same last-minute mechanism rarely comes through for a Judger. It's unreliable, at best.

Simply put, in last-minute situations, Perceivers can pull a rabbit out of a hat while Judgers can get overwhelmed and lock up. But that's not how either would self-identify or describe themselves.

As a final note, there are times when Judgers are sloppy and unorganized and Perceivers are meticulous and planned. For example, a Judger may have an organized life but a messy bedroom. The return on investment on cleaning their bedroom may not be high on the list of priorities since no one but themselves will see it. A Perceiver may have integrated the importance of a clean house or car and not allow themselves to have a single item out of place. These are exceptions, however, and tied more to the specific cognitive functions an individual is using.

There is an approximately 55/45 split in the population between Judgers and Perceivers, favoring Judgers.

Here's what to look for as you are determining whether you are a Judger or Perceiver:

JUDGER	PERCEIVER
• Uncomfortable when they don't know what to expect	• Focused when they don't know what to expect
• Tends to follow plans	• Tends to follow impulses
• Is usually better at long-term planning	• Is usually better at responding to crisis
• Tends to be early or on time	• Tends to be on time or late
• Takes pleasure in finishing projects	• Takes pleasure in starting projects
• Thinks often about the future or past	• Focuses on the present moment
• Is distracted by a chaotic environment	• Is indifferent to or energized by a chaotic environment
• Is at their best in familiar environments	• Is at their best in stimulating environments
• Is frustrated by open loops	• Is frustrated by restricted options
• Understands social structure, and is more likely to be compliant	• Is more likely to be counterculture and rebellious about social rules
• Usually wants to avoid risks	• Usually enjoys the thrill of uncertainty

What bothers you more: when your life is disorganized or your options are limited?

_____

Do you like to plan ahead or prefer to be spontaneous?

_____

Are you better at starting projects or finishing projects?

_____

Dichotomies: In Conclusion

There are sixteen possible combinations of the four dichotomies. We will go into the qualities of each of these types later in the book. They are:

ESTJ	ESTP	ENTJ	ENTP
ESFJ	ESFP	ENFJ	ENFP
ISTJ	ISTP	INTJ	INTP
ISFJ	ISFP	INFJ	INFP

Now that we've established the qualities of the dichotomies, let's plunge deeper into the next layer of Myers-Briggs: Jungian cognitive functions.

If you haven't yet taken the Myers-Briggs test on page 427, please take a moment to discover your type.

Imagine an iceberg. Until now, we've been looking at the part of the iceberg peaking above the water line: the four dichotomies. In the next chapter, we will plunge under the water and examine the part of the iceberg below the surface, the eight Jungian cognitive functions. This is where things can get a little confusing for some people. We will clarify the confusion as we go as best as we can. However, the full picture will emerge in the following chapter as we put the entire system together. Hang in there.

CHAPTER 3

The Cognitive Functions

Cognitive functions are the ways in which your mind is naturally wired to take in new information and determine the worth or value of that information. They are divided into perceiving functions and judging functions. We all need a way to take in new information (perceive), and a way to determine the worth or value of that information (judge).

There are eight cognitive functions. Of the eight cognitive functions, four are perceiving functions, and four are judging functions.

Cognitive Function Nickname	Cognitive Function Technical Name	Judging or Perceiving Function
Perspectives	Introverted Intuition	Perceiving
Exploration	Extraverted Intuition	Perceiving
Memory	Introverted Sensing	Perceiving
Sensation	Extraverted Sensing	Perceiving
Effectiveness	Extraverted Thinking	Judging
Accuracy	Introverted Thinking	Judging

Cognitive Function Nickname	Cognitive Function Technical Name	Judging or Perceiving Function
Harmony	Extraverted Feeling	Judging
Authenticity	Introverted Feeling	Judging

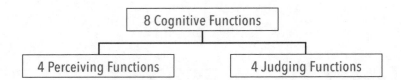

"Time out!" you might say. "I thought you just said above that someone was either a Judger or a Perceiver. Are you now saying that there are four types of Judgers and four types of Perceivers?"

This is where people begin to find themselves confused, because the same word is being used to denote two different concepts. In fact, you will notice this pattern all through this next section. The same words are used to convey different meanings.

The first concept, dichotomies, refers to a person: a Judger or a Perceiver. In a dichotomy, there are only two options. For example, if you look at the fourth letter in the Myers-Briggs code, an ESTJ is a Judger, while an INFP is a Perceiver.

The second concept, cognitive function, refers to a mental process or a quality a person possesses.

- A judging function aids in decision making and evaluation, which is something all people need to be able to do, not just Judgers. There are four judging cognitive functions.

- A perceiving function influences what captures our attention and what we find interesting. Everyone needs a perceiving function, not just Perceivers. There are four perceiving cognitive functions.

We'll talk more about the qualities of both judging and perceiving functions. The important thing for you to remember is this: Do not conflate Judgers and Perceivers (dichotomy) with judging and perceiving functions (cognitive function). Later, we'll reveal the relationship between the dichotomy of Judgers/Perceivers and the eponymous cognitive functions.

Learning Point Pause

Describe in your words the difference between a Judger and a judging cognitive function.

A Judger is _____

_____

A judging cognitive function is _____

_____

Describe in your words the difference between a Perceiver and a perceiving cognitive function.

A Perceiver is _____

_____

A perceiving cognitive function is _____

_____

The perceiving functions are split into two categories: sensing and intuition. These are based on our preference for either perceiving the world through our senses (sensing) or through a "sixth sense" (intuition), which we consider a type of advanced pattern recognition.

Again, we're not talking here about the Sensor/iNtuition dichotomy. Here, the terms *sensing* and *intuition* refer to the cognitive functions, the mental processes through which we understand the world.

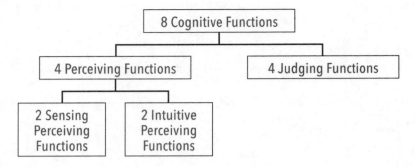

The judging functions are also split into two subcategories: feeling and thinking. These are based on our preference for judging information: by either how people will be impacted by our decisions (feeling) or how the numbers, metrics, and logic will play out (thinking). As above, the terms *feeling* and *thinking* in this context refer to the cognitive functions, not the Feeler/Thinker dichotomy.

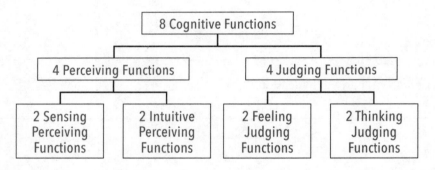

Finally, sensing, intuition, thinking, and feeling are each split into either an introverted or extraverted attitude. You've probably noticed the pattern here: We're not talking about the Introvert/Extravert dichotomy, but rather which direction the cognitive function is aimed—the outer world or the inner world. This is technically called its *attitude*.

When discussing cognitive functions, *introversion* and *extraversion* don't describe people or behaviors. They don't refer to the need to be the life of the party and/or to stay at home with your cat and read Charlotte Bronte. (Or whatever other stereotypes play in your head.) Introversion is a way to get in touch with one's inner world. Extraversion is a way to get outer-world feedback. When talking about cognitive functions, that's essentially all they mean.

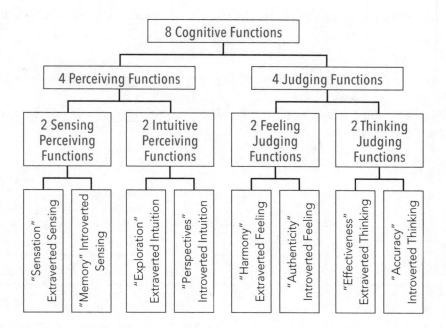

We take in and perceive the world through sensing and intuition, but not all of us use these processes in the same way. Some of us are more focused on our inner worlds when we perceive, and others are more focused on the outer world when we perceive.

		Introverted Attitude	Extraverted Attitude
Perceiving Functions	**Sensing Functions**	Introverted Sensing (Memory)	Extraverted Sensing (Sensation)
	Intuition Functions	Introverted Intuition (Perspectives)	Extraverted Intuition (Exploration)
Judging Functions	**Feeling Functions**	Introverted Feeling (Authenticity)	Extraverted Feeling (Harmony)
	Thinking Functions	Introverted Thinking (Accuracy)	Extraverted Thinking (Effectiveness)

Each of these eight functions has its own unique characteristics, which we'll outline in a later chapter.

Learning Point Pause

Use these questions to help you take what we just talked about and anchor it for the next section.

List the four perceiving functions.

1. _____

2. _____

3. _____

4. _____

List the four judging functions.

1. _____

2. _____

3. _____

4. _____

What is an attitude?

_____

What is the difference between a perceiving function and a judging function?

_____

_____

Congratulations! You've made it past the first sticking point—that dichotomies and cognitive functions share similar names but are different concepts. You should go to the kitchen and get yourself a treat.

The Four Cognitive Functions You Use

Your personality type is made up of four cognitive functions in descending order of strength. You have access to all eight of the functions discussed on the previous pages, and everyone uses all eight all the time. But, for you, only four of these processes have specific significance and a predictable influence. We'll focus on those four, which are technically called your cognitive function *stack*: a dominant and auxiliary function (strengths, or natural talents), and a tertiary and inferior function (weaknesses). All four play important roles.

Cognitive Function Strengths

These first two cognitive functions help make you a complete person. If we only ever judged, we would make terrible decisions since we would be working with limited information. If we only ever perceived, we wouldn't make decisions at all and the world would run us over. Similarly, we need a way to engage with the world inside of us (introvert), as well as get real-world feedback (extravert).

The first two functions in your stack are designed to fill all four of these needs. Let's explain how this works. (This is the next sticking point. Might want to grab another snack.)

If your judging function has an extraverted attitude, your perceiving function will *automatically* have an introverted attitude. The converse is also true.

This means if your judging function is Extraverted Thinking (Effectiveness) or Extraverted Feeling (Harmony), your perceiving function will be Introverted Sensing (Memory) or Introverted Intuition (Perspectives). On the other hand, if your judging function is Introverted Thinking (Accuracy) or Introverted Feeling (Authenticity), your perceiving function is Extraverted Sensing (Sensation) or Extraverted Intuition (Exploration).

This is a favor your brain has done for you. If both your functions were extraverted, you'd be a crazy person who only reacted to external stimuli, unable to know your inner self at all. If both your functions were introverted, you'd be equally crazy, but more likely to walk around downtown, perpetually talking to yourself.

Let's pick a cognitive function at random to illustrate this further. If you're using the Extraverted Feeling (Harmony) process, you have access to the world around you (extraversion) and are capable of making decisions (judging). You've just knocked out two of your four needs.

Extraverted Feeling (Harmony)	
• Access to the world around you • Making decisions (judging)	?

But you're still not complete. You need access to your inner world (introversion) and a way to take in new information (perceiving). So, you need a secondary process to help you meet all four needs. In this case, let's choose Introverted Sensing.

Extraverted Feeling (Harmony)	Introverted Sensing (Memory)
• Accessing the world around you (extraversion) • Making decisions (judging)	• Accessing your inner world (introversion) • Taking in new information (perceiving)

Let's choose another cognitive function at random.

If you're using the Introverted Intuition process, you have access to your inner world (introversion) and can take in new information (perceiving). You are still missing two of your four needs.

Introverted Intuition (Perspectives)	
• Access your inner world • Taking in new information (perceiving)	?

You still need access to your outer world (extraversion) and a way to make decisions (judging). So, you need a secondary, or auxiliary, process to meet all four of your needs. In this case, let's choose Extraverted Thinking.

Introverted Intuition (Perspectives)	Extraverted Thinking (Effectiveness)
• Accessing your inner world (introversion) • Taking in new information (perceiving)	• Accessing the outer world (extraversion) • Making decisions (judging)

Are you seeing a pattern? Certain functions pair with certain other functions in order to fulfill all four requirements: introversion, extraversion, perceiving, and judging.

Learning Point Pause

Use these questions to help you take what we just talked about and anchor it for the next section.

List the four needs all people have.

1. _____

2. _____

3. _____

4. _____

Why can't two introverted functions be paired together? What might happen?

_____

_____

_____

Why can't two extraverted functions be paired together? What might happen?

_____

_____

_____

List the two cognitive functions that can be paired with Introverted Feeling (Authenticity).

_____

_____

_____

Pairing Cognitive Functions with Myers-Briggs Types

Think of the dichotomies in the Myers-Briggs system as a sandwich: two pieces of meat in the middle, two pieces of bread on the outside.

The meat pieces in the middle are the foundation for the functions. Sensing/Intuition and Thinking/Feeling are the basis for the cognitive functions, and they are always represented by the middle two letters in the four-letter code. Notice the pattern in all sixteen types:

ESTJ	ESTP	ENTJ	ENTP
ESFJ	ESFP	ENFJ	ENFP
ISTJ	ISTP	INTJ	INTP
ISFJ	ISFP	INFJ	INFP

Which Cognitive Function Are You Extraverting?

This is another big sticking point for people, so listen up: You are considered a Judger or a Perceiver based on which cognitive function you are extraverting, and therefore which function is obvious to others.

It's important to be aware that extraverting a function does not necessarily mean that you are an Extravert. It means that this function is the *part* of you that is extraverted. The attitude of that particular function is directed toward the outer world, not your inner world.

If you are a Judger, that means you always extravert your judging function. If you are a Perceiver, you always extravert your perceiving function. In other words, you are considered a Judger or Perceiver based upon what you show to the world, not which function you prefer the most.

We'll annotate which function is being extraverted by adding a little (e) next to that function.

Since all Judgers extravert their judging function (thinking or feeling), then all Judgers look like this:

E S T(e) J	E N T(e) J	Extraverted Thinking (Effectiveness)
E S F(e) J	E N F(e) J	Extraverted Feeling (Harmony)
I S T(e) J	I N T(e) J	Extraverted Thinking (Effectiveness)
I S F(e) J	I N F(e) J	Extraverted Feeling (Harmony)

Since all Perceivers extravert their perceiving function (sensing or intuition), then all Perceivers look like this:

E S(e) T P	E S(e) F P	Extraverted Sensing (Sensation)
I S(e) F P	I S(e) T P	Extraverted Sensing (Sensation)
E N(e) T P	E N(e) F P	Extraverted Intuition (Exploration)
I N(e) F P	I N(e) T P	Extraverted Intuition (Exploration)

As mentioned earlier, everyone needs a way to get in touch with the outer world (extravert) and the inner world (introvert). Once you know which cognitive function in the meat of the sandwich is extraverted, you simply apply introversion to the other function. We use (i) to show introversion.

E S(i) T(e) J	E N(i) T(e) J	E S(e) T(i) P	E S(e) F(i) P
E S(i) F(e) J	E N(i) F(e) J	I S(e) F(i) P	I S(e) T(i) P
I S(i) T(e) J	I N(i) T(e) J	E N(e) T(i) P	E N(e) F(i) P
I S(i) F(e) J	I N(i) F(e) J	I N(e) F(i) P	I N(e) T(i) P

So, now you know which cognitive function you're extraverting and which function you're introverting. But how do you know which is your dominant (or preferred) function, and which is your auxiliary (or supportive) function?

Dominant and Auxiliary Functions

The first slice of bread in the four-letter code, E or I, determines which cognitive function is dominant:

- If you are an Extravert, then whichever function is extraverted is your dominant.

- If you are an Introvert, then whichever function is introverted is your dominant.

Therefore, it follows:

- If you are an Extravert, whichever function is introverted is your auxiliary.

- If you are an Introvert, whichever function is extraverted is your auxiliary.

As we discussed on page 37, your personality type is made up of four of the cognitive functions in a descending order of strength. If you know your Myers-Briggs personality type, you can figure out your dominant and auxiliary processes. These are the first two—and the strongest—cognitive functions in your cognitive function stack.

The last two functions are weaker processes, and are technically called your tertiary and inferior functions.

Use these questions to help you take what we just talked about and anchor it for the next section.

If you are a Judger, that means you always extravert your _____ function.

If you are a Perceiver, you always extravert your _____ function.

If your judging function is extraverted, your perceiving function must have an _____ attitude.

If your judging function is introverted, your perceiving function must have an _____ attitude.

If the first letter in your Myers-Briggs code is E, your dominant function's attitude is _____.

If the first letter in your Myers-Briggs code is I, your dominant function's attitude is _____.

If the first letter in your Myers-Briggs code is E, your auxiliary function's attitude is _____.

If the first letter in your Myers-Briggs code is I, your auxiliary function's attitude is _____.

───── ▬▬▬▬ ─────

Tertiary and Inferior Functions

To discover which cognitive functions are your tertiary and inferior, we use the principle of *polarities* by reversing the dominant and auxiliary. The inferior cognitive function is the polarity opposite of the dominant, whereas the tertiary function is the polarity opposite of the auxiliary.

Each of the cognitive functions has an opposite function it pairs with to create a polarity, or pairing of opposites. You don't have to look far—the polarities are all there in the eight functions.

Introversion is opposite of extraversion, sensing is opposite of intuition, thinking is opposite of feeling. Their polarity matches become:

COGNITIVE FUNCTION	POLARITY OPPOSITE
Introverted Sensing (Memory)	Extraverted Intuition (Exploration)
Introverted Intuition (Perspectives)	Extraverted Sensing (Sensation)
Introverted Thinking (Accuracy)	Extraverted Feeling (Harmony)
Introverted Feeling (Authenticity)	Extraverted Thinking (Effectiveness)

If one cognitive function is a strength, its polar opposite is, by definition, not getting as much time and attention in development. But they are intrinsically linked, so where one is present, the other also resides. Think of them as two sides to the same coin, with one side weighted to come up over and over again in your coin flips. The other is still there and has a percentage chance of surfacing.

This is important to know when determining your cognitive function stack, or the descending order of the four functions that influence you most.

It's easiest to grasp this using what we call the Car Model, discussed in the next chapter.

CHAPTER 4

The Car Model

Since 2009, we've been using a simple tool to teach cognitive functions; we named it the Car Model. It's been a powerful tool in our coaching, programs, and content. We feel it is the best way to grasp the full extent of your personality.

Imagine your mind as a four-passenger vehicle. In the front of the car, you have a Driver, and next to the Driver sits a Copilot. Directly behind the Copilot is a 10-Year-Old, and sitting behind the Driver is a 3-Year-Old. These passengers represent the cognitive stack.

It would look like this:

DRIVER	COPILOT
• Your greatest natural talent • Your flow state • Where you recharge your batteries and feel most like yourself • The mental process you feel compelled to use most; you will become depressed and lethargic if you cannot use it enough	• Your second strongest talent • Your growth state: You will get the biggest bang for your buck, developmentally, if you focus on exercising this process • Though you will not feel compelled to use this process, if it is well developed, you can enter your *genius* state
3-YEAR-OLD	**10-YEAR-OLD**
• Your biggest weakness; the opposite of your greatest strength • Your mental blind spot • Usually expressed in moments of stress or overload; when you feel like you are not yourself • Use sparingly and simply, with intention	• A weakness; the opposite function of your Copilot • Usually used when you feel defensive and don't want to deal with something; an escape into cognitive dissonance • Should not be used for major decisions • Best used in times of play, R&R, and intimacy

Now let's take what we learned in the last chapter and apply it here. We're going to show you how to use this tool to give you deeper insight into how your mind is wired. We are going to work clockwise.

First, place your dominant function in the position of the Driver. Next, make your auxiliary function the Copilot. Then, place the opposite of the Copilot (the tertiary) in the position of the 10-Year-Old. Finally, place the opposite of the Driver (the inferior) in the position of the 3-Year-Old.

This is how you determine all four cognitive functions in your personality, a.k.a. the four passengers in your car.

Let's illustrate this using a real-life example.

Determining Cognitive Function from Type

Antonia is an ENTP. First, let's isolate the two middle dichotomies in Antonia's four-letter code, or what we referred to in the last chapter as the meat in the sandwich. Her two middle dichotomies are iNtuition and Thinking.

Antonia is a Perceiver, which means she is extraverting her perceiving function, making it obvious to others. As an ENTP, her perceiving function is iNtuition. That means iNtuition is the process she is extraverting. We can add the annotation of (e) next to her perceiving process, *N* for iNtuition. To be a complete person, Antonia needs an introverted process. Therefore, her judging process, thinking, must be introverted. We can add the annotation of (i) next to *T* for thinking.

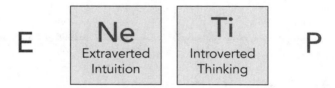

We've now determined Antonia's two primary cognitive functions. But we haven't determined which is dominant (the Driver).

We use the first dichotomy, Extraversion vs. Introversion, to determine which function is the Driver. As an ENTP, Antonia is an Extravert, meaning her dominant function is Extraverted Intuition. This means her introverted function is auxiliary, or the Copilot. In this case, the Copilot is Introverted Thinking.

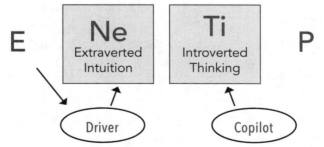

Now that we've established Antonia's two main functions, the dominant Driver and auxiliary Copilot, it's simply a matter of filling out the 10-Year-Old and the 3-Year-Old. We do this by using the principles of polarities (see page 44).

If her Driver is Extraverted Intuition (Ne), her 3-Year-Old is the opposite: Introverted Sensing (Si). If her Copilot is Introverted Thinking (Ti), her 10-Year-Old is the opposite: Extraverted Feeling (Fe).

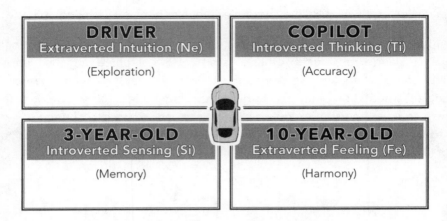

DRIVER Extraverted Intuition (Ne)	**COPILOT** Introverted Thinking (Ti)
(Exploration)	(Accuracy)
3-YEAR-OLD Introverted Sensing (Si)	**10-YEAR-OLD** Extraverted Feeling (Fe)
(Memory)	(Harmony)

Learning Point Pause

Use these questions to help you translate your Myers-Briggs type to your Car Model.

Step 1: Write your four-letter code here. If you are unfamiliar with your code, take the Myers-Briggs quiz on page 427.

E/I: _____

S/N: _____

T/F: _____

J/P: _____

Step 2: Focus on the two middle letters and determine which cognitive function you extravert. If you are a Perceiver, put an (e) next to the S/N. If you are a Judger, put an (e) next to the T/F.

_____ _____ _____ _____

Step 3: Now, put an (i) next to the other letter in the middle. If you are a Perceiver, put an (i) next to the T/F. If you are a Judger, put the (i) next to the S/N.

_____ _____ _____ _____

Step 4: Determine which function is your dominant by circling the cognitive function (S/N or T/F) that matches the first letter (E/I) in your four-letter code.

_____ _____ _____ _____

Step 5: Place the dominant function in the top-left square below.

Step 6: Place the auxiliary function in the top-right square.

Step 7: Using the principle of polarities, place the opposite function of the Copilot in the bottom-right square.

Step 8: Place the opposite function of the Driver in the bottom-left square.

DOMINANT (Driver)	AUXILIARY (Copilot)
_____	_____
INFERIOR (3-Year-Old)	TERTIARY (10-Year-Old)
_____	_____

Applying the Car Model to your personality requires you to understand two main things:

1. The characteristics of each of the eight cognitive functions

2. How they change depending upon where they fit in the Car Model

Before we take a deep dive into each of the eight cognitive functions, we'll first look at *type dynamics*, the relationship each function has to the other functions depending upon where it sits in the Car.

Driver (Dominant)

The Driver is the part of your personality that you identify with the most. If we were to ask you to describe yourself, you would spend 80 percent of your time describing this part of you. When you're using this cognitive function, you're in what we call your "flow state." It's the go-to tool in your cognitive toolbox.

But there is a difference between talent and skill. Talent is natural ability, whereas skill is conscious development. As author and educator Stephen Covey would say, honing a skill is like "sharpening the saw." Just because you have natural talent in something doesn't mean you have developed skill.

For example, you may find yourself in a family that doesn't understand or validate your Driver process. You may have been given the message that it's unacceptable to use and it may even be unconsciously sabotaged by people in your life whenever you attempt to develop it.

Or, you may find yourself in the opposite situation, when everyone in your family overvalues your Driver function and uses it to their advantage. Given no resistance, you receive positive feedback for using it, even if it's not very well-developed.

Either way, it's your responsibility to manage the Driver function by scheduling plenty of time for its use *and* development. If you don't clock enough time using it, you will find yourself dysthymic and depressed. If you don't build skill, you will find yourself ineffectual, and the go-to tool in your cognitive toolbox will not be up to the challenges life throws at you.

In his book *Flow*, author Mihaly Csikszentmihalyi writes about getting into a Flow State. One can experience flow by being fully immersed in an activity with energized focus and enjoyment. When in this state, most people report losing track of space and time. It's been our experience that people often enter this state of flow when they are fully and actively using their Driver process in an increasingly proficient way.

Copilot (Auxiliary)

The Copilot is a part of your personality that you identify with, but not nearly as strongly as with the Driver. It's an incredibly important part of yourself that you may tend to undervalue. When you're using your auxiliary cognitive function, you're in what we call your "growth state."

While the Copilot function is also a natural talent for you, you are less likely to build skill in this process than in the Driver process. It's usually circumstances that prevent development of the Driver, but with the Copilot, it's your own introverted/extraverted attitude preferences that get in the way.

If you recall, your Driver process, depending on your type, is either introverted or extraverted. Your Copilot process is the opposite attitude by design; it allows you access to the other "world" as a form of balance. Being 100 percent introverted or extraverted would be a form of pathology, and we don't know if any healthy person actually occupies that space. But that doesn't mean you don't have a strong preference for one of those worlds, and the process that encourages you to explore the other world may be seen as threatening.

If you are deeply introverted, you may avoid your extraverted Copilot to evade a scary outer world that gives you sensory overload or negative feedback that makes you feel like your thoughts and feelings are wrong and that you aren't enough. On the other hand, if you are highly extraverted, your introverted Copilot may force you to face uncomfortable introspection, including painful memories, trauma you haven't worked through, or unfamiliar and unexplored parts of yourself.

Here in the Copilot seat, there is also a difference between talent and skill. You might only use the Copilot's talent when you absolutely need to, resulting in limited skill development.

It's the combination of the Driver and Copilot functions that gets you where you want to go. Remember, together they meet all four needs a human has to be complete: One of these functions will have an introverted attitude and one will have an extraverted attitude; and, one of these functions will perceive information and one will make judgments on that information.

This makes both the Driver and the Copilot functions crucial for development.

You will always favor the Driver over the Copilot, but the more conscientious work you do to develop the Copilot, the more traction you'll get as you gain the necessary mechanisms for dealing with life: information gathering, decision making, inner-world introspection, and outer-world feedback.

We will talk more about using your Copilot cognitive function for growth in coming sections. For now, remember that this is usually your single best leverage point for growing yourself.

Learning Point Pause

Let's anchor what we've learned to apply it to the next section. Use these questions to help guide you:

Your Driver function is _____ .

Your Copilot function is _____ .

When looking at the Driver and Copilot, one needs to be introverted and the other needs to be _____ .

Briefly explain in your own words why it is important to have one introverted function and one extraverted function.

_____

_____

When one function judges information, the other function _____ information.

Briefly explain in your own words why you need both a judging function and a perceiving function.

_____

_____

Briefly explain in your own words the difference between talent and skill.

_____

_____

Why is skill development important for both the Driver and the Copilot functions?

_____

_____

_____

_____

———————— ▬▬▬▬▬ ————————

10-Year-Old (Tertiary)

You have a push/pull relationship with your 10-Year-Old process; it both crosses and supports each personality type. Sometimes you think you're good at it, sometimes it trips you up. When you're using the 10-Year-Old process, we call it the "defensive position."

The backseat passengers are less sophisticated than those in the front seat, but it's important to remember they can serve us in many ways. We've decided to call them "children" to give a sense of their place in the "family" of functions: valued, loved, even contributing, but still childlike in their perspectives and capabilities. Like children, these functions can have moments of brilliance, but they are less experienced than their parents are and they get overwhelmed easily. And as children often do, these functions can overestimate their abilities.

The 10-Year-Old process can be a helper in many ways, but only in the service of the front-seat passengers. Striking the right balance between the 10-Year-Old and the Copilot process greatly enriches a person's life. When the 10-Year-Old serves the Copilot function, it helps a person plan for the future, gain personal insight, and seek meaning in life. Trouble brews when the Driver process calls upon the 10-Year-Old instead of the Copilot.

Why would the Driver do that? Because the 10-Year-Old allows the Driver to stay in its preferred attitude of extraversion or introversion. If you notice, the attitude of the 10-Year-Old matches that of the Driver. That is to say, if the Driver is introverted, the 10-Year-Old will be introverted. If the Driver is extraverted, the 10-Year-Old will be extraverted. So, it will be easy for someone to identify with their 10-Year-Old function, which matches the attitude of their primary function.

DRIVER (Extraverted)	COPILOT (Introverted)
3-YEAR-OLD (Introverted)	10-YEAR-OLD (Extraverted)

DRIVER (Introverted)	COPILOT (Extraverted)
3-YEAR-OLD (Extraverted)	10-YEAR-OLD (Introverted)

When the Driver skips the wisdom of the Copilot to favor that of the 10-Year-Old, this is called getting caught in a *loop*, and you will only be meeting three of the four needs of a complete person. You'll be getting your perceiving and judging needs met, but if you're an Introvert, you'll be missing vital extraverted feedback, or if you're an Extravert, you'll lose out on necessary introspection.

It's the equivalent of two parents arguing in front of their 10-Year-Old kid when one of them turns to the kid to ask, "You agree with ME, right, Johnny?" Of course, the kid agrees. He doesn't have enough experience to disagree, nor does he know that it's inappropriate for the adult to use him as reinforcement. He's more flattered than appalled because he doesn't know any better.

Of course, none of this means that the 10-Year-Old is a bad part of you. It's a very valuable part, as are all of the pieces that make up who you are. Just like in any family, you would love and value the 10-Year-Old, but you wouldn't trust it in the decision-making process. However, when two adults provide a united front and make the rest of the family aware of their decision or insight, the 10-Year-Old can lean into the relationship and add a helping hand, maybe even provide wisdom in that "kids say the darnedest things!" sorta way. By this, we mean that sometimes, your 10-Year-Old can be an unexpected source of insight.

As you read your type's profile in Section Two, look out for ways the Driver and 10-Year-Old can get stuck in a loop. You can avoid these loops if you sharpen your Copilot by building skill in it as often as possible, especially during key moments of life.

Learning Point Pause

Let's anchor what we've learned to apply it to the next section. Use these questions to help guide you:

Your 10-Year-Old function is _____ .

Why are your Driver and 10-Year-Old likely to "join forces" and get caught in a loop?

_____

_____

If your Driver process is extraverted, your 10-Year-Old process will be

_____

If your Driver process is introverted, your 10-Year-Old process will be

_____

List the four things each person needs to be a complete person:

1) Need to get in touch with their _____ world to see inside themselves.

2) Need to get in touch with their _____ world to see what's going on outside themselves.

3) Need to _____ information to learn.

4) Need to _____ information to make good decisions.

When you get caught in a Driver/10-Year-Old Loop, you only have met _____ of the four needs to be a complete person.

Which function should you build skill around to avoid the loop in your personality?

_____

3-Year-Old (Inferior)

The 3-Year-Old is the most unsophisticated part of you, and so you have a tendency not to see it. It often influences you from the shadows until it makes its presence known, usually through inner turmoil. When you're using the 3-Year-Old function, we call it the "blind spot."

As the least sophisticated function in your stack, the 3-Year-Old process influences you in a number of ways, some good and some bad. You probably won't identify with descriptions of your 3-Year-Old cognitive function. When it exerts its influence on you and you find yourself in what's technically called its *grip,* you may be appalled or embarrassed by your behavior and make comments like "I wasn't myself."

Like being stuck in the loop, being in the grip of the 3-Year-Old occurs when you are not in control of your personality-type dynamics. This can be evident in two primary circumstances:

1. When the Driver process is exhausted

2. When you've neglected the 3-Year-Old for far too long and it will no longer be ignored

You use the Driver process as often as possible. It's the go-to tool in your toolbox, but it's not always the best tool for any given job.

For example, with some time and practice, you can open a bottle with a screwdriver, but a screwdriver is not designed for this use and you may get frustrated if it's not working. The same is true with your Driver process. You use it for almost everything, including tasks for which it wasn't designed. Usually, you just avoid things out of your wheelhouse, delegating them to other people when you can get away with it. But sometimes that's not possible, and you're left "using a screwdriver to open a bottle."

If your Driver function becomes too exhausted while problem-solving and doesn't get a break, it will nod off at the wheel, so to speak. Your mind unconsciously knows that the best way to give your Driver a break is to call upon its opposite process, the Copilot, providing it with plenty of space to rest. But if you don't pull over to the side of the road, you'll just hand the wheel to a 3-Year-Old, which will yield predictable results.

When this happens, you experience tantrums, breakdowns, and moments of pure paranoia or paralysis. These are the moments you don't really share with anyone other than people who will forgive you afterward, and if these behaviors are seen in public, you feel deeply ashamed or embarrassed. They are your toddler moments.

Fortunately, these moments are preventable if you understand the unique way your own 3-Year-Old manifests. You can learn to recognize your red flags: the moments you need to pull the car over to the side of the road to rest and let your 3-Year-Old run around a tree for a while. We'll discuss this for each of the individual personality types.

The other scenario where you might find yourself in the grip is when you've been neglecting the 3-Year-Old for too long.

We've been living with a toddler, our daughter Piper, for the past five years, and she pretty much entertains herself when we're driving...until she suddenly demands attention. If she has to call for us too many times, the bids for attention will turn into whining, then crying, then screaming.

Your 3-Year-Old process works similarly. It will allow itself to be ignored for long periods of time, but not indefinitely. And you really don't want to ignore it if it can be helped. We recommend giving it the same attention you would an exercise regimen—thirty minutes a day, three days a week at minimum. We will give you specific ways to do this in the section for your personality type.

Your 3-Year-Old function is not all bad news. It's where you get in touch with the most fragile, precious aspects of yourself. It also holds your aspirations, as only a child who hasn't been touched by cynicism can. There are a couple of reasons for this.

First, the childlike part of you has childlike dreams and longings. Your 3-Year-Old function has a wonder and excitement that has truly never grown up. It's unburdened by the trappings of adulthood.

Second, there are challenges the world throws at you that people of other types seem to solve effortlessly. They may have your 3-Year-Old cognitive function as a Driver or Copilot function, and they expertly apply that function to solve challenges. But when you try to do the same, the function is insufficient and clumsy in your hands. For you to solve these same challenges, you must take a different approach, which is often a clever strategy that your Driver and Copilot cook up.

For example, an INTJ who has experienced challenges with their 3-Year-Old function of Extraverted Sensing (Sensation) and finds themselves struggling with health and wellness may seek out non-traditional methods such as cryogenic freezing. This would appeal to their future-pacing Driver function of Introverted Intuition (Perspectives), and the "whatever works" mentality of their Copilot of Extraverted Thinking (Effectiveness). They may even discover a completely new strategy of wellness that can be shared with the public.

Like the INTJ in this example, your 3-Year-Old weakness must be navigated around. It becomes a catalyst to find new solutions to challenges you personally face. It is the source of invention and creativity, and you may be in a position to gift the world with your ingenious solution. When referring to how your 3-Year-Old influences you in this way, it is technically called your *aspiration*.

If you see someone working in their passion, purpose, or mission, there's almost always some aspect of their 3-Year-Old function whispering in their ear, breathing fire and determination, keeping the coals of their purpose warm. When we utilize the process as a guide for our life's work, we're on the right track.

Learning Point Pause

Let's anchor what we've learned to apply it to the next section. Use these questions to help guide you:

Your 3-Year-Old function is _____

What are the two reasons people may find themselves in a 3-Year-Old grip?

_____

_____

What are the two primary reasons that your 3-Year-Old function holds your aspirations?

_____

_____

———————————————

Understanding the relationship each of these positions has with the others is key to optimizing your cognitive wiring. In the next chapter, we are going to detail the characteristics of the eight functions themselves.

CHAPTER 5

Cognitive Functions in Detail

Now that we've explored how to figure out your function stack and the dynamics between the cognitive functions, let's discuss the functions in more detail.

A major part of our mission at Personality Hacker is to make powerful concepts accessible and simple. Not because people aren't intelligent, but because people are busy and many things vie for our attention. We came up with nicknames to help make it easier to grasp the cognitive functions, as you may have noticed in the previous two chapters. Here is a guide:

JUDGING OR PERCEIVING	COGNITIVE FUNCTION	NICKNAME	ABBREVIATION
Perceiving	Extraverted Sensing	Sensation	(Se)
Perceiving	Introverted Sensing	Memory	(Si)
Perceiving	Extraverted Intuition	Exploration	(Ne)
Perceiving	Introverted Intuition	Perspectives	(Ni)

JUDGING OR PERCEIVING	COGNITIVE FUNCTION	NICKNAME	ABBREVIATION
Judging	Extraverted Thinking	Effectiveness	(Te)
Judging	Introverted Thinking	Accuracy	(Ti)
Judging	Extraverted Feeling	Harmony	(Fe)
Judging	Introverted Feeling	Authenticity	(Fi)

Perceiving Functions

There's a classic story of an elephant that was brought to a town full of blind people. The townspeople had never heard of an elephant before. They decided to use their sense of touch to explore this creature and determine its characteristics. The first man placed his hands on the tail and described the elephant as a rope. A woman ran her hands up the length of the trunk and claimed it was like a snake. A little boy standing to the side of the creature described it to the town as a textured wall. A small girl hugged the leg and explained it as like a tree trunk. All were experiencing the same creature from their unique perceptive vantage points, ages, heights, and understandings.

We use our perceiving functions to take in information and perceive our world. Each person is wired to be attracted to different sources of stimulation. Similar to the illustration of the blind people and the elephant, your perceiving function informs what you become focused on, as well as how you experience it. Are you past, present, or future oriented? Do you pick up details in the moment, or do you capture information for later review? Your perceiving process points to the things that are of greatest interest to you and determines when you will collate the information that arrests your attention.

Extraverted Sensing: Sensation (Se)

Sensation is the Driver of ESTPs and ESFPs. It is the Copilot of ISTPs and ISFPs.

When you live for the present moment, when you don't miss a detail of what's going on around you and you're tapped into all of your senses, you're using the Sensation process. Sensation is favored by people who want verifiable information to help them determine the truth of something for themselves.

If you identify with Sensation, from the time you were a little kid, you've had an extraordinary ability to process sensory information. Not only do you process large amounts of sensory data, you also see, taste, smell, feel, and hear nuances other people miss. For example, people of your type are often extraordinary chefs, artists, and performers. You pick up a huge array of subtlety in flavors, colors, musical notes, and physical movements.

Sensation users have high kinesthetic awareness and strong body-mapping abilities. It's not uncommon for Sensation users to quickly remap their bodies to include tools like musical instruments, athletic equipment, weapons, and vehicles, making it appear as if these tools are simply extensions of their own bodies.

Joel's brother, Jason, is an ESFP. His relationship with his body has always been impressive. He easily picked up snowboarding as a teenager, making dangerous and complicated maneuvers appear effortless. He can play multiple musical instruments though he has had very little formal training. Now in his late 30s, he has become a powerlifter and fitness trainer who spends hours a day in the gym. He recently deadlifted over 600 lbs.

According to research done by Dario Nardi (author, speaker, and expert in the fields of neuroscience and personality), when a Sensation user is observed via an EEG machine, there's a phenomenon unique to the Sensation process called the "tennis hop." Just like tennis players bounce from one foot to another to anticipate any possible trajectory of a tennis ball, someone favoring the Sensation process is always anticipating the need to act. There's no need to overcomplicate problems that can be dealt with immediately. If there is no action to respond to, the Sensation process can become frustrated and disinterested. Often, this feeling of anticipation encourages Sensation users—especially Sensation Drivers—to invent action. Many emergency early responders use Sensation as a Driver or Copilot process, as do many entertainers and athletes.

Introverted Sensing: Memory (Si)

Memory is the Driver of ISTJs and ISFJs. It is the Copilot of ESTJs and ESFJs.

As with Sensation, those who use Memory prefer reliable information. But unlike Sensation users, who trust information inputs in real time, Memory users prefer to capture information for later review. What's more reliable than both experiencing a situation and carefully ruminating on it, combing through the memory for personal significance?

If you have a strong Memory process, even from the time you were a little kid, it was very important for you to do things carefully and correctly. You prefer to take your time and to consider how your current experience is similar to what you've experienced in the past.

This is why we call this process Memory. A careful and cautious person seeks a reliable source, and what's more reliable than what's already happened? Over time, people with a strong Memory process can develop an absolutely amazing memory for both the details and impressions of their experiences. They often say that when they're caught up in a memory, it's as if the past is happening again. Colors, feelings, smells, tastes, and sounds can be replicated with amazing accuracy, and these get placed in a large Rolodex of memories you can reference when the need arises.

Memory users are also concerned with carefulness, which manifests in a desire for safety and precedence. There's an imperative to do things the proper way, but as Memory is a perceiving process, Memory users don't come to conclusions about how things should be. Rather, these individuals are information gatherers and look to experts and tradition to inform the judging process. If there's a standard for how something has been done, they will use that as a reference for how things could continue to be done. The tendency to organize information, not for evaluation, but for reference, gives Memory users the superpower of creating procedures and processes for replication.

Since Memory users are focused on review, they have a tendency to be more interested in the past than the present. The present is interesting, too, but can be overwhelming.

An ISFJ friend of ours, Scott, is a big Harry Potter fan, and Joel accompanied him to the Harry Potter exhibit at Universal Studios in Orlando, Florida, this past year. The first time through, Scott struggled to enjoy the experience, and eventually admitted that he was rather overwhelmed. He and Joel left for a different part of the park to grab a drink and chill for a few minutes. After about an hour, Scott said he wanted to go back to the exhibit. He'd had time to post-process the original experience and was then able to enjoy it much more the second time through. The initial impression was simply too much, but once he could integrate the experience, it was familiar, and he was able to get into the moment.

Memory users recognize that not everyone picks up the same information to post-process. In particular, Memory Drivers are fairly open to individual idio-syncrasies people develop based on their unique experiences. A Memory friend of ours regularly says, "You can tell a lot about a person by the family they were raised in," and for her, that's completely true. Memory is crafted by the familiar, and its users tend to become masters of niche information and quirky collections based on childhood imprints.

At their best, Memory users have the greatest natural talent for acceptance. True acceptance includes letting go of judgment and blame (including of oneself) and instead addressing situations with tolerance and forgiveness, finding peace within.

Extraverted Intuition: Exploration (Ne)

Exploration is the Driver of ENTPs and ENFPs. It is the Copilot of INTPs and INFPs.

Exploration, as an intuitive process, relies on pattern recognition to specu-late what's going on behind the curtain. Unlike those who rely on the sensory processes, who prefer reliable and verifiable information, Exploration users are totally comfortable hypothesizing what could be.

If you strongly identify with Exploration, ever since you were a little kid, you've been driven to mess with your environment in order to figure out how things work. You viewed the entire world as a laboratory filled with things to discover. This gave you an interesting advantage, since it allowed you to watch how patterns emerged from the various buttons you pushed. It also helped you see relationships between things that other people didn't even realize were connected.

As you've matured and become more sophisticated in both your experiences and learning, so has the Exploration process. Over time, the world has become a huge spider web of connections and relationships, and you've gotten really good at both seeing these connections and speculating on how things could be connected. And the process has gotten faster.

As an extraverted process, Exploration involves pattern recognition in the outside world. The easiest way to spot new patterns is to mess with the environment: pull levers, push buttons, walk in restricted areas. These can be misinterpreted as acts of rebellion, but they're really attempts to interrupt the current patterns everyone seems to be taking for granted. There's nothing more satisfying to Exploration users than finding new ways to do old things.

We are both Exploration Drivers, and have noticed that when people tell jokes, we've discovered the punchline before they can deliver it. Since we can't carefully verify information while also accessing information at these speeds, we end up speculating a lot. We often trust our gut instincts about people and opportunities. Sometimes we're terribly wrong, but more often than not, our speculations bear out.

Questions starting with "What if…" generate deeply satisfying discussions for users of Exploration. There's nothing quite like a brainstorming conversation with a group of creative people, all furiously writing ideas on a whiteboard.

Someone who identifies with Exploration becomes bored if situations are too familiar. Repetitive tasks can become mind-numbing and maddening, and an Exploration user may change a perfectly workable system just to prevent their own boredom.

Introverted Intuition: Perspectives (Ni)

Perspectives is the Driver of INTJs and INFJs. It is the Copilot of ENTJs and ENFJs.

Like Exploration, Perspectives is an intuitive process that involves looking for complex patterns. It is an introverted process, however, and is inwardly focused, recognizing patterns inside the mind. This can be difficult to explain, and even Perspectives users have trouble putting their own process into words.

The number of different patterns inside of us is only limited by the number of humans on the planet. But there are patterns to these patterns, and the Perspectives user naturally enjoys digging into the different ways people interpret reality.

If you identify strongly with Perspectives, even from the time you were a little kid, you've been at least a little removed or disconnected from your own perspective. This gave you an interesting advantage, since it allowed you to watch how your mind formed connections. Over time, as you watched your own mind making connections, you also started to see patterns emerge. Every person creates their own unique pattern for how they experience the world. By observing other people exhibit the same patterns that you had watched your own mind form, you began to figure out there was a pattern to the patterns.

Perspectives users naturally shift perspectives to solve problems until the solution becomes clear. If they become adept at using Perspectives, they may be able to guess at another person's mood, problem, or mindset. The other person might feel uncomfortable about the accuracy of the Perspectives user's speculation, almost as if that person were using ESP.

Our friend Charis, an INFJ, told us of a dream she had related to our business that heavily featured an octopus. Within six months, a business opportunity presented itself in the form of an entity named Tako, intentionally named after the Japanese word for octopus. While it may have been entirely inci-dental, experiencing and making meaning from synchronicities is the natural focus of Perspectives users.

The ability of Perspectives users to notice these internal patterns and follow them has been likened to a bloodhound on the scent. If they lose the scent, become distracted, or get thrown off from observing a new *a-ha*, it could be lost forever. This is why Perspectives users often seek alone time to get their best creative thinking done.

In contrast with those who identify with Sensation, who seem to have excess energy and are always looking for opportunities to expend it, Perspectives users lack energy and are always looking for ways to conserve it. Living in the moment and being reactive is a massive energy suck. People who identify with Perspectives teach themselves the strategy of future-pacing (using mental imagery to predict future outcomes) in order to identify low-stamina actions that will have a big impact. Over time, Perspectives users unconsciously integrate future-pacing as a way of understanding life, making it the most future-oriented of the four perceiving functions.

Judging Functions

The judging functions are what we use to make decisions and evaluate information. When we make "should" statements, they are the result of our judging functions determining how the world should operate, how we should think, how we should treat each other, and what our values should be.

Extraverted Thinking: Effectiveness (Te)

Effectiveness is the Driver of ENTJs and ESTJs. It is the Copilot of INTJs and ISTJs.

Effectiveness is the function that asks, "Does this work?" When systems need to be put in place to accomplish goals, it's Effectiveness that figures it out. When you see how resources can be managed and manipulated to make something happen, and when you're making a cost/benefit analysis, you're using Effectiveness as decision-making criteria.

If you strongly identify with Effectiveness, from the time you were a little kid, you've been aware of what works and what doesn't work, what passes tests and what fails them. The ultimate goal is to be effective—to design a system or a tool that works in the face of changing circumstances and conditions. You may have even been considered destructive as a child, but you know your goal wasn't to ruin things (though sometimes a good explosion is deeply satisfying). It was to discover the stress point of objects and systems, to tag that information for later when it was your turn to produce objects and systems.

McDonald's franchises around the world primarily employ teenagers and other people with limited work experience. Despite this, McDonald's restaurants remain some of the most lucrative franchise businesses to own. Why? The systems themselves are so elegant and so effective that they require very little individual talent to maintain.

People who use Effectiveness are far more driven by outcomes than personal feelings. Getting an outcome accomplished means orchestrating a lot of resources, and when an Effectiveness user is in project-management mode, people can become resources, too. That doesn't mean they're cold-hearted. Being able to make the tough call is a gift, and Effectiveness users understand that personal feelings get in the way of making things happen. They're willing to be the bad guy in order to serve the common good, and many Effectiveness users have been willing to risk demonization by society in order to do the "right thing."

That means considering options that other people may find distasteful. Personal feelings are fickle and clash with each other. So, at decision time, it takes a thick skin to make a choice that is bound to offend someone's sensibilities. This includes being willing to "stress test" both people and situations.

Antonia's brother Ty, an ENTJ, used to make spaceships out of Legos only to immediately destroy them with industrial-size rubber bands he had from his job as a paperboy. He wasn't trying to ruin his creation. His goal was to see how much impact the spaceship could withstand in order to make the best, most sturdy version. If the spaceship couldn't pass the test of a rubber band assault, it failed. If the wing fell off, that meant the wing must be reinforced. If the wheels collapsed, then they would have to be attached better. Once the weaknesses had been exposed and improved upon, his next spaceship had all the components the original ship was missing. If in the next barrage of rubber bands the spaceship held up, then the structure passed.

From this desire to test and improve is born a fascination with measurements of all kinds. Aristotle's position was that if something wasn't measurable, it wasn't controllable, and therefore not real. This is the basic tenet of people that share the Effectiveness process. What can be measured can be controlled, and what can be controlled can be made to pass any tests that it may come across.

At their best, Effectiveness users mobilize large teams of people and resources to accomplish truly remarkable things. CEO positions and the military's top brass are teeming with Effectiveness users who find nothing so satisfying as checking boxes off their to-do lists.

Introverted Thinking: Accuracy (Ti)

Accuracy is the Driver of INTPs and ISTPs. It is the Copilot of ENTPs and ESTPs.

Accuracy users ask, "Does this make sense?" When data is incongruent or when it doesn't add up, you're using Accuracy to sort it out. When you make a decision based upon logical analysis at the cost of beloved personal truths or social conventions, you're using Accuracy as decision-making criteria.

Accuracy is far more driven by facts than by people. Personal desires and emotions get in the way of clean data, and in order to pursue logic, sometimes other people become data points. But Accuracy users aren't necessarily cold-hearted. Seeking truth is the ultimate virtue, but everyone's interpretation of truth is subjective, as any Accuracy user will tell you.

If you strongly identify with this function, from the time you were a little kid, you were extremely aware of incongruities and inconsistencies, especially inconsistencies of thought. When you were younger, this usually showed up as the difference between what people said and what they did. If an adult or an authority figure gave you a command but did not observe this command themselves, the discrepancy was immediately obvious to you, and you felt compelled to point it out.

People of your type often report that they were called disrespectful and anti-authoritarian as children. This wasn't the intent. The intent was to have consistency of thought, and if an authority figure could have explained in a clear way why they as an adult didn't have to follow the same rules as children, then all would have been forgiven. But explanations like "because I'm the adult" or "because I'm in charge" didn't really fly. As you can guess, Accuracy is also where you get your sense of fair play. Accuracy, at its core, is looking to fix inconsistencies, and that means sorting through a lot of ideally unpolluted data to see as clear a picture as possible. People's emotions are sticky—definitely not unpolluted. So, when it comes to decision time, emotions take a back seat.

An archetypal example of Accuracy is the child in the classic fairy tale *The Emperor's New Clothes,* a story that illustrates how society can collectively favor group delusion to maintain each individual's personal position and status. In the story, the child points out what is obvious to him—that the emperor is naked—disregarding the fear of going against the collective delusion. Social position, personal desires, and fear of censure are completely unimportant to him in the face of logic and observable fact.

At their best, Accuracy users will look at their own minds to cull information and beliefs that don't pass their stringent criteria. Like a computer programmer spotting bugs, Accuracy users seek to remove all lines of code that could corrupt the rest of the program. If you're mistaken and an Accuracy-oriented person corrects you, it's not personal. They honestly would want that information themselves and they expect you to want it, too.

Extraverted Feeling: Harmony (Fe)

Harmony is the Driver of ENFJs and ESFJs. It is the Copilot of INFJs and ISFJs.

Harmony users ask, "Is everyone getting their needs met?" Knowing how interpersonal dynamics impact the culture of a room, family, and society as a whole is the province of Harmony.

Harmony users possess an almost uncanny ability to understand social dynamics, unwritten social rules, and culture. This emerges from a lifetime of focusing on everyone's feelings and needs. Since it's impossible to meet every single person's needs all the time, Harmony users instead set up conditions to meet the needs of the collective. This often manifests as etiquette.

If you strongly identify with Harmony, even from the time you were a little kid, you've had other people's emotions on your radar, especially what they approved and disapproved of. This gave you an interesting advantage, since it allowed you to quickly read other people's responses in a variety of situations.

As you matured and became more sophisticated in your experience and learning, so did the Harmony process. For example, it may have started out by registering the approval your mother gave you when you presented her with a handful of flowers you picked. You stored that information for later, and as you aged, you realized it wasn't just your actions that have significance for other people. In fact, you learned that everyone's actions are interconnected and warrant an emotional response. Your ability to read a single person's approval and disapproval grew to understanding entire social systems between people.

This process continues to encompass more and more people: understanding school dynamics, corporate settings, and eventually, entire cultures. That's why people of your type can spot the highest-status person in a room very quickly, as well as intuitively comprehend the social rules we expect everyone to abide by.

Oprah, who we suspect to be an ENFJ, is an excellent example of the Harmony function. She invites everyone to benefit from her hospitality, and she's created a rabid fan base doing so. She is masterful at bringing an audience together and helping them meet their needs by introducing them to experts who can help them in areas of their lives.

Harmony users determine the value of information they're given based on whether it brings people together or breaks connection. They're hesitant to pass information along that will hurt someone's feelings, even if that information is true. When they must confront another person, they will often go to great lengths to be diplomatic. At their best, they're the quintessential "hosts" of the world: warm, inviting, and wired to keep morale high.

Introverted Feeling: Authenticity (Fi)

Authenticity is the Driver of INFPs and ISFPs. It is the Copilot of ENFPs and ESFPs.

Authenticity asks, "Does this feel right to me?" When we need to make a decision that is true and honest to who we are, it's Authenticity that guides us. When you understand how an action or word will impact the subjective human experience, or when you feel conviction, you're using Authenticity as decision-making criteria.

The archetype of the reluctant hero fits well with the Authenticity function: the humble and ordinary person, thrust into circumstances "bigger" than they are, compelled to face the extraordinary based solely on a personal responsibility to good, staying to the bitter end even if they don't make it out alive.

Authenticity users are far more driven by personal conviction than any other consideration. In fact, it is sometimes difficult to motivate an Authenticity user unless they are personally touched or inspired. Once committed, however, they are a powerhouse and oftentimes unstoppable.

If you strongly identify with Authenticity, from the time you were a little kid, you've been extremely aware of the emotional impact events have on you as a person, or how they make you feel. As you matured and became more sophisticated in your experience and learning, so did the Authenticity process. Since you've experienced a variety of situations with a variety of responses, then your type, more than any other, comes to understand the huge array and nuance of human motivations.

Conflicting emotions within the Authenticity user represent different hopes, fears, desires, and agendas. As Authenticity matures, it learns to interact with these inner voices as a counsel, with the ego at the head of the table. It learns to listen for the deepest ethic, even if there are other dissenting internal voices and motivations. At its most refined, Authenticity avoids becoming hijacked by more expedient or demanding inner voices in the counsel.

In the final battle scene of the movie *Return of the Jedi,* Luke Skywalker (who we suspect to be an INFP) has to determine which motivation will win out in a formidable and pivotal moment. Which voice will he listen to? The one that wants revenge in behalf of his friends? The one that is seduced by power? The voice that is pained and angered by an abandoning father, or the one that stays true to the ethics molded by his Jedi training and mentors? In the end, Luke follows his highest ethic and the other motivations must fall in line behind it.

Conviction can take Authenticity users in idealistic directions, believing something to be possible because they first felt it on the inside. Outside considerations are not nearly as interesting or compelling as internal feelings, and so they are often strangers, or even blind, to metrics. A dream can be accomplished because they believe it can be, and others will stand in admiration as an Authenticity user moves mountains to accomplish their vision.

Throughout this book, we discuss the unique ability Authenticity users have as "emotional aikido." Morihei Ueshiba, the founder of the martial art *aikido*, often described this art as being like the flow of water, moving gently around obstacles, working with the current rather than fighting against it. Aikido aims to turn anger, defensiveness, and the tendency to meet aggression with aggression into compassion, empathy, and even love. Those who master the Authenticity function find themselves having a similar effect on other people. They are able to work with others and their own emotional energies to create qualities that are more positive. At their best, they are a true inspiration to others, congruent with all of their inner voices and aligned toward a mission.

The Good News and Bad News

We've explained the foundation of each function and what it looks like when it's being used well. However, two things will impact how the cognitive functions show up: the emotional and mental health of the person using the function and the development of the cognitive function itself.

If your emotional or mental state is undeveloped or unhealthy, you may use your cognitive functions as a weapon. Those who are naturally talented at wielding a hammer can use it to build a house or to bludgeon someone to death. The healthier you are, the more likely you are to use the tools in your cognitive tool belt for building. The less healthy you are, the more likely you are to "bludgeon others" with your natural talents.

Here's a quick guide to how each cognitive function looks in its healthy and unhealthy states:

	HEALTHY	UNHEALTHY
SENSATION	Understands the body. Learns through movement and activity. Is fully present and in the moment. Loves pushing the body and environment to their limits. Gets ahead of problems by quickly taking action.	Becomes kinesthetically self-indulgent. Wants to feed cravings, such as food, sex, alcohol, drugs, exercise. Won't consider future consequences or how actions impact others. Can be reckless.
MEMORY	Works like an autobiographer/memoirist, recording experiences and their impact. Honors precedent, and will create order if not present. Desires and understands stability and tradition.	Seeks psychological comfort, often retreating to comfort zones. Gets stuck in unhealthy ruts. Refuses to venture out of the familiar.
EXPLORATION	Sees patterns in the outer world and makes connections between disparate things. Learns quickly by trying new combinations and experimenting. Is extremely optimistic, seeing new possibilities everywhere.	Impulsive. Wants a change of any kind to escape current discomfort. Flighty and cannot be pinned down. May also use pattern recognition functions to justify erroneous conclusions.
PERSPECTIVES	Dives deep into the subconscious to see patterns within the human mind. Shifts perspectives to understand self and others. Sees into the future.	Paranoid. May become fearful of the future, assuming worst case scenarios. May become fearful of everything.
EFFECTIVENESS	Organizes people and resources to accomplish goals. Scouts out talent and delegates. Able to make tough calls.	Controlling. Pushes to make something happen. Will do anything to get their own way, from angry outbursts to passive-aggressive behavior. Will do "what works" at any cost.

	HEALTHY	UNHEALTHY
ACCURACY	Understands frameworks and analyzes empirically to inform choices. Exerts tremendous focus on single subject/object. Uses radical honesty to communicate.	Thinking patterns of "what makes sense" become small and myopic. Cannot be reasoned with; will only see their own logic. Thinking patterns become small/myopic. Becomes cold, removed, and focused on self-preservation.
HARMONY	Understands people's needs and meets them through organized efforts. Connects emotionally with others. Understands culture and promotes unspoken social contracts.	Emotional and manipulative. Uses emotions to bully others or to garner sympathy. "Getting needs met" becomes entirely self-serving: focuses on *my needs, right now.*
AUTHENTICITY	Recognizes how events impact individual emotions, starting with their own, and makes choices accordingly. Taps into motivations. Uses art or expression to communicate and replicate inner emotions and motivations.	Self-obsessed. Convinced of rightness, regardless of evidence. Conviction without rationale. Self-indulgent—wants to feel comforted. "What feels right" becomes "What feels good."

As we walk through each of the sixteen Myers-Briggs personality types in Section Two, ask yourself:

1. "How can I utilize my cognitive functions in healthy ways?"

2. "How can I exercise my functions to better serve others and myself?"

Section Two

THE SIXTEEN TYPES

Now let's dive deeper into the sixteen Myers-Briggs personality types. While each of the sixteen types has recognizable patterns of thought and behavior, you experience your type as a unique individual. So each chapter has recommended exercises and journal prompts to encourage understanding and growth for your personality type in your unique expression.

As mentioned earlier, there is redundancy in these upcoming chapters. For types that share the same cognitive functions, similar language has been used to describe both the characteristics and the exercises recommended for growth. This was a stylistic choice to allow you, the reader, to focus on your type description with an uninterrupted flow, without needing to constantly reference other parts of the book.

CHAPTER 6

ENTP Personality Type

ENTPs have a deep desire to contribute through innovative thought. They often work out their ideas through debate, which can at times appear to be a self-centered need to proclaim the flawed thinking of others. But at their core, they are teachers and mechanics of difficult concepts.

If a subject is too complex, the ENTP simplifies it for their audience. If it's a difficult truth, they make it funny to cushion the blow. ENTPs see the importance, as well as the absurdity, of a shared reality. They recognize that people actually want good data and information. They become comedians, coaches, inventors, and teachers to maneuver around social resistances and hit the target of what people will accept.

ENTPs may become jaded or cynical if they receive too much hostile or negative feedback in response to the truths they attempt to impart. They might not have the self-awareness to recognize that their harsh reactions are still attempts to connect with others. If allowed to fester for too long, ENTPs may resort to cavalier or even caustic behavior as an attempt to reflect the absurd nature of reality back to humanity.

ENTPs can develop strategies for teaching hard truths while remaining connected to people by first learning to be brutally honest with themselves. Once they can do this, their radical honesty with others is better received, because it meets the rigorous standards the ENTP sets.

ENTP CAR MODEL OVERVIEW

DRIVER
Exploration (Ne)

- Innovates
- Recognizes patterns in behaviors and processes
- Sees between the lines and makes connections

COPILOT
Accuracy (Ti)

- Prunes out logical inconsistencies and incongruities
- Practices integrity and radical honesty
- Focus and skill mastery

3-YEAR-OLD
Memory (Si)

- References the past to mark growth
- Realizes where it has come from, but may feel trapped by past choices
- Becomes overwhelmed, fatalistic, or adopts limited beliefs when feeling threatened

10-YEAR-OLD
Harmony (Fe)

- Unsure whether, and to what extent, feedback of others is valid
- Emotional outbursts or manipulation when stressed
- Desire to positively contribute to social conditioning

The ENTP Driver Is Exploration (Ne)

It's important to remember that the Exploration process is a talent. This means that not every ENTP will have the same skill level or use it in a healthy way. Developing Exploration as a healthy process is crucial to becoming an amazing ENTP.

Exploration, when developed and sharpened, allows you three very unique gifts. It lets you identify patterns, possibilities, and opportunities; gives you excitement, fuel, and optimism; and helps you leave comfort zones to enter into new, undiscovered territory.

Pattern Recognition

Exploration, as an intuitive process, uses advanced pattern recognition to see connections other people miss. It wants to know what's going on behind the curtain, what it can't directly access. As it gets more sophisticated, Exploration's predictive powers improve, and the Exploration user eventually becomes adept at not only seeing what others miss, but imagining what could exist. Whiteboard sessions, or meetings where ideas are shared and built upon with other creative minds, are moments where this ability truly shines. Feeding off the energy of other people's suggestions, Exploration will come up with truly novel and unique ideas that transform the mundane into the extraordinary.

But pattern recognition gets better over time only if the Exploration user lets themselves experience the world at large. Reading and researching are part of the process, but they are not a complete expression of Exploration. Theories have to be acted upon to get real-world feedback, and if the theory was wrong, it has to be revised.

Exploration benefits from the process of testing and iterating. When the Exploration user finds that they are wrong, they view it as an opportunity for expanding their understanding, learning even greater possibilities, and transforming this amazing talent into real opportunities. Instead of getting defensive when they learn their original idea was wrong, the ENTP can say a mental "thanks!" to the universe for giving them the gift of calibration.

Exercise

Get good at pattern recognition by making quick predictions about how a mystery movie will end. Mystery movies follow a limited set of plot twists. Use your Exploration process to not only predict an individual movie's ending, but to identify the types of plot twists movie scripts use.

Reflection

Name three times your pattern recognition was confirmed to be accurate:

_____

_____

_____

Name three times your pattern recognition was confirmed to be wrong:

_____

_____

_____

The next time I'm wrong, I'm going to learn to enjoy the process by:

_____

_____

_____

_____

Excitement, Fuel, and Optimism

The Exploration function burns a lot of fuel, so it must also generate a lot fuel. According to Dario Nardi, author of *Neuroscience of Personality*, Extraverted Intuition is the cognitive function that takes the longest to get into a flow state but, once there, it's the most difficult to slow down.

ENTPs are wired to have energy to burn when they tap into the Exploration function. They ride on the feeling of optimism and being fully engaged. There are so many things the world has to offer, so many possibilities for improvement. The sheer brightness of it all can be contagious.

There can be challenges, of course. Possibility thinking can be seen as threatening to some people, and those who use Exploration may feel they have to fight to represent it. Fortunately, Exploration is unfazed by negative feedback. Its job isn't to accept defeat but to see all the different ways to make something happen.

The greatest gift ENTPs can give themselves is permission to continue using Exploration in the face of opposition. Part of Exploration's genius is finding new ways to present itself. If one style doesn't work, it will modify its strategy to become what the situation needs it to be. This is why Exploration users are often highly charismatic.

Exercise

Keep life exciting! A simple exercise is to practice jumping out of bed. In the middle of the day, lay down under your covers and set your alarm for 1 minute. When the alarm goes off, jump out of bed fast and put a huge smile on your face. Do this seven times in a row. Immediately follow this exercise with an activity you love and look forward to doing. Each day for seven days, practice this technique. By the end of the week, see if you are jumping out of bed in the morning, too.

Reflection

Name the most exciting thing in your life right now:

_____

_____

_____

Name something that always gives you joy, just by thinking about it. How can you include this in your life every single day? Be creative with how you can introduce this activity daily:

_____

_____

Leaving Comfort Zones

Exploration loves novelty and blazing new trails. It faces six-foot-tall grass holding a machete, screaming, "tigers be damned!" Getting fully into this function means being willing to leave comfort zones, physically, psychologically, and emotionally.

It can be difficult if circumstances seem to be hindering adventure. But as an ENTP, it's important to make sure you engage in some novelty every day. Exploring the world gives the ENTP true open-mindedness. Beliefs and ideas ENTPs may be attached to must be reevaluated in the face of new information and patterns.

Conveniently, as comfort zones are expanded, anxiety and fear of the unknown turn into the excitement of what could be. All growth happens outside of comfort zones, and the feeling of growing can become a healthy addiction. ENTPs know they've fully developed this function when growth becomes the new normal.

Exercise

Practice getting out of your comfort zone by seeking out new situations you would not normally pursue. If there's a question of doing something that feels right to you, but may include some hassle or an "unsafe" element, practice taking the risk instead of playing it safe. It's common for people of your type, once they get past the scary part of a new experience, to say "Was that it?" Most of your growth happens by being adventurous and letting go of the belief that you must live the way others want you to live.

Reflection

Today, I will get outside of my comfort zone by:

_____

_____

_____

I will make this a daily practice by:

_____

_____

_____

Setting Up the Right Conditions

The enemy of Exploration is the mundane. Exploration is fueled by novelty and new experiences. If day-to-day life has become rote or is in a rut, the energy of the Exploration function will run out as if it has a slow leak.

As your ENTP Driver, Exploration is your flow state, and if you're not using this process enough, you'll eventually run out of energy and may become depressed. Set up your daily conditions to access this mental process often. For example, if each day seems to be bleeding into the next, add novelty to it by taking a new class, gathering friends for an idea-generating conversation, eating at an exotic restaurant, or simply getting lost in a new part of your city that you'll have to navigate back from. Starting a daring new project or entrepreneurial endeavor will require the need to be innovative every day.

When the Exploration function is young, Exploration users can be unrealistic about themselves, others, and the world. Hungry for opportunity and perpetually optimistic, they may take on too much, becoming overwhelmed. Young Exploration Drivers expect too much out of themselves and other people and are disappointed when no one seems to be meeting their potential fast enough. They can be callous and have trouble understanding their true impact on other people. Without ballast, they struggle with time management, irresponsibility, and boredom.

ENTPs and ENFPs especially must recognize that the only time change happens is when they work with the system. There is benefit in both optimism and making a sober assessment. These types can increase their impact by being focused, accurate, and grounded.

UNDEVELOPED EXPLORATION (Ne)	DEVELOPED EXPLORATION (Ne)
Avoid:	Work Toward:
• Arbitrary action	• Testing and iterating ideas
• Idealism and unrealistic expectations	• Optimism with sober assessments
• Boredom and callousness	• Growth and self-improvement

Reflection

The talents Exploration can give me are:

_____

_____

_____

The ways I usually use Exploration are:

_____

_____

_____

I'm going to develop Exploration more by:

_____

_____

_____

List three activities that put you into flow:

_____

_____

_____

The ENTP Copilot Is Accuracy (Ti)

Without an introverted judging process, the ENTP is not complete. Without developing a strong inner character, the ENTP will become overly reactive to feedback from the world. They may be too susceptible to pressure from peers or family members, simultaneously feeling a need to be rebellious and overly compliant.

An introverted judging process empowers the ENTP to find their own sense of integrity, remove beliefs that are limiting or illogical, and call out truths that are obvious to them but ignored by others.

It's important to remember that, like the Driver function, the Copilot process is a talent. But that doesn't mean every ENTP will have the same skill level or use it in a healthy way. Developing Accuracy as a healthy process is crucial to becoming an amazing ENTP.

It can be difficult to actively develop an introverted function as an Extravert. For an ENTP, working on Accuracy won't be as natural as working on Exploration, so discipline and a focus on the rich rewards Accuracy brings will be key.

Prune Out Logical Inconsistencies and Incongruities

People with a strong Accuracy process often have no problem slicing through emotionally difficult circumstances in order to see the situation as presented. Accuracy users have the ability to spot logical fallacies and biases. That said, it's far easier to see other people's biases than our own. The more an ENTP develops Accuracy, the more the function will enable an ENTP to spot their own biases and dissonance.

Accuracy is a subjective function. This means the Accuracy user asks, "What makes sense to *me*?" When the function is in its infancy, it can rationalize nearly anything. Over time, as the process develops and matures, Accuracy users begin spotting incongruities not only in what others are saying, but also in their own thinking. Like a programmer working through lines of code, an Accuracy user's first job is to clean up corrupt script within their own mind.

This can be challenging. Once a mental code is discovered to be faulty, it can seem like the mind is being ripped apart in an effort to dismantle the flawed idea. This may manifest as an existential crisis, and can be as emotionally impactful as the death of a loved one. But the more you build the skill of Accuracy, the more survivable the surgical removal of faulty code becomes. Eventually, the rewards of clean thinking are felt, and removing cognitive dissonance and bias becomes part of your identity as an ENTP.

Reflection

What if there were no right answers, only better questions? If you were able to craft your own ideas from scratch, what would they be? Do you fear losing your competency if you lose your thoughts? Can you ever truly lose who you are, or are you constantly changing, anyway?

At its best, Accuracy learns to say, "I don't know," without being disturbed by uncertainty. Reflect on the following questions:

What thought or belief have I not been looking at too carefully? If I looked at it critically, would it survive an honest analysis? Do I fear letting it go? What else would I have to look at critically if I let this one go?

_____

_____

_____

Being kind to myself, I'm going to address this belief by:

_____

_____

_____

Integrity and Radical Honesty

Well-developed Accuracy allows you to express truths no matter how hurtful they can be. While truth can hurt, it doesn't have to be unkind or cruel. In fact, Accuracy users intend to be kind when speaking harsh truths, and are usually appreciative when others do them the service of being honest. Accuracy users would much rather know the truth now than be deluded and taken off guard later.

Young Accuracy users can feel like they're always on the wrong side of the conversation. It's not uncommon for ENTPs to get the feedback that they're always saying the wrong thing or being offensive. The world has a push-pull relationship with the idea of truth, and ENTPs can sometimes find themselves grasping at how to say something.

As the function matures, however, Accuracy becomes less about forcing truth on others and develops a skill in sharing truths. Complete truths are almost always welcomed by others, and eventually ENTPs get better at giving context to their messages. ENTPs often master the art of comedy as a way to deliver these truths while breaking down resistances.

It's also important for ENTPs to develop radical honesty with themselves, ensuring that they stay true to their values. Sometimes that means being honest about what their values truly are, especially if they differ from conventional society's, as well as owning up to transgressions and mistakes. However, if an ENTP hasn't first been honest with themselves, then their views can instead be antisocial opinions, which are rarely welcome.

Exercise

Observe how often you lie to other people. According to a study done by the University of Massachusetts at Amherst, 60 percent of people tell an average of two to three lies in a ten-minute conversation.

For example, when people ask how you're doing, do you answer honestly? Do you feign interest in conversations that are boring to you? Do you hide the truth to avoid hurt feelings? While you watch yourself lie in conversation, don't judge or justify yourself by saying, "I have to lie in this situation because...." Just observe.

Now that you've watched the different ways you tend to lie, turn this inward. Watch how often you lie to yourself. Keep a finger on the pulse of your cognitive dissonance.

Reflection

How could I be more honest with others and myself? Am I willing to speak the truth even if it's hurtful? Do others find me condescending when I do this? How can I learn to speak complete truths?

_____

_____

_____

_____

_____

Focus and Mastery

Accuracy offers an amazing ability to focus, which is represented in a huge variety of ways. It's seen in the best athletes, philosophers, and mechanics. A basketball player using Accuracy can spend endless hours practicing 3-point shots, ever so slightly altering the angle of their wrist until they can shoot a perfect 3-point shot each time. This same talent starts with noticing incongruities of thoughts as a child. The same process takes place in the mind and on the court: When something doesn't line up, keep working until it lines up perfectly. Philosophers and scientists often use Accuracy when breaking down ideas and beliefs.

It's important to discipline the mind to focus on mastering practical skills, not simply pleasurable activities. It's easy to focus on things that are fun and engaging, but ENTPs make a true difference when they can use their skill of focus on mundane or "boring" activities. Using focus and skill mastery to improve yourself and fulfill duties creates a rewarding life.

When we focus our eyes, we zero in on a single object and allow everything else to become fuzzy around it. That object becomes very clear and sharp, and if we focus long enough, we'll begin to see the object in detail. All of the object's parts become obvious.

Do this with your mind. Work on a problem while allowing everything outside the problem to become fuzzy. This could be anything from trying to master a musical refrain to working out a complex mathematical problem. As you spend more time focusing your attention, you will start to see its parts, such as the notes in the refrain to the formulas of the math problem.

Reflection

How can I discipline my mind to be 5 percent more focused today?

_____

_____

_____

_____

Copilot Growth

Accuracy allows you as an ENTP to make self-directed decisions. Accuracy encourages you to ignore social pressure and status, focusing instead on radical honesty and what makes logical sense. However, you will lose your sense of integrity and ability to be persuasive if you conflate the talent of out-arguing others with critical thinking.

Growing your Accuracy can be a challenge for you as an ENTP. It takes maturity to stop using other people's feedback as a sign you're on the right track, and instead develop the ability to spot inconsistencies and be willing to point them out when appropriate.

Every personality type tends to avoid growing their Copilot mental process. But here lies the power of understanding your personality. Don't see your

Accuracy as a hindrance. Rather, embrace the slower pace of getting into this mental process because it gives you the opportunity to build impressive skills.

It makes sense to focus on your inner truth. It's smart to focus on your true internal logic. Similarly, it should make sense that the more rigor you use to vet information and conclusions—and the more polarizing you are willing to be—the more impact your ideas will have.

To help develop your Accuracy Copilot, start asking yourself, "What *actually* makes sense in this situation?" Spend focused, introverted time ruminating about what strikes you as true, both for yourself and for others.

Each time you are faced with a decision, close your eyes and ask yourself what is most logical, not what will make others happy. Practice finding holes in your own logic, and in the middle of disagreements, pay attention to your own bullshit meter. Pay attention to the validity of your own thoughts before calling bullshit on the ideas of others. Do what it takes to access your inner truth while ruthlessly rooting out internal inconsistencies in your own logic. Start seeing your own cognitive dissonance as being completely unacceptable. In doing this, you will become a leader of social conditioning as opposed to being at its mercy.

Reflection

The talents Accuracy can give me are:

_____

_____

_____

The ways I usually use Accuracy are:

_____

_____

_____

I'm going to develop Accuracy more by:

_____

_____

_____

List three ways you can start growing your Accuracy process today:

_____

_____

_____

————————

The ENTP 10-Year-Old Is Harmony (Fe)

The Harmony function encourages compassion, helps us take care of each other, and allows us to make strong emotional connections. It provides an instinctive understanding of people's needs and how to get them met. Harmony users tap into social dynamics to make sure personal boundaries are honored, which keeps morale high.

ENTPs can use the Harmony function to commit to their relationships. Harmony can help an ENTP develop warmth and kindness. It can also help them persuade others through humor and other positive shared emotions. Additionally, Harmony helps ENTPs remember their responsibility to a bigger community and encourages them to contribute positively.

As an extraverted function, Harmony allows the ENTP to access a judging process while avoiding their inner world. This can be okay at times, but if the ENTP gets used to relying on Harmony to support their perceptions, they can rationalize skipping development of their introverted judging Copilot, Accuracy. And that's when the trouble starts. For ENTPs, overreliance on Harmony usually manifests as seeking approval from other people to avoid troubling inner truths.

Harmony is, in a large part, about checking in with other people. Harmony users consult with how others are feeling to vet their own opinions. People who have Harmony as a strength are usually pretty good at it, and they use this function to influence society and meet the needs of others. But you're an ENTP, meaning you're wired to be at your best when consulting your personal logic, not the influence of other people.

If your 10-Year-Old gets to have the final call without consulting the Copilot, it's going to see the world like a child would. Children aren't great at judging the validity of others' opinions, and without the radically honest analysis of the situation provided by Accuracy, the ENTP may hand over too much power to their relationships or other people's opinions.

The 10-Year-Old Harmony can manifest by letting other people set the tone of how the ENTP should live their life or how they should feel about themselves. Frustrated by the feeling of disempowerment, they may use emotions to manipulate or to bully people, and relationships can become codependent. However it shows up, its motive is to protect the perceptions of Exploration and, ultimately, the ENTP's very identity.

The Driver/10-Year-Old Loop

There are three ways an ENTP experiences the loop, the echo chamber–like relationship between the Driver and 10-Year-Old functions. The way to get out of a loop is the same in all cases: focus on developing the Accuracy function.

Short-term loop. This may last for a few moments up to a few days. Feeling the discomfort of their own contradictory thoughts and wanting to silence both the inner voice and whatever triggered it, the ENTP will use emotion defensively. This can show up many ways, but it usually looks like either anger or a joking dismissiveness toward others. Plugging into a shared emotional experience renders introspective, analytic thinking impossible for the ENTP. Once the cognitive dissonance retreats back into a deeper place and can be ignored, the ENTP will be back in good humor.

Long-term loop. In order to manage troubling thoughts, the ENTP will rely too heavily on intimate relationships to set the tone for their lives. They will outsource their important beliefs and values to others, fearing to follow their own logic to its conclusion. They will believe in partial truths that sound logical on the surface and pursue answers to questions only as long as those answers remain nonthreatening to their lifestyle and the people in their lives. This loop is often marked by codependent relationships.

Habitual loop. Instead of determining their own sense of worth using subjective, radically honest criteria, the ENTP compulsively seeks praise to bolster their self-esteem. Sometimes there is enough self-awareness to realize that out-and-out bragging is considered distasteful, but regardless, the ENTP will compulsively put themselves at the center of attention. They may single out another person or group of people to make fun of, pick fights to showcase their own intelligence, or argue everything to exhibit intellectual dominance. The ENTP will categorize people into "smart" and "stupid," and seek approval from those deemed smart. The worse the loop, the more people are dehumanized, only seen as valuable if they offer positive feedback. Any puncturing of the ENTP's self-image is met with anger and, in the worst cases, banishment.

Reflection

The ways Exploration and Harmony can loop in an ENTP are:

_____

_____

_____

The ways I find myself looping are (include behaviors and situations):

_____

_____

_____

I'm going to work on breaking my loop(s) by:

_____

_____

_____

How to Best Use Harmony

If you find yourself compromising your truth in favor of unhealthy relationships or feedback, this is a bad use of the Harmony function. Tap into Accuracy and ask yourself, "What kind of life do I have if it's built on a lie?"

That said, if you want to share yourself fully with another person, connecting with them based on who you truly are and what you truly believe, Harmony can help guide you. It can help you deliver hard truths with compassion. Just don't let it fool you into becoming dishonest.

You can also engage your 10-Year-Old in times of play, love, and intimacy. People of your type love connecting with friends, being intimate, and helping everyone have a good time. You can also use Harmony to feel motivated by your compassion, reach out to those less fortunate, and be generous for a social cause.

The ENTP 3-Year-Old Is Memory (Si)

Memory creates a sense of continuity. It references past experiences and knowledge to establish standards, traditions, and customs. It's gradual, patient, accepting, and consistent. It understands how we are shaped by our past. As a 3-Year-Old process, Memory is the part of the ENTP that whispers from the shadows. Normally indifferent to traditions, benchmarks, and what's come before, suddenly the ENTP will seek comfort in the familiar, or feel trapped by past decisions.

There are three ways an ENTP experiences the grip, those moments when your Driver process is stressed out, needs a break, and the 3-Year-Old function takes over the wheel of the car.

Short-term grip. This occurs when the ENTP truly feels like a child. They start to feel anxious and uncertain when they don't know the rules or whether they're doing something wrong. For example, what if they make a mistake when filling out a government or bank form that requires a lot of minute attention? If asked to follow dietary restrictions that require heightened discipline, where do they start? Who would even know this information? What if they make it worse somehow? The result is avoidance and hoping the answer will magically appear or, alternatively, that the problem will somehow go away.

Long-term grip. The ENTP will adopt a sense of fatalism, the idea that the Fates have cursed them into a bad situation that will last forever. It is marked by emotions like pessimism, hopelessness, and depression. The ENTP no longer experiences the joy of life, and may be cynical that others seem to be getting away with not having followed the rules and face no consequences. It can be focused on health, career, family, or relationships. Memory is quirky and attaches to random things, so whatever the ENTP has decided is fated will be unique to them.

Habitual grip. The strategy is attachment to a limiting belief, which is a bastardized version of Memory's superpower, acceptance. Unlike fatalism, this type of grip is rarely emotional. It simply roots into the ENTP and becomes the catch-all excuse for why they can't build the life they want. Whatever it is—a codependent relationship, body issues, a paradigm or belief structure—it is unlikely to be truly permanent, but the ENTP is convinced that it will be. This grip isn't as intense as the previous two styles of grip experiences, and so it is much easier for the ENTP to become attached to it. Ultimately, it becomes the excuse to perpetually seek comfort, be in fear, and live a retracted life.

How to Best Use Memory

The best way to use Memory as a 3-Year-Old is to exercise it regularly, which will help prevent the grip from occurring. In this case, reconnect with the part of you who has stayed the same throughout time. Watch a movie you've seen a hundred times. Listen to music you grew up with. Share memories with family members about how things used to be and how much they've changed.

Remember, Memory is an introverted process, so make sure you have plenty of uninterrupted ruminating time. Thirty minutes should be long enough, but feel free to take as long as needed to de-stress. If you're still not feeling settled, make a diary entry or vlog about who you were and who you've become.

The goal is to give yourself a break from feeling the need to have an immediate creative solution. Make sure you're diving deeply into the positive tethers to your past. Once your Driver has had enough of a break, you can usually come back to the situation with a whole new outlook. Then, take small, manageable steps to feel back in control.

Using Memory in this way can also provide a source of aspiration, the voice that whispers in the back of your mind. Memory as an aspiration can encourage ENTPs to track the progress of their lives and have realistic expectations for change. People of your type can be true change agents, but they have to play nice with the institutions that exist and remember what has been tried and what has come before.

Reflection

The ways Memory can grip an ENTP are:

_____

_____

_____

The ways I find myself being in the grip are (include behaviors and situations):

_____

_____

_____

I'm going to control the process by:

_____

_____

_____

My 3-Year-Old inspires me/is my aspiration in these ways:

_____

_____

_____

CHAPTER 7

ENFP Personality Type

ENFPs love to outwardly express themselves. By observing the way others react to their expressions, ENFPs learn more about their inner selves.

Self-expression creates a feedback loop for ENFPs. Over time, they adapt and craft their identity to become clearer on who they are and who they are meant to be. They do this by building a map of their own core motivations and contrasting them with other people's motivations.

Balancing their charm and energy with a clear internal value system is the lifelong growth work for ENFPs. When ENFPs express themselves without a goal, cause, or self-development focus, they can become attention seeking, manipulative, and even cruel. It's important for ENFPs to use their natural performance abilities to become more empathetic and encouraging, rather than exploitative or conniving. When an ENFP has self-discipline as well as vision for their life, they reflect back to others what's possible for them to become.

ENFP CAR MODEL OVERVIEW

DRIVER Exploration (Ne)	COPILOT Authenticity (Fi)
• Innovates • Recognizes patterns in behaviors and processes • Sees between the lines and makes connections	• Lives by core values and ethics • Has inner alignment and conviction • Sympathy, art, and emotional aikido
3-YEAR-OLD Memory (Si)	10-YEAR-OLD Effectiveness (Te)
• References the past to mark growth • Realizes where it has come from, but may feel trapped by past choices • Becomes overwhelmed, fatalistic, or adopts limited beliefs when feeling threatened	• Places too much weight on efficiency • Forceful outbursts when stressed • Driven, with a desire to lead

The ENFP Driver Is Exploration (Ne)

It's important to remember that the Exploration process is a talent. This means that not every ENFP will have the same skill level or use it in a healthy way. Developing Exploration as a healthy process is crucial to becoming an amazing ENFP.

Exploration, when developed and sharpened, allows you three very unique gifts. It lets you identify patterns, possibilities, and opportunities; gives you excitement, fuel, and optimism; and helps you leave comfort zones to enter into new, undiscovered territory.

Pattern Recognition

Exploration, as an intuitive process, uses advanced pattern recognition to see connections other people miss. It wants to know what's going on behind the curtain, what it can't directly access. As it gets more sophisticated, Exploration's predictive powers improve, and the Exploration user eventually becomes adept at not only seeing what others miss, but imagining what could exist. Whiteboard sessions, or meetings where ideas are shared and built upon with other creative minds, are moments where this ability truly shines. Feeding off the energy of other people's suggestions, Exploration will come up with truly novel and unique ideas that transform the mundane into the extraordinary.

But pattern recognition gets better over time only if the Exploration user lets themselves experience the world at large. Reading and researching are part of the process, but they are not a complete expression of Exploration. Theories have to be acted upon to get real-world feedback, and if the theory was wrong, it has to be revised.

Exploration benefits from the process of testing and iterating. When the Exploration user finds that they are wrong, they view it as an opportunity for expanding their understanding, learning even greater possibilities, and transforming this amazing talent into real opportunities. Instead of getting defensive when they learn their original idea was wrong, the ENFP can say a mental "thanks!" to the universe for giving them the gift of calibration.

Exercise

Get good at pattern recognition by making quick predictions about how a mystery movie will end. Mystery movies follow a limited set of plot twists. Use your Exploration process to not only predict an individual movie's ending, but to identify the types of plot twists movie scripts use.

Reflection

Name three times your pattern recognition was confirmed to be accurate:

_____

_____

_____

Name three times your pattern recognition was confirmed to be wrong:

_____

_____

_____

The next time I'm wrong, I'm going to learn to enjoy the process by:

_____

_____

_____

_____

Excitement, Fuel, and Optimism

The Exploration function burns a lot of fuel, so it must also generate a lot fuel. According to Dario Nardi, author of *Neuroscience of Personality*, Extraverted Intuition is the cognitive function that takes the longest to get into a flow state but, once there, it's the most difficult to slow down.

ENFPs are wired to have energy to burn when they tap into the Exploration function. They ride on the feeling of optimism and being fully engaged. There are so many things the world has to offer, so many possibilities for improvement. The sheer brightness of it all can be contagious.

There can be challenges, of course. Possibility thinking can be seen as threatening to some people, and those who use Exploration may feel they have to fight to represent it. Fortunately, Exploration is unfazed by negative feedback. Its job isn't to accept defeat but to see all the different ways to make something happen.

The greatest gift ENFPs can give themselves is permission to continue using Exploration in the face of opposition. Part of Exploration's genius is finding new ways to present itself. If one style doesn't work, it will modify its strategy to become what the situation needs it to be. This is why Exploration users are often highly charismatic.

Exercise

Keep life exciting! A simple exercise is to practice jumping out of bed. In the middle of the day, lay down under your covers and set your alarm for 1 minute. When the alarm goes off, jump out of bed fast and put a huge smile on your face. Do this seven times in a row. Immediately follow this exercise with an activity you love and look forward to doing. Each day for seven days, practice this technique. By the end of the week, see if you are jumping out of bed in the morning, too.

Reflection

Name the most exciting thing in your life right now:

_____

_____

_____

Name something that always gives you joy, just by thinking about it. How can you include this in your life every single day? Be creative with how you can introduce this activity daily:

_____

_____

_____

Leaving Comfort Zones

Exploration loves novelty and blazing new trails. It faces six-foot-tall grass holding a machete, screaming, "tigers be damned!" Getting fully into this function means being willing to leave comfort zones, physically, psychologically, and emotionally.

It can be difficult if circumstances seem to be hindering adventure. But as an ENFP, it's important to make sure you engage in some novelty every day. Exploring the world gifts the ENFP with true open-mindedness. Beliefs and ideas ENFPs may be attached to must be reevaluated in the face of new information and patterns.

Conveniently, as comfort zones are expanded, anxiety and fear of the unknown turn into the excitement of what could be. All growth happens outside of comfort zones, and the feeling of growing can become a healthy addiction. ENFPs know they've fully developed this function when growth becomes the new normal.

Exercise

Practice getting out of your comfort zone by seeking out new situations you would not normally pursue. If there's a question of doing something that feels right to you, but may include some hassle or an "unsafe" element, practice taking the risk instead of playing it safe. It's common for people of your type, once they get past the scary part of a new experience, to say, "Was that it?" Most of your growth happens by being adventurous and letting go of the belief that you must live the way others want you to live.

Reflection

Today, I will get outside of my comfort zone by:

_____

_____

_____

I will make this a daily practice by:

_____

_____

_____

———————— ▭ ————————

Setting Up the Right Conditions

The enemy of Exploration is the mundane. Exploration is fueled by novelty and new experiences. If day-to-day life has become rote or is in a rut, the energy of the Exploration function will run out as if it has a slow leak.

As your ENFP Driver, Exploration is your Flow state, and if you're not using this process enough, you'll eventually run out of energy and may become depressed. Set up your daily conditions to access this mental process often. For example, if each day seems to be bleeding into the next, add novelty to it by taking a new class, gathering friends for an idea-generating conversation, eating at an exotic restaurant, or simply getting lost in a new part of your city that you'll have to navigate back from. Starting a daring new project or entrepreneurial endeavor will require the need to be innovative every day.

When the Exploration function is young, Exploration users can be unrealistic about themselves, others, and the world. Hungry for opportunity and perpetually optimistic, they may take on too much, becoming overwhelmed. Young Exploration Drivers expect too much out of themselves and other people and are disappointed when no one seems to be meeting their potential fast enough. They can be callous and have trouble understanding their true impact on other people. Without ballast, they struggle with time management, irresponsibility, and boredom.

ENTPs and ENFPs especially must recognize that the only time change happens is when they work with the system. There is benefit in both optimism and making a sober assessment. These types can increase their impact by being focused, accurate, and grounded.

UNDEVELOPED EXPLORATION (Ne)	DEVELOPED EXPLORATION (Ne)
Avoid:	Work Toward:
• Arbitrary action	• Testing and iterating ideas
• Idealism and unrealistic expectations	• Optimism with sober assessments
• Boredom and callousness	• Growth and self-improvement

Reflection

The talents Exploration can give me are:

_____

_____

_____

The ways I usually use Exploration are:

_____

_____

_____

I'm going to develop Exploration more by:

_____

_____

_____

List three activities that put you into flow:

_____

_____

_____

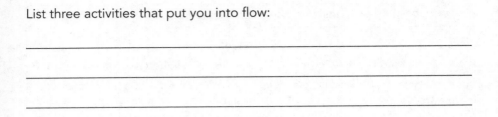

The ENFP Copilot Is Authenticity (Fi)

Without an introverted judging process, the ENFP is not complete. Without developing a strong inner character, the ENFP will become overly reactive to feedback from the world. They may feel like they're missing out or moving too slow to make the impact they wish to make. By trying to do too much, they end up accomplishing little.

An introverted judging process empowers the ENFP to find their own sense of identity, slow down enough to listen to their deepest motivations, and get a sense of what's true for them.

It's important to remember that, like the Driver function, the Copilot process is a talent. But that doesn't mean every ENFP will have the same skill level or use it in a healthy way. Developing Authenticity as a healthy process is crucial to becoming an amazing ENFP.

It can be difficult to actively develop an introverted function as an Extravert. For an ENFP, working on Authenticity won't be as natural as working on Exploration, so discipline and attention on the rich rewards Authenticity brings will be key.

Core Values and Ethics

Being aware of one's emotional responses at all times creates an ethical complication. A person may feel one way in one situation but completely different in a seemingly identical situation. They must learn to judge the

context of their reactions: Are their responses fully subjective, or are they based on certain principles that can be used to guide future behaviors?

What is a truly ethical action? When an ENFP feels the full emotional force of all behaviors, they ask this question frequently to create a personal list of what's ethical and what isn't. Since the majority of behaviors fall on a spectrum, ENFPs are pretty laid back about most actions people take. A person may be insensitive or obtuse, but unless they offend one of the ENFP's core values or true principles, the behavior is likely to be forgotten or even go unnoticed.

Once a core value has been upset, however, the Authenticity process will immediately register the offending action as unacceptable, and the ENFP will have to figure out how to deal with the offense. At this point, they may become uncharacteristically impassioned, outraged, and aggressive.

This is why it is incredibly important to know one's core values and revise them frequently. It's important for an Authenticity user to not simply default to whatever feels good in the moment, or get locked into values formed at a less sophisticated age. When one's core values are set in youth and not reviewed, a person can show up as self-absorbed, indulgent, and fixated on their own experience. A truly healthy Authenticity function will draft a set of values that are both meaningful and adaptable. Just like people change and grow, one's core values should change and grow with them. As an ENFP gets to know themselves better over time, their core values will be a natural emergent of greater self-knowledge.

Exercise

Core values are guiding principles. In all situations, core values determine right or wrong and let you know if you're on the right path. Take a sheet of paper and write down all behaviors you believe are either right or wrong, regardless of the situation. Give yourself plenty of time to do this exercise: hours, days, even weeks. Feel free to revisit this list on a regular basis and refine it as you learn more about yourself.

Reflection

My top five core values are … because…:

1. _____

_____

_____

2. _____

_____

_____

3. _____

_____

_____

4. _____

_____

_____

5. _____

_____

_____

Five core values that I have reevaluated and adapted over the years are:

_____

_____

_____

_____

_____

Inner Alignment and Conviction

Everyone has experienced inner conflict, but the Copilot Authenticity function knows that being of two minds is just the tip of the iceberg. Focused on being true to themselves, ENFPs know there isn't just one self; rather, there's a legion of voices inside, all vying for attention. It's difficult to know what to do when listening intently to all those voices, each with their own agenda.

The task of Authenticity is to listen closely to what each part of this inner council is saying and prioritize based on what's true, what's right, and what will get needs or desires met.

If the burden of Authenticity is to listen to one's inner council, the responsibility of Authenticity is to lead those voices into alignment. Or, if they can't be in full chorus, Authenticity must determine which parts should have the stage at any given time.

The easiest decisions are ones that present no inner conflict, which could be said to align with convictions. The moments when all inner voices are in full agreement are beautiful moments and produce such momentum that the ENFP can feel unstoppable. It's difficult for Authenticity users to feel motivated when they feel uncertain, but once certainty is on the table, the ENFP becomes an unstoppable force capable of extraordinary feats.

Managing the inner council of voices and ideas is a skill that must be built, similar to managing groups of people. It's imperative for an ENFP to learn to prioritize their needs and desires based on core values and a code of ethics, not simply what feels good in the moment.

Self-confidence comes from seeking out dissenting voices and sitting with them, asking difficult questions, and considering what the answers mean for the ENFP's identity. If some of those voices are unhealthy and have ill intent, it becomes the ENFP's responsibility to heal that part of themselves, or even allow the toxic parts of themselves to die. It's a painful process that can feel like literal death to Authenticity users, but it is a crucial aspect of self-management and self-leadership.

Exercise

Think of a decision you've been ruminating on, maybe even putting off. Listen for any internal conflict. Imagine yourself in a council room where each voice comes up with a compelling argument. Allow them plenty of time to get through their concerns, considerations, and valid points. After each voice has stated their case, pull out your list of core values. Ask yourself which arguments are most in alignment with your core values, and why some of the voices may be counter to your values. If this is a values-based decision, why are some of the voices representing a solution that runs counter to your values? Are these less mature or unhealed parts of yourself? What would persuade them to stay consistent with your values? Alternatively, is it a decision that isn't values based? Is more information needed and are the voices stumped? Do you need to learn more and revisit the council later?

Reflection

What parts of yourself have you been avoiding listening to? Is it because they aren't saying things of value, or because what they have to say represents changes for which you may not feel ready?

_____

_____

_____

_____

Being kind to myself, I'm going to address these parts by:

_____

_____

_____

_____

Sympathy, Art, and Emotional Aikido

So much of the human experience is impossible to express using verbal language. Despite that, all of us have a need to understand each other and to be understood. When Authenticity is in its infancy, a person can be quite self-absorbed. Without sharpening the function, an ENFP will stay fixated on their own experience, unable to surface long enough to feel sympathy with others.

Over time and with development, Authenticity users recognize that other people's experiences are incredibly real to them, and so they offer their compassion and sympathy. People with Authenticity Copilots know that to understand a person's inner workings is to demonstrate their emotions and motivations back to them, showing that all people share these things in common and can also experience them on a deeply personal level. The most powerful medium through which humans accomplish this task is art and self-expression.

All throughout history, Authenticity users have found themselves unable to convey their own subjective emotional experience in conversation, which has driven them to become artists. They have become great at replicating an aspect of humanity in a single, time-bound piece of art: painting, song, poem, statue, choreographed dance, performance, or even their lifestyle. The foundation of art is the expression of universal human experiences, honoring that it will be personalized by the receiver.

Authenticity uses art to perform emotional aikido (page 73), transforming one person's energy into a shared experience. It's difficult to deny the poignancy of a shared experience, or to judge it harshly. Authenticity encourages onlookers to see themselves and the world with sympathy.

Exercise

Communicate an emotion to a friend without using words. You may use hand gestures, facial expressions, drawings, noises, and sounds. Ask your friend if they understood the emotion you were trying to share, and if they were able to replicate the emotion within themselves by linking it to their own experience.

How can I use my chosen art form to help me better understand others and myself?

_____

_____

_____

If you do not currently have an art form, what is a style of art you've always been attracted to? What is the lowest barrier of entry to begin engaging in this art form?

_____

_____

_____

Copilot Growth

Authenticity allows you as an ENFP to make decisions that resonate with your core identity and inner wisdom. When you evaluate decisions, Authenticity allows you to ask the question, "Does this feel right to me?" It's a feeling process concerned with identity, motivation, and consistency of core values.

Authenticity encourages you as an ENFP to ignore expedience and instead choose meaning and alignment. An ENFP will lose their direction and true path in life if they do the opposite.

Growing your Authenticity can be a challenge for you as an ENFP. It takes maturity to stop using outer-world results as a sign you're on the right track, and instead develop the ability to find the projects and tasks that are the right fit for your heart.

Every personality type tends to avoid growing their Copilot mental process. But here lies the power of understanding your personality. Don't see your Authenticity as a hindrance. Rather, embrace the slower pace of getting into this mental process because it gives you the opportunity to slow down and become present as an ENFP.

For you, it feels right to focus on your core values, true internal motivations, and desires. It should feel in alignment that to continue doing the right things, you'll need to look inward to discover what really matters to you on a core level. Start asking yourself, "What emotional impact do I want to create in my life?" Spend some focused introverted time thinking about how you personally feel.

- See if you can map your emotions to parts of your body.

- Each time you are faced with a decision, close your eyes and ask yourself what feels right in that moment.

- In the middle of a disagreement, pay attention to how you are feeling in the moment.

As an ENFP, you will bring the best version of yourself to the world when you get inside your heart and map your inner values and motivations. And, most importantly, you will become a strong leader of people as opposed to being at their mercy.

Reflection

The talents Authenticity can give me are:

_____

_____

_____

The ways I usually use Authenticity are:

_____

_____

_____

I'm going to develop Authenticity more by:

_____

_____

_____

List three ways you can start growing your Authenticity process today:

1. _____

2. _____

3. _____

The ENFP 10-Year-Old Is Effectiveness (Te)

When you use Effectiveness, you make decisions based on what works. The process is focused on structure, project management, and getting things done. It desires organization and systems that are self-managing, and can provide the motivation to work hard and see fruits for its labor.

The ENFP can use the Effectiveness function to set goals and build resources. Effectiveness can help them optimize their skills and talents, while inspiring others to work on bigger projects that the ENFP can't accomplish alone. It gives them leadership qualities and drive. However, as a 10-Year-Old function, Effectiveness can prioritize expedience at the expense of authentic expression.

As an extraverted function, Effectiveness allows the ENFP to access a judging process while avoiding their inner world. This can be okay at times, but if the ENFP gets used to relying on Effectiveness to support their perceptions, they can rationalize skipping development of their introverted judging Copilot, Authenticity. And that's when the trouble starts. For ENFPs, this usually manifests as letting other people's expectations define their value system.

Effectiveness is, in large part, about creating a shared system of values based on what gets things done. People who have Effectiveness as a strength are usually pretty good at it, and they use this function to accomplish big things. But you're an ENFP, meaning you're wired to be at your best when creating a value system based on your feelings, not when you're conforming to the world's expectations.

If your 10-Year-Old gets to have the final call without consulting the Copilot of Authenticity, it's going to see the world like a child would. Children aren't great at prioritizing their lives based on enterprise. If an ENFP doesn't know what's authentic to them and instead prioritizes based on what a larger network deems effective, they may allow their values and life direction to be determined by other people's agendas. Losing a grip on their identity, an ENFP may bury themselves in a flurry of activity to avoid self-reflecting on how distanced they are from their true selves.

However it shows up, the motive of Effectiveness as a 10-Year-Old is to protect the Driver's perceptions and, ultimately, the ENFP's self-worth.

The Driver/10-Year-Old Loop

There are three ways an ENFP experiences the loop, the echo chamber–like relationship between the Driver and 10-Year-Old functions. The way to get out of a loop is the same in all cases: focus on developing the Authenticity process.

Short-term loop. The ENFP will become forceful to protect themselves. This often manifests as actual aggression—punching walls, yelling at others, even becoming physically or verbally violent. In this way, the ENFP communicates that they're unstable, even crazy, and forces others to back down. By focusing on intimidation, the ENFP has no room for introspection or other people's experiences.

Long-term loop. This strategy is perpetual busyness. Preoccupied with a whirlwind of tasks and results, the ENFP can't slow down enough to ask if what they're working on is what they really want. In this case, all attention is focused on the outside world. If in a position of authority, the ENFP may become a micromanager, certain that others are being lazy, incompetent, and wasteful. Nitpicking the activities of others leaves no time to self-assess.

Habitual loop. To be seen as competent, the ENFP will align their values and identity with whatever society expects. Over time, they completely lose track of who they are as they seek to receive feedback that they're doing the right thing, staying on the right track, and impressing everyone. Unable to trust their self-evaluation, they base their self-respect on the opinions of others. This is the most difficult loop to interrupt, as most cultures celebrate the results that come with Effectiveness and often criticize the "wastefulness" of Authenticity. The ENFP loses who are they are in exchange for approval.

Reflection

The ways Exploration and Effectiveness can loop in an ENFP are:

_____

_____

_____

The ways I find myself looping are (include behaviors and situations):

_____

_____

_____

I'm going to work on breaking my loop(s) by:

_____

_____

_____

How to Best Use Effectiveness

If you find yourself compromising your values and identity in favor of productivity or praise, this is a bad use of the Effectiveness function. Tap into Authenticity and ask yourself, "Who have I become? Who am I becoming? Is this the person I truly want to be?"

That said, in times that you feel inspired to lead yourself and others toward healthy goals in life or to streamline and problem-solve challenges, Effectiveness can help guide you. It can help you set and accomplish goals. Just don't get fooled into losing yourself.

You can also engage your 10-Year-Old in times of play, love, and intimacy. People of your type often enjoy team sports, entrepreneurship, emceeing, organizing fun events, and hosting parties. You can also use this process to get big projects done and organize social causes.

The ENFP 3-Year-Old Is Memory (Si)

Memory creates a sense of continuity. It references past experiences and knowledge to establish standards, traditions, and customs. It's gradual, patient, accepting, and consistent. It understands how we are shaped by our past. As a 3-Year-Old process, Memory is a part of the ENFP that whispers from the shadows. Normally indifferent to traditions, benchmarks, and what's come before, suddenly the ENFP will seek comfort in the familiar, or feel trapped by past decisions.

There are three ways an ENFP experiences the grip, those moments when your Driver process is stressed out, needs a break, and the 3-Year-Old function takes over the wheel of the car.

Short-term grip. This occurs when the ENFP truly feels like a child. They start to feel anxious and uncertain when they don't know the rules or whether they're doing something wrong. For example, what if they make a mistake when filling out a government or bank form that requires a lot of minute attention? If asked to follow dietary restrictions that require heightened discipline, where do they start? Who would even know this information? What if they make it worse somehow? The result is avoidance and hoping the answer will magically appear or, alternatively, the problem will somehow go away.

Long-term grip. The ENFP will adopt a sense of fatalism, the idea that the Fates have cursed them into a bad situation that will last forever. It is marked by emotions like pessimism, hopelessness, and depression. The ENFP no longer experiences the joy of life, and may be cynical that others seem to be getting away with not having followed the rules and face no consequences. It can be focused on health, career, family, or relationships. Memory is quirky and attaches to random things, so whatever the ENFP has decided is fated will be unique to them.

Habitual grip. The strategy is attachment to a limiting belief, which is a bastardized version of Memory's superpower, acceptance. Unlike fatalism, this type of grip is rarely emotional. It simply roots into the ENFP and becomes the catch-all excuse for why they can't build the life they want. Whatever it is—a codependent relationship, body issues, a paradigm or belief structure—it is unlikely to be truly permanent, but the ENFP is convinced that it will be. This grip isn't as intense as the previous two styles of grip experiences, and it is much easier for the ENFP to become attached to it. Ultimately, it becomes the excuse to perpetually seek comfort, be in fear, and live a retracted life.

How to Best Use Memory

The best way to use Memory as a 3-Year-Old is to exercise it regularly, which will help prevent the grip from occurring. In this case, reconnect with the part of you who has stayed the same throughout time. Watch a movie you've seen a hundred times. Listen to music you grew up with. Share memories with family members about how things used to be and how much they've changed.

Remember, Memory is an introverted process, so make sure you have plenty of uninterrupted ruminating time. Thirty minutes should be long enough, but feel free to take as long as needed to de-stress. If you're still not feeling settled, make a diary entry or vlog about who you were and who you've become.

The goal is to give yourself a break from feeling the need to have an immediate creative solution. Make sure you're diving deeply into the positive tethers to your past. Once your Driver has had enough of a break, you can usually come back to the situation with a whole new outlook. Then, take small, manageable steps to feel back in control.

Using Memory in this way can also provide a source of aspiration, the voice that whispers in the back of your mind. Memory as an aspiration can encourage ENFPs to track the progress of their lives and have realistic expectations for change. People of your type can be true change agents, but they have to play nice with the institutions that exist and remember what has been tried and what has come before.

Reflection

The ways Memory can grip an ENFP are:

_____

_____

_____

The ways I find myself being in the Grip are (include behaviors and situations):

_____

_____

_____

I'm going to control the process by:

_____

_____

_____

My Memory 3-Year-Old inspires me/is my aspiration in these ways:

_____

_____

_____

CHAPTER 8

ESTP Personality Type

ESTPs are playful and magnetic. They can be powerfully attractive to others, which gives them the ability to be charismatic leaders.

ESTPs see the value in high-energy shared physical experiences. They recognize that people want to feel connected and enjoy an active life, so they often find themselves in roles where they are avatars for others like politicians, athletes, or performers.

If an ESTP feels too much societal pressure to conform, they may purposely behave in antisocial ways. Sometimes they can exhibit indulgent behavior to escape the pressure of the social expectations placed upon them.

If an ESTP can avoid feeling overwhelmed by social expectations, develop healthy ways to manage their image, and take full responsibility for their own actions, they can become powerful voices that represent the people they lead.

ESTP CAR MODEL OVERVIEW

DRIVER	COPILOT
Sensation (Se)	**Accuracy (Ti)**
• Simplifies problems and takes action • Realistic, but playful • Stays present in a situation	• Prunes out logical inconsistencies and incongruities • Practices integrity and radical honesty • Focus and skill mastery

3-YEAR-OLD	10-YEAR-OLD
Perspectives (Ni)	**Harmony (Fe)**
• Desires a life of meaning • Looks to the future but fears what it might hold • Becomes withdrawn, paranoid, or suspicious when feeling threatened	• Unsure whether, and to what extent, feedback of others is valid • Emotional outbursts or manipulation when stressed • Desires to positively contribute to social conditioning

The ESTP Driver Is Sensation (Se)

It's important to remember that the Sensation process is a talent, and that means not every ESTP will have the same skill level or use it in a healthy way. Developing Sensation as a healthy process is crucial to becoming an amazing ESTP. Sensation, when developed and sharpened, allows you to simplify problems and take action; be present, realistic, and playful; and push your limits.

Simplify Problems

Healthy Sensation users don't have a problem with overanalyzing; instead, they reduce situations down to their fundamentals and address them head-on. They take action immediately, happy to have something on which to expend their energy. In this way, Sensation Drivers handle problems quickly without letting them stack up. While there are complexities in life that must be addressed as such, ESTPs know that much of life is a matter of simply showing up and carving a direct path. They enjoy a sense of responsibility and getting things done, as opposed to being self-indulgent with their time. Taking action also helps an ESTP develop a wide variety of skills. They can become excellent early responders, whether professionally or voluntarily.

Exercise

Turn your cell phone's voicemail off for a week, only allowing yourself to take calls as they come. This lets you remove a "to-do" item from your list (calling people back) in favor of handling business in the moment.

Reflection

Name three tasks you've been avoiding that you could take care of immediately:

1. _____

2. _____

3. _____

Name a skill (like playing a musical instrument) you've been dreaming about starting but have been putting off:

_____

_____

Make a commitment with yourself to finish these tasks and then begin building that skill by this date: _____

Be Present and Playful

"Seeing is believing," as it's often said, and the Sensation process is always scanning for the facts that can be directly experienced. Tapping into the real-time feedback of the world means ESTPs notice most details about people, places, and things. For example, all people betray what's going on inside of themselves with "tells," unique actions that flag their internal condition. When the Sensation function is present in the moment, other people's tells are obvious, and much of relationship building is based on the ESTP's ability to read body language.

The ability to be present lets ESTPs look at life through a philosophical lens. They may feel that life is unpredictable and has to be met with flexibility. It doesn't really serve people to be too finicky about their experience. Though they might be able to anticipate the future, they still can't foresee it. Complaining is a waste of time. It's much better to roll with the punches and see if something better can be made of it. Because of this viewpoint, Sensation Drivers usually have a pretty good sense of humor and a strong playful spirit. Life is to be lived, not endlessly contemplated. An ESTP might say, "Don't let the future rob you of your present."

Exercise

Find a partner. Have a conversation with them where you get to talk but they can only use nonverbal cues. Find out how far into the conversation you can get and still be accurate about what they're trying to communicate to you.

Reflection

I am going to live more in the present moment by:

_____

_____

_____

_____

Push the Limit

Sensation users love to push imposed physical limitations. Their ability to improvise quickly as well as their heightened awareness helps them become excellent athletes, if that's where they choose to focus their attention. Tools become extensions of their body, from cars to musical instruments, and ESTPs can become the best in the world at using these tools, coupled with quick reflexes and the ability to think well under pressure. If the ESTP is more interested in science than athletics, they can use the Sensation function to push themselves cerebrally by becoming surgeons, chemists, and entrepreneurs. Developing this aspect of Sensation increases the ESTP's self-esteem and brings inspiration to others.

Exercise

You are probably already doing an activity that stretches you: participating in some type of sport, playing a musical instrument, or stretching yourself in your business. Add a new physical limitation to your hobby or craft, and/or use equipment in a new way. For example, practice trick shots with a basketball or when playing pool, learn to play a full song on your musical instrument with just one hand, etc. If you do not currently have a hobby or craft that is using this aspect of Sensation, begin one immediately. Pushing your body with exercise is the easiest and healthiest one to introduce.

Reflection

I am going to test my limits, push myself, and increase my self-esteem by:

_____

_____

_____

_____

Setting Up the Right Conditions

The enemy of Sensation is inactivity. If you're not using this process enough, you'll eventually run out of energy and may become depressed. Being chained to a desk, forced to do too much planning, or engaged in esoteric meaning-making causes the function to atrophy.

As your ESTP Driver, Sensation is your flow state, so set up your daily conditions to access this mental process often. For example, picking up new skills, talking with a variety of people, and having a daily exercise routine are all great ways to keep life exciting and interesting.

When Sensation is young, it can show up as impulsiveness, rebellion, and superficiality. Unsure where to direct its energy, the function can engage you in high-octane and dangerous activities, becoming addicted to the adrenaline rush. Tapped into the body's responses, addictions to food, alcohol, and other substances can take over. Sensation users can also become overly concerned with their appearance, unable to read other people's body language without fear of being judged.

ESTPs must get in touch with their integrity, becoming less reactive to outerworld feedback. Inside of themselves, they'll find character and depth.

UNDEVELOPED SENSATION (Se)	DEVELOPED SENSATION (Se)
Avoid:	Work Toward:
• Rebelliousness	• Responsibility to get things done
• Addictions, self-indulgence	• Being present and playful
• Superficiality	• Self-esteem

Reflection

The talents Sensation can give me are:

_____

_____

_____

The ways I usually use Sensation are:

_____

_____

_____

I'm going to develop Sensation more by:

_____

_____

_____

List three activities that put you into flow:

1. _____

2. _____

3. _____

The ESTP Copilot Is Accuracy (Ti)

Without an introverted judging process, the ESTP is not complete. Without developing a strong inner character, the ESTP will become overly reactive to feedback from the world. They may be too susceptible to pressure from peers or family members, simultaneously feeling a need to be rebellious and overly compliant.

An introverted judging process empowers the ESTP to find their own sense of integrity, remove beliefs that are limiting or illogical, and call out truths that are obvious to them but ignored by others.

It's important to remember that, like the Driver function, the Copilot process is a talent. But that doesn't mean every ESTP will have the same skill level or use it in a healthy way. Developing Accuracy as a healthy process is crucial to becoming an amazing ESTP.

It can be difficult to actively develop an introverted function as an Extravert. For an ESTP, working on Accuracy won't be as natural as working on Sensation, so discipline and a focus on the rich rewards Accuracy brings should be kept in mind.

Prune Out Logical Inconsistencies and Incongruities

People with a strong Accuracy process often have no problem slicing through emotionally difficult circumstances in order to see the situation as presented. Accuracy users have the ability to spot logical fallacies and biases. That said, it's far easier to see other people's biases than our own. The more an ESTP develops Accuracy, the more the function will enable an ESTP to spot their own biases and dissonance.

Accuracy is a subjective function. This means the Accuracy user asks, "What makes sense to *me*?" When the function is in its infancy, it can rationalize nearly anything. Over time, as the process develops and matures, Accuracy users begin spotting incongruities not only in what others are saying, but also in their own thinking. Like a programmer working through lines of code, an Accuracy user's first job is to clean up corrupt script within their own mind.

This can be challenging. Once a mental code is discovered to be faulty, it can seem like the mind is being ripped apart in an effort to dismantle the flawed idea. This may manifest as an existential crisis, and can be as emotionally impactful as the death of a loved one. But the more you build the skill of Accuracy, the more survivable the surgical removal of faulty code becomes. Eventually, the rewards of clean thinking are felt, and removing cognitive dissonance and bias becomes part of your identity as an ESTP.

Reflection

What if there were no right answers, only better questions? If you were able to craft your own ideas from scratch, what would they be? Do you fear losing your competency if you lose your thoughts? Can you ever truly lose who you are, or are you constantly changing, anyway?

At its best, Accuracy learns to say, "I don't know," without being disturbed by uncertainty. Reflect on the following questions:

What thought or belief have I not been looking at too carefully? If I looked at it critically, would it survive an honest analysis? Do I fear letting it go? What else would I have to look at critically if I let this one go?

_____

_____

_____

Being kind to myself, I'm going to address this belief by:

_____

_____

_____

Integrity and Radical Honesty

Well-developed Accuracy allows you to express truths no matter how hurtful they can be. While truth can hurt, it doesn't have to be unkind or cruel. In fact, Accuracy users intend to be kind when speaking harsh truths, and are usually appreciative when others do them the service of being honest. Accuracy users would much rather know the truth now than be deluded and taken off guard later.

Young Accuracy users can feel like they're always on the wrong side of the conversation. It's not uncommon for ESTPs to get the feedback that they're always saying the wrong thing or being offensive. The world has a push-pull relationship with the idea of truth, and ESTPs can sometimes find themselves grasping at how to say something.

As the function matures, however, Accuracy becomes less about forcing truth on others and develops a skill in sharing truths. Complete truths are almost always welcomed by others, and eventually ESTPs get better at giving context to their messages. ESTPs often master the art of comedy as a way to deliver these truths while breaking down resistances.

It's also important for ESTPs to develop radical honesty with themselves, ensuring that they stay true to their values. Sometimes that means being honest about what their values truly are, especially if they differ from conventional society's, as well as owning up to transgressions and mistakes. However, if an ESTP hasn't first been honest with themselves, then their views can instead be antisocial opinions, which are rarely welcome.

Exercise

Observe how often you lie to other people. According to a study done by the University of Massachusetts at Amherst, 60 percent of people tell an average of two to three lies in a ten-minute conversation.

For example, when people ask how you're doing, do you answer honestly? Do you feign interest in conversations that are boring to you? Do you hide the truth to avoid hurt feelings? While you watch yourself lie in conversation, don't judge or justify yourself by saying, "I have to lie in this situation because...." Just observe.

Now that you've watched the different ways you tend to lie, turn this inward. Watch how often you lie to yourself. Keep a finger on the pulse of your cognitive dissonance.

Reflection

How could I be more honest with others and myself? Am I willing to speak the truth even if it's hurtful? Do others find me condescending when I do this? How can I learn to speak complete truths?

_____

_____

_____

_____

_____

Focus and Mastery

Accuracy offers an amazing ability to focus, which is represented in a huge variety of ways. It's seen in the best athletes, philosophers, and mechanics.

A basketball player using Accuracy can spend endless hours practicing 3-point shots, ever so slightly altering the angle of their wrist until they can shoot a perfect 3-point shot each time. This same talent starts with noticing incongruities of thoughts as a child. The same process takes place in the mind and on the court: When something doesn't line up, keep working until it lines up perfectly. Philosophers and scientists often use Accuracy when breaking down ideas and beliefs.

It's important to discipline the mind to focus on mastering practical skills, not simply pleasurable activities. It's easy to focus on things that are fun and engaging, but ESTPs make a true difference when they can use their skill to focus on mundane or "boring" activities. Using focus and skill mastery to improve yourself and fulfill duties creates a rewarding life.

Exercise

When we focus our eyes, we zero in on a single object and allow everything else to become fuzzy around it. That object becomes very clear and sharp, and if we focus long enough, we'll begin to see the object in detail. All of the object's parts become obvious.

Do this with your mind. Work on a problem while allowing everything outside the problem to become fuzzy. This could anything from trying to master a musical refrain to working out a complex mathematical problem. As you spend more time focusing your attention, you will start to see its parts, such as the notes in the refrain or the formulas of the math problem.

Reflection

How can I discipline my mind to be 5 percent more focused today?

_____

_____

_____

_____

Copilot Growth

Accuracy allows you as an ESTP to make self-directed decisions. It encourages you to ignore social pressure and status, focusing instead on radical honesty and what makes logical sense. However, you will lose your sense of integrity and ability to be persuasive if you conflate the talent of out-arguing others with critical thinking.

Growing your Accuracy can be a challenge for you as an ESTP. It takes maturity to stop using other people's feedback as a sign you're on the right track, and instead develop the ability to spot inconsistencies and be willing to point them out when appropriate.

Every personality type tends to avoid growing their Copilot mental process. But here lies the power of understanding your personality. Don't see your Accuracy as a hindrance. Rather, embrace the slower pace of getting into this mental process because it gives you the opportunity to build impressive skills.

It makes sense to focus on your inner truth. It's smart to focus on your true internal logic. Similarly, it should make sense that the more rigor you use to vet information and conclusions—and the more polarizing you are willing to be—the more impact your ideas will have.

To help develop your Accuracy Copilot, start asking yourself, "What *actually* makes sense in this situation?" Spend focused, introverted time ruminating about what strikes you as true, both for yourself and for others.

Each time you are faced with a decision, close your eyes and ask yourself what is most logical, not what will make others happy. Practice finding holes in your own logic, and in the middle of disagreements, pay attention to your own bullshit meter. Pay attention to the validity of your own thoughts before calling bullshit on the ideas of others. Do what it takes to access your inner truth while ruthlessly rooting out internal inconsistencies in your own logic. Start seeing your own cognitive dissonance as being completely unacceptable. In doing this, you will become a leader of social conditioning as opposed to being at its mercy.

Reflection

The talents Accuracy can give me are:

_____

_____

_____

The ways I usually use Accuracy are:

_____

_____

_____

I'm going to develop Accuracy more by:

_____

_____

_____

List three ways you can start growing your Accuracy process today:

1. _____

2. _____

3. _____

The ESTP 10-Year-Old Is Harmony (Fe)

The Harmony function encourages compassion, helps us take care of each other, and allows us to make strong emotional connections. It provides an instinctive understanding of people's needs and how to get them met. Harmony users tap into social dynamics to make sure personal boundaries are honored, which keeps morale high.

ESTPs can use the Harmony function to commit to their relationships. Harmony can help an ESTP develop warmth and kindness. It can also help them persuade others through humor and other positive shared emotions. Additionally, Harmony helps ESTPs remember their responsibility to a bigger community and encourages them to contribute positively.

As an extraverted function, Harmony allows the ESTP to access a judging process while avoiding their inner world. This can be okay at times, but if the ESTP gets used to relying on Harmony to support their perceptions, they can rationalize skipping development of their introverted judging Copilot, Accuracy. And that's when the trouble starts. For ESTPs, this usually manifests as seeking approval from other people to avoid troubling inner truths.

Harmony is, in a large part, about checking in with other people. Harmony users consult with how others are feeling to vet their own opinions. People who have Harmony as a strength are usually pretty good at it, and they use this function to influence society and meet the needs of others. But you're an ESTP, meaning you're wired to be at your best when consulting your personal logic without the disruption of other people's influence.

If your 10-Year-Old gets to have the final call without consulting the Copilot, it's going to see the world like a child would. Children aren't great at judging the validity of other's opinions, and without the radically honest analysis of the situation provided by Accuracy, the ESTP may hand over too much power to their relationships or other people's opinions.

The 10-Year-Old Harmony can manifest by letting other people set the tone of how the ESTP should live their life or how they should feel about themselves. Frustrated by the feeling of disempowerment, they may use emotions to manipulate or to bully people, and relationships can become codependent. However it shows up, its motive is to protect the perceptions of Sensation and, ultimately, the ESTP's very identity.

The Driver/10-Year-Old Loop

There are three ways an ESTP experiences the loop, the echo chamber–like relationship between the Driver and 10-Year-Old functions. The way to get out of a loop is the same in all cases: focus on developing the Accuracy function.

Short-term loop. This may last for a few moments up to a few days. Feeling the discomfort of their own contradictory thoughts and wanting to silence both the inner voice and whatever triggered it, the ESTP will use emotion defensively. This can show up many ways, but it usually looks like either anger or a joking dismissiveness toward others. Plugging into a shared emotional experience renders introspective, analytic thinking impossible for the ESTP. Once the cognitive dissonance retreats back into a deeper place and can be ignored, the ESTP will be back in good humor.

Long-term loop. The second style of looping is a more long-term strategy. In order to manage troubling thoughts, the ESTP will rely too heavily on intimate relationships to set the tone for their lives. They will outsource their important beliefs and values to others, fearing to follow their own logic to its conclusion. They will believe in partial truths that sound logical on the surface and pursue answers to questions only as long as those answers remain nonthreatening to their lifestyle and the people in their lives. This loop is marked by codependent relationships.

Habitual loop. The third style of looping is a mindset and lifestyle made up of compulsive praise seeking. Instead of determining their own sense of worth using subjective, radically honest criteria, the ESTP compulsively seeks praise to bolster their self-esteem. Sometimes there is enough self-awareness to realize that out-and-out bragging is considered distasteful, but regardless, the ESTP will compulsively put themselves at the center of attention. They may single out another person or group of people to make fun of, pick fights to showcase their own intelligence, or argue everything to exhibit intellectual dominance. The ESTP will categorize people into "smart" and "stupid," and seek approval from those deemed smart. The worse the loop, the more people are dehumanized, only seen as valuable if they offer positive feedback. Any puncturing of the ESTP's self-image is met with anger and, in the worst cases, banishment.

Reflection

The ways Sensation and Harmony can loop in an ESTP are:

_____

_____

_____

The ways I find myself looping are (include behaviors and situations):

_____

_____

_____

I'm going to work on breaking my loop(s) by:

_____

_____

_____

How to Best Use Harmony

If you find yourself compromising your truth in favor of unhealthy relationships or feedback, this is a bad use of the Harmony function. Tap into Accuracy and ask yourself, "What kind of life do I have if it's built on a lie?"

That said, if you want to share yourself fully with another person, connecting with them based on who you truly are and what you truly believe, Harmony can help guide you. It can help you deliver hard truths with compassion. Just don't let it fool you into becoming dishonest.

You can also engage your 10-Year-Old in times of play, love, and intimacy. People of your type love connecting with friends, being intimate, and helping everyone have a good time. You can also use Harmony to feel motivated by your compassion, reach out to those less fortunate, and be generous for a social cause.

The ESTP 3-Year-Old Is Perspectives (Ni)

As a 3-Year-Old process, Perspectives for the ESTP is the part of them that whispers from the shadows. Normally indifferent to future implications, deeper meaning, and esoteric topics, suddenly the ESTP will obsess about a dark future, or become paranoid about forces out to get them.

There are three ways an ESTP experiences the grip, the moments when the Driver process is stressed out, needs a break, and gives the 3-Year-Old function control of the car. This is most likely to happen when the ESTP behaves in an overly impulsive or cavalier way, creating problems for themselves that immediate action can't solve.

Short-term grip. Though the ESTP is usually active, social, and optimistic, the 3-Year-Old will cause them to withdraw and show up feeling pessimistic, irritable, and joyless. The ESTP will feel a need to be alone to ruminate over their thoughts, but to their disappointment, solutions aren't found. This leads to a grumpy isolation, where the ESTP stews in their own misery.

Long-term grip. This is marked by paranoia and suspicion. Though less debilitating than the first grip experience, it can be drawn out to become a general attitude about life. The ESTP may project ill intent onto other people, believing that a person or group or people is out to get them or their kind. There also may be some paranoia about impersonal threats, like germs, which may result in excessive hand washing or showering. This grip experience robs the ESTP of their usually generous attitude.

Habitual grip. This is particularly insidious, and can claim an ESTP for much of their lives. The 3-Year-Old Perspectives function attempts to make meaning from the confusing, unpleasant, and sometimes traumatic experiences the ESTP has faced. Unsure how to proceed, the Perspectives function may cause the ESTP to apply cosmic or universal meaning to a situation without any merit. For example, in response to a trauma: "I deserve this," or, "I know too much." The 3-Year-Old may aim to spiritually balance the scales, leading the ESTP to believe a bad situation is somehow divine justice or in alignment with the will of God. Since this grip is less intense but more persistent, if confronted, the ESTP may claim to be happy. Ultimately, this grip is the result of indecision and fearing the dire consequences of doing wrong.

How to Best Use Perspectives

The best way to use Perspectives as a 3-Year-Old is to exercise it regularly, which will help prevent the grip from occurring. In this case, get inside a safer space inside your mind. Do a simple meditation where you focus on your breathing. Do some yoga. Pray to whichever deity you worship. Talk to yourself as you would a friend you're coaching through a tough time. If you're having trouble focusing on your mind, take a shower while you're meditating or praying.

Remember, Perspectives is an introverted process, so make sure you have plenty of uninterrupted alone time. Thirty minutes should be long enough, but feel free to take as long as needed to de-stress. If you're still not feeling settled, take a nap or set aside an entire day to just walk and ruminate.

The goal is to give yourself a break from feeling as if you have to do something. Make sure you're getting as far into your mind as possible. Once your Driver has taken enough of a break, you can usually come back to the situation with a whole new outlook. Then, take small, manageable steps to feel back in control.

Using Perspectives in this way can also provide a source of aspiration, the voice that whispers in the back of your mind. Perspectives as an aspiration can encourage ESTPs to plunge their own hidden depths and live a life of meaning. People of your type are inspirations as athletes, celebrities, entrepreneurs, and early responders, but they have to reach out for it and believe in themselves.

Reflection

The ways Perspectives can grip an ESTP are:

1. _____

2. _____

3. _____

The ways I find myself being in the grip are (include behaviors and situations):

_____

_____

_____

I'm going to control the process by:

_____

_____

_____

My Perspectives 3-Year-Old inspires me/is my aspiration in these ways:

_____

_____

_____

CHAPTER 9

ESFP Personality Type

ESFPs are almost always likable people. They can be energetic, fun, good natured, open, and expressive. They have the ability to master their bodies and use them as an art form. They showcase deep emotional truths through physical engagement and activity.

Because the need for expression lives deep in the heart of the ESFP, they are one of the most magnetic, energetic, and physically expressive types. ESFPs have an incredible talent for reading body language and understanding others by observing their nonverbal cues. They often enjoy high-octane activities that make them feel fully alive. On the other hand, they can become bored when forced to be quiet and still in order to produce outer-world results.

If the ESFP doesn't slow down enough to get in touch with their most important core values, they can end up losing their sense of identity to an ever-growing world of outer stimulation. Over time, if the ESFP spends too much time in motion, they may become resentful or detached and forget who they truly are.

The best ESFPs maintain a healthy balance between living their core values and expressing their identity in a dynamic and energetic fashion.

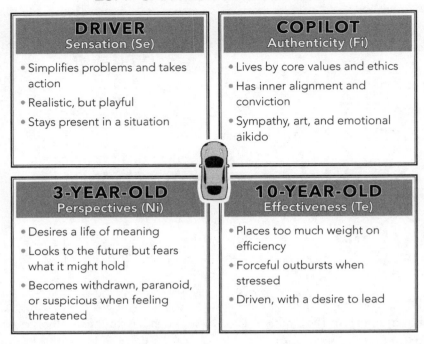

DRIVER
Sensation (Se)

- Simplifies problems and takes action
- Realistic, but playful
- Stays present in a situation

COPILOT
Authenticity (Fi)

- Lives by core values and ethics
- Has inner alignment and conviction
- Sympathy, art, and emotional aikido

3-YEAR-OLD
Perspectives (Ni)

- Desires a life of meaning
- Looks to the future but fears what it might hold
- Becomes withdrawn, paranoid, or suspicious when feeling threatened

10-YEAR-OLD
Effectiveness (Te)

- Places too much weight on efficiency
- Forceful outbursts when stressed
- Driven, with a desire to lead

The ESFP Driver Is Sensation (Se)

It's important to remember that the Sensation process is a talent, and that means not every ESFP will have the same skill level or use it in a healthy way. Developing Sensation as a healthy process is crucial to becoming an amazing ESFP. Sensation, when developed and sharpened, allows you to simplify problems and take action; be present, realistic, and playful; and push your limits.

Simplify Problems

Healthy Sensation users don't have a problem with overanalyzing; instead, they reduce situations down to their fundamentals and address them head-on. They take action immediately, happy to have something on which to expend their energy. In this way, Sensation Drivers handle problems quickly without letting them stack up. While there are complexities in life that must be addressed as such, ESFPs know that much of life is a matter of simply showing up and carving a direct path. They enjoy a sense of responsibility and getting things done, as opposed to being self-indulgent with their time. Taking action also helps an ESFP develop a wide variety of skills. They can become excellent early responders, whether professionally or voluntarily.

Exercise

Turn your cell phone's voicemail off for a week, only allowing yourself to take calls as they come. This lets you remove a "to-do" item from your list (calling people back) in favor of handling business in the moment.

Reflection

Name three tasks you've been avoiding that you could take care of immediately:

_____

_____

_____

Name a skill (like playing a musical instrument) you've been dreaming about starting but have been putting off:

_____

Make a commitment with yourself to finish these tasks and then begin building that skill by this date: _____

Be Present and Playful

"Seeing is believing," as it's often said, and the Sensation process is always scanning for the facts that can be directly experienced. Tapping into the real-time feedback of the world means ESFPs notice most details about people, places, and things. For example, all people betray what's going on inside of themselves with "tells," unique actions that flag their internal condition. When the Sensation function is present in the moment, other people's tells are obvious, and much of relationship building is based on the ESFP's ability to read body language.

The ability to be present lets ESFPs look at life through a philosophical lens. They may feel that life is unpredictable and has to be met with flexibility. It doesn't really serve people to be too finicky about their experience. Though they might be able to anticipate the future, they still can't foresee it. Complaining is a waste of time. It's much better to roll with the punches and see if something better can be made of it. Because of this viewpoint, Sensation Drivers usually have a pretty good sense of humor and a strong playful spirit. Life is to be lived, not endlessly contemplated. An ESFP might say, "Don't let the future rob you of your present."

Exercise

Find a partner. Have a conversation with them where you get to talk but they can only use nonverbal cues. Find out how far into the conversation you can get and still be accurate about what they're trying to communicate to you.

Reflection

I am going to live more in the present moment by:

_____

_____

_____

Push the Limit

Sensation loves to push imposed physical limitations. Their ability to improvise quickly as well as their heightened awareness helps them become excellent athletes, if that's where they choose to focus their attention. Tools become extensions of their body, from cars to musical instruments, and ESFPs can become the best in the world at using these tools, coupled with quick reflexes and the ability to think well under pressure. If the ESFP is more interested in science than athletics, they can use the Sensation function to push themselves cerebrally by becoming surgeons, chemists, and entrepreneurs. Developing this aspect of Sensation increases the ESFP's self-esteem and brings inspiration to others.

Exercise

You are probably already doing an activity that stretches you: participating in some type of sport, playing a musical instrument, or stretching yourself in your business. Add a new physical limitation to your hobby or craft, and/ or use equipment in a new way. For example, practice trick shots with a basketball or when playing pool, learn to play a full song on your musical instrument with just one hand, etc. If you do not currently have a hobby or craft that is using this aspect of Sensation, begin one immediately. Pushing your body with exercise is the easiest and healthiest one to introduce.

Reflection

I am going to test my limits, push myself, and increase my self-esteem by:

_____

_____

_____

Setting Up the Right Conditions

The enemy of Sensation is inactivity. If you're not using this process enough, you'll eventually run out of energy and may become depressed. Being chained to a desk, forced to do too much planning or esoteric meaning-making causes the function to atrophy.

As your ESFP Driver, Sensation is your Flow state, so set up your daily conditions to access this mental process often. For example, picking up new skills, talking with a variety of people, and having a daily exercise routine are all great ways to keep life exciting and interesting.

When Sensation is young, it can show up as impulsiveness, rebellion, and superficiality. Unsure where to direct its energy, the function can engage you in high-octane and dangerous activities, becoming addicted to the adrenaline rush. Tapped into the body's responses, addictions to food, alcohol, and other substances can take over. Sensation users can also become overly concerned with their appearance, unable to read other people's body language without fear of being judged.

ESFPs must get in touch with their identity, becoming less reactive to outerworld feedback. Inside of themselves, they'll find character, depth, and integrity.

UNDEVELOPED SENSATION (Se)	DEVELOPED SENSATION (Se)
Avoid: • Rebelliousness • Addictions, self-indulgence • Superficiality	Work Toward: • Responsibility to get things done • Being present and playful • Self-esteem

Reflection

The talents Sensation can give me are:

_____

_____

_____

The ways I usually use Sensation are:

_____

_____

_____

I'm going to develop Sensation more by:

_____

_____

_____

List three activities that put you into flow:

1. _____

2. _____

3. _____

The ESFP Copilot Is Authenticity (Fi)

Without an introverted judging process, the ESFP is not complete. Without developing a strong inner character, the ESFP will become overly reactive to feedback from the world. They may feel like they're missing out or moving too slow to make the impact they wish to make. By trying to do too much, they end up accomplishing little.

An introverted judging process empowers the ESFP to find their own sense of identity, slow down enough to listen to their deepest motivations, and get a sense of what's true for them.

It's important to remember that, like the Driver function, the Copilot process is a talent. But that doesn't mean every ESFP will have the same skill level or use it in a healthy way. Developing Authenticity as a healthy process is crucial to becoming an amazing ESFP.

It can be difficult to actively develop an introverted function as an Extravert. For an ESFP, working on Authenticity won't be as natural as working on Sensation, so discipline and attention on the rich rewards Authenticity brings will be key.

Core Values and Ethics

Being aware of one's emotional responses at all times creates an ethical complication. A person may feel one way in one situation but completely different in a seemingly identical situation. They must learn to judge the context of their reactions: Are their responses fully subjective, or are they based on certain principles that can be used to guide future behaviors?

What is a truly ethical action? When one feels the full emotional force of all behaviors, they ask this question frequently to create a personal list of what's ethical and what isn't. Since the majority of behaviors fall on a spectrum, ESFPs are pretty laid back about most actions people take. A person may be insensitive or obtuse, but unless they offend one of the ESFP's core values or true principles, the behavior is likely to be forgotten or even go unnoticed.

Once a core value has been upset, however, the Authenticity process will immediately register the offending action as unacceptable, and the ESFP will have to figure out how to deal with the offense. At this point, they may become uncharacteristically impassioned, outraged, and aggressive.

This is why it is incredibly important to know one's core values and revise them frequently. It's important for an Authenticity user to not simply default to whatever feels good in the moment, or get locked into values formed at a less sophisticated age. When one's core values are set in youth and not reviewed, a person can show up as self-absorbed, indulgent, and fixated on their own experience. A truly healthy Authenticity function will draft a set of values that are both meaningful and adaptable. Just like people change and grow, one's core values should change and grow with them. As an ESFP gets to know themselves better over time, their core values will be a natural emergent of greater self-knowledge.

Exercise

Core values are guiding principles. In all situations, core values determine right or wrong and let you know if you're on the right path. Take a sheet of paper and write down all behaviors you believe are either right or wrong, regardless of the situation. Give yourself plenty of time to do this exercise: hours, days, even weeks. Feel free to revisit this list on a regular basis and refine it as you learn more about yourself.

Reflection

My top five core values are ... because...:

1. _____

2. _____

3. _____

4. _____

5. _____

Five core values that I have reevaluated and adapted over the years are:

1. _____

2. _____

3. _____

4. _____

5. _____

Inner Alignment and Conviction

Everyone has experienced inner conflict, but the Copilot Authenticity function knows that being of two minds is just the tip of the iceberg. Focused on being true to themselves, ESFPs know there isn't just one self; rather, there's a legion of voices inside, all vying for attention. It's difficult to know what to do when listening intently to all those voices, each with their own agenda.

The task of Authenticity is to listen closely to what each part of their inner council is saying and prioritize based on what's true, what's right, and what will get needs or desires met.

If the burden of Authenticity is to listen to one's inner council, the responsibility of Authenticity is to lead those voices into alignment. Or, if they can't be in full chorus, Authenticity must determine which parts should have the stage at any given time.

The easiest decisions are ones that present no inner conflict, which could be said to align with convictions. The moments when all inner voices are in full agreement are beautiful moments and produce such momentum that the ESFP can feel unstoppable. It's difficult for Authenticity users to feel motivated when they feel uncertain, but once certainty is on the table, the ESFP becomes an unstoppable force capable of extraordinary feats.

Managing the inner council of voices and ideas is a skill that must be built, similar to managing groups of people. It's imperative for an ESFP to learn to prioritize their needs and desires based on core values and a code of ethics, not simply what feels good in the moment.

Self-confidence comes from seeking out dissenting voices and sitting with them, asking difficult questions, and considering what the answers mean for the ESFP's identity. If some of those voices are unhealthy and have ill intent, it becomes the ESFP's responsibility to heal that part of themselves, or even allow the toxic parts of themselves to die. It's a painful process that can feel like literal death to Authenticity users, but it is a crucial aspect of self-management and self-leadership.

Exercise

Think of a decision you've been ruminating on, maybe even putting off. Listen for any internal conflict. Imagine yourself in a council room where each voice comes up with a compelling argument. Allow them plenty of time to get through their concerns, considerations, and valid points. After each voice has stated their case, pull out your list of core values. Ask yourself which arguments are most in alignment with your core values, and why some of the voices may be counter to your values. If this is a values-based decision, why are some of the voices representing a solution that runs counter to your values? Are these less mature or unhealed parts of yourself? What would persuade them to stay consistent with your values? Alternatively, is it a decision that isn't values based? Is more information needed and are the voices stumped? Do you need to learn more and revisit the council later?

What parts of yourself have you been avoiding listening to? Is it because they aren't saying things of value, or because what they have to say represents changes for which you may not feel ready?

_____

_____

_____

_____

Being kind to myself, I'm going to address these parts by:

_____

_____

_____

_____

Sympathy, Art, and Emotional Aikido

So much of the human experience is impossible to express using verbal language. Despite that, all of us have a need to understand each other and to be understood. When Authenticity is in its infancy, a person can be quite self-absorbed. Without sharpening the function, an ESFP will stay fixated on their own experience, unable to surface long enough to feel sympathy with others.

Over time and with development, Authenticity users recognize that other people's experiences are incredibly real to them, and so they offer their compassion and sympathy. People with Authenticity Copilots know that to understand a person's inner workings is to demonstrate their emotions and motivations back to them, showing that all people share these things in common and can also experience them on a deeply personal level. The most powerful medium through which humans accomplish this task is art and self-expression.

Throughout history, Authenticity users have found themselves to be unable to convey their own subjective emotional experience in conversation, which has driven them to become artists. They have become great at replicating an aspect of humanity in a single, time-bound piece of art: painting, song, poem, statue, choreographed dance, performance, or even their lifestyle. The foundation of art is the expression of universal human experiences, honoring that it will be personalized by the receiver.

Authenticity uses art to perform emotional aikido (page 73), transforming one person's energy into a shared experience. It's difficult to deny the poignancy of a shared experience, or to judge it harshly. Authenticity encourages onlookers to see themselves and the world with sympathy.

Exercise

Communicate an emotion to a friend without using words. You may use hand gestures, facial expressions, drawings, noises, and sounds. Ask your friend if they understood the emotion you were trying to share, and if they were able to replicate the emotion within themselves by linking it to their own experience.

Reflection

How can I use my chosen art form to help me better understand others and myself?

_____

_____

_____

If you do not currently have an art form, what is a style of art you've always been attracted to? What is the lowest barrier of entry to begin engaging in this art form?

_____

_____

_____

Copilot Growth

Authenticity allows you as an ESFP to make decisions that resonate with your core identity and inner wisdom. When you evaluate decisions, Authenticity allows you to ask the question, "Does this feel right to me?" It's a feeling process concerned with identity, motivation, and consistency of core values.

Authenticity encourages you as an ESFP to ignore expedience and instead choose meaning and alignment. An ESFP will lose their direction and true path in life if they do the opposite.

Growing your Authenticity can be a challenge for you as an ESFP. It takes maturity to stop using outer-world results as a sign you're on the right track, and instead develop the ability to find the projects and tasks that are the right fit for your heart.

Every personality type tends to avoid growing their Copilot mental process. But here lies the power of understanding your personality. Don't see your Authenticity as a hindrance. Rather, embrace the slower pace of getting into this mental process because it gives you the opportunity to slow down and become present as an ESFP.

For you, it feels right to focus on your core values, true internal motivations, and desires. It should feel in alignment that to continue doing the right things, you'll need to look inward to discover what really matters to you on a core level. Start asking yourself, "What emotional impact do I want to create in my life?" Spend some focused introverted time thinking about how you personally feel. Do what it takes to access your inner wisdom.

- See if you can map your emotions to parts of your body.

- Each time you are faced with a decision, close your eyes and ask yourself what feels right in that moment.

- In the middle of a disagreement, pay attention to how you are feeling in the moment.

As an ESFP, you will bring the best version of yourself to the world when you get inside your heart and map your inner values and motivations. And, most importantly, you will become a strong leader of people as opposed to being at their mercy.

The talents Authenticity can give me are:

_____

_____

_____

The ways I usually use Authenticity are:

_____

_____

_____

I'm going to develop Authenticity more by:

_____

_____

_____

List three ways you can start growing your Authenticity process today:

1. _____

2. _____

3. _____

The ESFP 10-Year-Old Is Effectiveness (Te)

When you use Effectiveness, you make decisions based on what works. The process is focused on structure, project management, and getting things done. It desires organization and systems that are self-managing, and can provide the motivation to work hard and see fruits of its labor.

The ESFP can use the Effectiveness function to set goals and build resources. Effectiveness can help them optimize their skills and talents, while inspiring others to work on bigger projects that the ESFP can't accomplish alone. It gives them leadership qualities and drive. However, as a 10-Year-Old function, Effectiveness can prioritize expedience at the expense of authentic expression.

As an extraverted function, Effectiveness allows the ESFP to access a judging process while avoiding their inner world. This can be okay at times, but if the ESFP gets used to relying on Effectiveness to support their perceptions, they can rationalize skipping development of their introverted judging Copilot, Authenticity. And that's when the trouble starts. For ESFPs, this usually manifests as letting other people's expectations define their value system.

Effectiveness is, in large part, about creating a shared system of values based on what gets things done. People who have Effectiveness as a strength are usually pretty good at it, and they use this function to accomplish big things. But you're an ESFP, meaning you're wired to be at your best when creating a value system based on your feelings, not when you're conforming to the world's expectations.

If your 10-Year-Old gets to have the final call without consulting the Copilot of Authenticity, it's going to see the world like a child would. Children aren't great at prioritizing their lives based on enterprise. If an ESFP doesn't know what's authentic to them and instead prioritizes based on what a larger network deems effective, they may allow their values and life direction to be determined by other people's agendas. Losing a grip on their identity, an ESFP may bury themselves in a flurry of activity to avoid self-reflecting on how distanced they are from their true selves.

However it shows up, the motive of Effectiveness as a 10-Year-Old is to protect the Driver's perceptions and, ultimately, the ESFP's self-worth.

The Driver/10-Year-Old Loop

There are three ways an ESFP experiences the loop, the echo chamber–like relationship between the Driver and 10-Year-Old functions. The way to get out of a loop is the same in all cases: focus on developing the Authenticity process.

Short-term loop. The ESFP will become forceful to protect themselves. This often manifests as actual aggression—punching walls, yelling at others, even becoming physically or verbally violent. In this, way the ESFP communicates that they're unstable, even crazy, and forces others to back down. By focusing on intimidation, the ESFP has no room for introspection or other people's experiences.

Long-term loop. This strategy is perpetual busyness. Preoccupied with a whirlwind of tasks and results, the ESFP can't slow down enough to ask if what they're working on is what they really want. In this case, all attention is focused on the outside world. If in a position of authority, the ESFP may become a micromanager, certain that others are being lazy, incompetent, and wasteful. Nitpicking the activities of others leaves no time to self-assess.

Habitual loop. To be seen as competent, the ESFP will align their values and identity with whatever society expects. Over time, they completely lose track of who they are as they seek to receive feedback that they're doing the right thing, staying on the right track, and impressing everyone. Unable to trust their self-evaluation, they base their self-respect on the opinions of others. This is the most difficult loop to interrupt, as most cultures celebrate the results that come with Effectiveness and often criticize the "wastefulness" of Authenticity. The ESFP loses who are they are in exchange for approval.

Reflection

The ways Sensation and Effectiveness can loop in an ESFP are:

_____

_____

_____

The ways I find myself looping are (include behaviors and situations):

_____

_____

_____

I'm going to work on breaking my loop(s) by:

_____

_____

_____

————

How to Best Use Effectiveness

If you find yourself compromising your values and identity in favor of productivity or praise, this is a bad use of the Effectiveness function. Tap into Authenticity and ask yourself, "Who have I become? Who am I becoming? Is this the person I truly want to be?"

That said, in times that you feel inspired to lead yourself and others toward healthy goals in life or to streamline and problem-solve challenges, Effectiveness can help guide you. It can help you set and accomplish goals. Just don't get fooled into losing yourself.

You can also engage your 10-Year-Old in times of play, love, and intimacy. People of your type often enjoy team sports, entrepreneurship, emceeing, organizing fun events, and hosting parties. You can also use this process to get big projects done and organize social causes.

The ESFP 3-Year-Old Is Perspectives (Ni)

As a 3-Year-Old process, Perspectives for the ESFP is the part of them that whispers from the shadows. Normally indifferent to future implications, deeper meaning, and esoteric topics, suddenly the ESFP will obsess about a dark future, or become paranoid about forces out to get them.

There are three ways an ESFP experiences the grip, the moments when the Driver process is stressed out, needs a break, and gives the 3-Year-Old function control of the car. This is most likely to happen when the ESFP behaves in an overly impulsive or cavalier way, creating problems for themselves that immediate action can't solve.

Short-term grip. Though the ESFP is usually active, social, and optimistic, the 3-Year-Old causes them to withdraw and show up feeling pessimistic, irritable, and joyless. The ESFP will feel a need to be alone to ruminate over their thoughts, but to their disappointment, solutions aren't found. This leads to a grumpy isolation, where the ESFP stews in their own misery.

Long-term grip. Marked by paranoia and suspicion, this is a less debilitating grip than the first experience, but it can be drawn out to become a general attitude about life. The ESFP may project ill intent onto other people, believing that a person or group or people is out to get them or their kind. There also may be some paranoia about impersonal threats, like germs, which may result in excessive hand washing or showering. This grip experience robs the ESFP of their usually generous attitude.

Habitual grip. This is particularly insidious, and can claim an ESFP for much of their lives. The 3-Year-Old Perspectives function attempts to make meaning from the confusing, unpleasant, and sometimes traumatic experiences the ESFP has faced. Unsure how to proceed, the Perspectives function may cause the ESFP to apply cosmic or universal meaning to a situation without any merit. For example, in response to a trauma: "I deserve this," or, "I know too much." The 3-Year-Old may aim to spiritually balance the scales, leading the ESFP to believe a bad situation is somehow divine justice or in alignment with the will of God. Since this grip is less intense but more persistent, if confronted, the ESFP may claim to be happy. Ultimately, this grip is the result of indecision and fearing the dire consequences of doing wrong.

How to Best Use Perspectives

The best way to use Perspectives as a 3-Year-Old is to exercise it regularly, which will help prevent the grip from occurring. In this case, get inside a safer space inside your mind. Do a simple meditation where you focus on your breathing. Do some yoga. Pray to whichever deity you worship. Talk to yourself as you would a friend you're coaching through a tough time. If you're having trouble focusing on your mind, take a shower while you're meditating or praying.

Remember, Perspectives is an introverted process, so make sure you have plenty of uninterrupted alone time. Thirty minutes should be long enough, but feel free to take as long as needed to de-stress. If you're still not feeling settled, take a nap or set aside an entire day to just walk and ruminate.

The goal is to give yourself a break from feeling as if you have to do something. Make sure you're getting as far into your mind as possible. Once your Driver has taken enough of a break, you can usually come back to the situation with a whole new outlook. Then, take small, manageable steps to feel back in control.

Using Perspectives in this way can also provide a source of aspiration, the voice that whispers in the back of your mind. Perspectives as an aspiration can encourage ESFPs to plunge their own hidden depths and live a life of meaning. People of your type are inspirations as athletes, celebrities, entrepreneurs, and early responders, but they have to reach out for it and believe in themselves.

Reflection

The ways Perspectives can grip an ESFP are:

_____

_____

_____

The ways I find myself being in the grip are (include behaviors and situations):

_____

_____

_____

I'm going to control the process by:

_____

_____

_____

My Perspectives 3-Year-Old inspires me/is my aspiration in these ways:

_____

_____

_____

CHAPTER 10

INTJ Personality Type

At the core of every INTJ is a desire for sustainability, an aim to make sure things work for the long term. There is an almost unstoppable desire to see how all operations can be improved.

When an INTJ observes an existing system—a business plan, a model, or even a concept—they instinctively seek to identify the failure or stress points. What elements are going to break down over time?

INTJs do not feel they have a lot of physical energy to burn or waste, but they possess almost endless amounts of mental energy: "If I can think about this long enough, if I can figure it out inside of my own mind, then when I implement it in the outside world, I can set it and forget it." There can be idealism around making a beautiful model that perpetually runs, and this can hamstring their ability to get things done. Their need to do "just a little more research" is both a strength and challenge to overcome.

The practice of future-pacing all possible outcomes is more than just utilitarian for INTJs; it's a pleasure. Many INTJs are futurists and are fascinated with emerging technologies, as well as the direction humankind is headed.

INTJs are more sensitive than others give them credit for, even when they attempt to marginalize this part of themselves. They are built somewhat like arthropods, with a hard exoskeleton over a gooey, nougat-like center.

Because of this, they can be self-protective and slow to build relationships, though they are fiercely loyal once they've invited someone into their heart.

INTJ CAR MODEL OVERVIEW

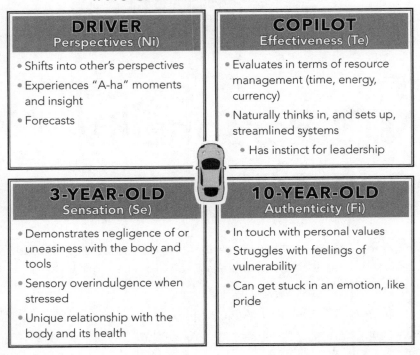

DRIVER
Perspectives (Ni)

- Shifts into other's perspectives
- Experiences "A-ha" moments and insight
- Forecasts

COPILOT
Effectiveness (Te)

- Evaluates in terms of resource management (time, energy, currency)
- Naturally thinks in, and sets up, streamlined systems
  - Has instinct for leadership

3-YEAR-OLD
Sensation (Se)

- Demonstrates negligence of or uneasiness with the body and tools
- Sensory overindulgence when stressed
- Unique relationship with the body and its health

10-YEAR-OLD
Authenticity (Fi)

- In touch with personal values
- Struggles with feelings of vulnerability
- Can get stuck in an emotion, like pride

The INTJ Driver Is Perspectives (Ni)

It's important to remember that the Driver process is a talent, but that doesn't mean every INTJ will have the same skill level or use it in a healthy way. Developing Perspectives as a healthy process is crucial to becoming an amazing INTJ.

The Perspectives function is the least-represented mental process in the population, and so often considered the most misunderstood. When it's fully developed, Perspectives helps the INTJ see the world from another person's point of view, receive deep insight, and see into the future.

Perspectives of Others

Since the Perspectives Driver watches its own mind form patterns, it builds the skill of detaching from its own perspective. In this detached space, it becomes easy to jump into the perspective of others.

Being able to see things from another person's worldview helps the INTJ explain why others do the things they do. Perspectives Drivers realize the simple truth that all actions, regardless of how confusing or distasteful they are to others, make sense to the person who committed them. It ceases to be a matter of explaining the behavior and becomes a matter of explaining how it made sense to the individual.

As an INTJ, getting inside other people's minds means recognizing not only how their experiences have shaped them, but the conclusions they've come to about how life works. This can include their beliefs, paradigms, and strategies of behavior.

Influencing people toward a better future, whether they have smaller or larger ambitions, means recognizing which mental patterns need to be improved upon and how to communicate in a way that impacts those patterns.

This doesn't mean that all INTJs must be consultants or thought leaders. However, there is a strong pull for INTJs to help organizations and structures carve a better path. Building the skills necessary for influence—writing, public speaking, creating models, and showing results-based evidence—also benefit INTJs internally. They can shine a light on those patterns within the INTJ that may be erroneous.

Exercise

Think of a heinous action or controversial person that you can't see yourself ever condoning. Instead of jumping to condemn the action, take a moment to really get inside the head of the person who performed the action. How did their action make complete sense to them at the time? Can you understand it so well you could defend it to another person? Don't focus on the act itself, but on the mind of the person who committed it.

Now that you are in a Perspectives frame of mind, fill out the following journal prompt. If you cannot think of anything immediately, feel free to ruminate on the question. It may guide you to some uncomfortable places, and that's okay. Developing your Perspectives process means getting outside your comfort zone. It also means applying this same generosity of spirit to yourself.

Reflection

What patterns are inside of me (beliefs, perspectives, strategies of behavior) that I've been avoiding looking at?

_____

_____

_____

Being kind to myself, I'm going to address these patterns by:

_____

_____

_____

Deep Insight

This type of pattern recognition is best done unconsciously, allowing the mind to wander wherever it needs to go. INTJs may find themselves getting their best ideas when they first wake up, or even while they dream. Attempting to direct these thoughts may actually interrupt the process. An insight in process can feel like a bloodhound on the scent, and it needs freedom to explore whatever is the next lead. The mind can offer up buried insights, if one is quiet enough to hear them.

Exercise

Create a gentle, quiet space for one full hour. Turn off all sensory stimulation, turn off lights, and deaden any noise. Ensure no one will interrupt you during this time. Consider your favorite quote. (For example, Carl Sagan said, "We are a way for the universe to know itself." Rumi said, "The wound is the place where the Light enters you.") Set a timer. When one hour is up, immediately write down where your mind took you.

Reflection

My most recent insight from one hour of quiet time is:

_____

_____

_____

———————————————

Future Perspectives

INTJs solve problems by shifting perspectives until the solution becomes clear. Running simulations becomes second nature, watching how each possible scenario plays out over time. Using their Driver process to do this, the INTJ will get into a flow state by future-pacing, and will clock many pleasurable hours considering the fate of relationships, business, politics, technology, and humanity itself.

This is a far healthier exercise than its bastard cousin, conspiracy theorizing. While some conspiracies are interesting thought exercises and may even have some foundation in truth, attempting to know the malevolent forces at work doesn't really help move the needle of humanity as much as it encourages paranoia. For INTJs to be the best version of themselves, asking what's possible for humanity is generally better than assuming humanity is doomed (and only the INTJ can see it).

Exercise

Personalize this skill by future-pacing. Theorize how an upcoming event or activity will pan out. Rehearse how you expect to behave in the situation and how others will respond to you. Continue to do this exercise with more complex situations—social encounters, romantic evenings, board meetings, etc. If you find yourself sabotaging situations in order to affirm your predictions (that is, expecting that nobody will talk to you at a party while spending the evening in a dark corner), whenever possible, future pace a positive outcome, the one you would love to experience. What are small actions that influence the trajectory of the outcome? Were they what you expected?

Reflection

Write down the five most recent predictions you made that came true.

1. _____

2. _____

3. _____

4. _____

5. _____

Setting Up the Right Conditions

The enemy of Perspectives is distraction. Perspectives is a delicate process, and requires as much sensory deprivation as you can afford to give it. Because this is your Driver, this is also the flow state, and if the process is not used often enough, the INTJ will eventually run out of juice and become depressed.

So, set up your conditions to access this mental process as much as possible. Find a quiet room in the house or office where you can go inside your mind and let it watch as connections form. This is when you are most creative, and how you solve your major problems.

Also, make sure you set up your office or work area facing the room, with your back to the wall. This is because distractions are jarring to the Perspectives process, and if your back is to the room, you end up dedicating a piece of mental real estate to making sure those distractions can't sneak up on you. The more distractions you can see coming, the less mental real estate you have to dedicate, and the more high-quality thinking you can get done.

UNDEVELOPED PERSPECTIVES (Ni)	DEVELOPED PERSPECTIVES (Ni)
Avoid:	Work Toward:
• Overreliance on baseless conclusions. • Fearing vulnerability. • Paranoia and assumptions that information will be used with ill intent.	• Influencing others with persuasive wording. • Plenty of alone time. • Future pacing and prediction.

Reflection

The talents Perspectives can give me are:

_____

_____

_____

The ways I usually use Perspectives are:

_____

_____

_____

I'm going to develop Perspectives more by:

_____

_____

_____

List three activities that put you into flow:

1. _____

2. _____

3. _____

The INTJ Copilot Is Effectiveness (Te)

Without an extraverted judging process, the INTJ is not complete. The patterns and insights that emerge may be uncalibrated and filled with bias. The INTJ will wonder, "Does this worldview, thought, or insight actually work in the outside world? Or is it an insular position that only works in limited contexts?" Without an answer, the INTJ will become paranoid of encroaching thoughts and stuck in their ways, losing insight in favor of feeling invulnerable to others. An extraverted judging process also empowers the INTJ to have a true impact in the world by moving beyond simple theorizing to building proof of concept. As opposed to sitting on the sidelines of life, they can become a proactive and empowered player.

It's important to remember that, like the Driver, the Copilot process is a talent. But that doesn't mean every INTJ will have the same skill level or use it in a healthy way. Developing Effectiveness as a healthy process is crucial to becoming an amazing INTJ.

It can be difficult to actively develop an extraverted function when one is an Introvert. It won't be as natural as working on Perspectives, so discipline and an eye on the rich rewards Effectiveness brings will be key.

Resource Management

Time, energy, money—everything that is built requires resources to build it. When it comes to determining which resources to use, the Effectiveness Copilot has a natural interest in return on investment (ROI). Is a certain resource worth the effort? To answer that question, Effectiveness also pays special attention to stress tests, which help determine if something can hold up in the long run.

Ultimately, INTJs use Effectiveness for sustainability. The least amount of effort for the most amount of return is great, but if it's going to break quickly and require more effort in the long run, it's not truly worth it. Thinking on a large scale helps inform whether or not something will pass the test of time.

Get good at determining the value of human or emotional factors. Time is often overlooked in ROI, as are things like emotional expense. When determining if something is worth effort, use monetary gain as only one consideration. Take into account enjoyment of process, learning, and quality of product. The standard ROI algorithm is ROI = (Gain − Cost) / Cost. Feel free to create your own algorithm to incorporate more factors.

———————— *Reflection* ————————

Name three soft factors you tend to either waste (or overprotect) that may be interrupting your ROI:

_____

_____

_____

Journal one area of your life where you would like to improve your ROI. Using the algorithm above (or one you have created), state an actionable plan that will help you get more out of the resource than you're putting into it:

_____

_____

_____

_____

_____

Streamlined Systems

If Effectiveness could be expressed in a single quote, it might be, "Freedom is defined as a system that runs so well, you no longer have to think about it."

Effectiveness, like Harmony, is about attempting to create an environment where people get their needs met. But unlike Harmony, the needs
of Effectiveness aren't emotional, they're logistical. Systems help groups
stay in a flow without participants getting in each other's way. Automobile
freeway systems are a great example of how streamlining keeps us all moving forward without having to really think about it. Once these systems are
in place, even bigger goals can be attained, since accomplishments build
upon themselves.

Exercise

The next time you perform a task, document the process with a goal of
streamlining the task. Consider that there are two types of processes: critical and optional. Which steps are necessary to the task, and which can be
cut? Which resources (time, money, energy) are necessary? Can you afford
to pare the resources down for outcome? Once you have a step-by-step
procedure, consult with others who have accomplished this same task and
discover if there was anything you missed.

Reflection

Name three resources you need to improve managing:

_____

_____

_____

Now, look at your schedule. What are you prioritizing that compromises the
proper management of those resources? Record three to five ideas on how
to recoup those resources into your weekly schedule.

_____

_____

_____

_____

Building Necessary Skills

Effectiveness Copilots can shut off personal feelings in order to get things done. In fact, it may be argued that this is the core competency of Effectiveness. Daily tasks aren't always pleasant, nor is skill building outside one's area of expertise. INTJs sometimes struggle with socializing, emotional intelligence, romantic partnerships, and interest in mundane chores. While it's easy to forget the need for these things on a day-to-day basis, eventually they can pile up. And at times, it's only obvious that these skills are underdeveloped when an opportunity for their use has already slipped by.

When an INTJ builds a strong relationship with their Effectiveness Copilot, they'll bite the bullet and focus on proficiency in areas that are necessary for life. Anything unnecessary can be delegated, as long as the resources have been built to hire them out or hand them off. But for anything that can't be delegated—cultivating friendships, finding love, maintaining physical health, performing household responsibilities—the INTJ can lean on Effectiveness to help them put their head down, muscle through, and make it happen, all the while building a sustainable system to keep the benefits of the hard work going.

Exercise

Identify one area of your life you care about improving but have been procrastinating. It could be getting into better physical shape, improving your diet, finding a spouse, doing public speaking, finding a better job, etc.… Make a list of why this is something you want, and identify what has been holding you back. Ask yourself how much more rewarding your life would be if you just started working toward it, even if it isn't optimal or ideal in the beginning. Paint a picture of what your life would look like if you were to succeed. Write this visualization out and put it on your refrigerator.

Reflection

Name one area of your life you would like to improve:

_____

_____

Name three activities you can begin immediately that would address this improvement:

_____

_____

_____

At the beginning of each day, write down what you are going to do that day to improve this area of your life by 5 percent:

_____

_____

_____

_____

At the end of each day, write down what you did to improve this area of your life by 5 percent:

_____

_____

_____

_____

Copilot Growth

Effectiveness is the highest leverage point for growth in your personality. It allows you as an INTJ to make decisions that will help you build something real by asking "What works? What can I do today that will improve each area of my life by 5 percent?"

Growing your Effectiveness can be a challenge for you as an INTJ. It can feel like a threat to your ideas to have them vetted in the real world. It's easy to spend a lot of time thinking and ruminating on how the world should be set up, but without testing your ideas and thoughts, they may be more hopeful fantasy than reality. Embrace the Effectiveness mental process, as it gives you the opportunity to put your ideas into action.

Effectiveness encourages an INTJ to get out of the perfectionism cycle, because it embodies the concept "done is better than perfect." No idea is ever perfect, and a plan can fail. But nobody's ever lived in a blueprint. If you want to quickly test and refine your ideas so they become strong and powerful, you will need to get out of your comfort zone.

Effectiveness encourages you to make something happen, like launching a project or building something. As an INTJ, your mind is already wired to make things happen. Don't ignore the natural talent that you possess; develop it into a skill. You will bring the best version of yourself to the world when you get outside your head and create something in the outer world. Don't hesitate to act; jump into your creative process to make the most of Effectiveness. For example, create rapid prototypes of products or services you've been pondering, or practice leadership skills by working on projects with other people.

Reflection

The talents Effectiveness can give me are:

_____

_____

_____

The ways I usually use Effectiveness are:

_____

_____

_____

I'm going to develop Effectiveness more by:

_____

_____

_____

List three ways you can start growing your Effectiveness process today:

1. _____

2. _____

3. _____

The INTJ 10-Year-Old Is Authenticity (Fi)

Authenticity is fascinated by the subjective human experience, which in its most simple form translates into *identity*. "Who am I?" "What am I feeling right now?" "What has meaning for me?" "What do I believe is right and true in the world and what does that say about me?" Sorting through these complicated questions is a big task, especially when an individual realizes the answers are ever-changing. As Authenticity matures, it accepts that more mature versions of oneself must replace younger versions.

As a 10-Year-Old process, Authenticity may struggle with the need to change, feeling that changing who they are makes them flaky or disingenuous. INTJs may be unaware that their inflexibility is more rooted in stubbornness than it is in staying true to self.

INTJs can use Authenticity to see contradictions within people, and understand how complicated people really are. While realizing that most people need much better tools, such as training, education, purpose, and competence, they also have an awareness that people are usually doing the best they can with what they have. Authenticity also gives INTJs an appreciation of aesthetics. The heart yearns for beauty, as long as that beauty is clean-lined and multipurpose.

As an introverted function, Authenticity allows the INTJ to access a judging process while avoiding the outer world. This can be okay at times, but if the INTJ gets used to relying upon Authenticity to help form conclusions, they can rationalize skipping development of their extraverted judging Copilot, Effectiveness. And that's when the trouble starts. This usually manifests as INTJs shutting down and digging in their heels, especially if they feel hurt.

Authenticity is, in a large part, about introspection and consulting your personal feelings on a matter. People who have it as a strength are usually pretty good at it, and they usually look at the bigger implications of how things affect both themselves and others. But as an INTJ, you're wired to be at your best when looking at situation objectively, not subjectively. This means that if you're in a defensive place and feeling threatened by information, you'll end up forging a wall between yourself and anything you don't want to listen to. You'll take things personally, misinterpret intent, and become intractable.

Another way Authenticity can manifest itself as a 10-Year-Old is by staying in emotional comfort zones, including ones that don't serve the INTJ. An example would be avoiding relationships to prevent getting hurt, but rationalizing it as good resource management.

You may tell yourself you don't have the time and effort to develop new relationships and so you avoid getting close to people, when really it's the fear that an unknown person, if they worm their way into your heart, may have the ability to hurt you.

The Driver/10-Year-Old Loop

There are three ways an INTJ experiences the loop, the echo chamber–like relationship between the Driver and 10-Year-Old functions. The way to get out of a loop is the same in all cases: focus on developing the Effectiveness process and letting the 10-Year-Old serve the Copilot.

Short-term loop. This may only last for a few moments up to a few days. Its intent is to protect the INTJ from information that could be emotionally distressing in the moment. If someone respected or close to them hurts their feelings, they can use the loop to build a fortress of pride. Instead of its usual role of understanding, Perspectives launches into conspiracy theorizing, and 10-Year-Old Authenticity supports the claims by believing the offender was either deliberately malicious or capriciously careless. Either way, pride won't allow the INTJ to crack in front of the culprit, even if that person happens to be a lover or trusted friend. Difficult conversations—the ones that would help smooth the situation over—are avoided, and the INTJ licks their wounds in private.

Long-term loop. The strategy of hiding from responsibility is usually applied in contexts when life requires something from the INTJ that feels bigger or more demanding than it "should be," causing the INTJ to become overwhelmed. This loop is marked by avoidance and a belief that they shouldn't have to do anything they don't feel like doing. They'll know when they're ready, they'll claim; don't push them. A little pride may show up here, too. If pushed too hard, the result can be a feeling of disdain. Avoiding responsibilities doesn't make them go away; it exacerbates them. What seems overwhelming at first can become a serious problem later in life. At its worst, it can turn into perpetual fretting.

Habitual loop. This is possibly the most challenging to overcome: perfectionism. This loop encourages the INTJ to stay in the realm of conceptualizing, becoming self-punishing if they aren't able to execute flawlessly the first time. The payoff? The more perfection an INTJ requires from their performance, the less physical energy is required.

The biggest challenge with perfectionism is that there's no incremental, measurable way to improve. Authenticity has become their metric: a desirable outcome is judged by how the INTJ feels about their performance. Even when feedback tells them they've done a completely acceptable, if not outstanding, job, the INTJ shrugs this off, knowing they haven't met their own immeasurable standards.

Reflection

The ways Perspectives and Authenticity can loop in an INTJ are:

_____

_____

_____

The ways I find myself looping are (include behaviors and situations):

_____

_____

_____

I'm going to work on breaking my loop(s) by:

_____

_____

_____

—————————————

How to Best Use Authenticity

If you find yourself getting overly sensitive, ignoring your tasks, or setting unrealistic expectations for yourself, this is a bad use of the Authenticity function. Tap into Effectiveness and ask yourself, "Yes, but what really works in this situation? Are these feelings getting in the way of me accomplishing my goals?"

That said, when you've carefully scrutinized what's objective and rational and your heart is still telling you something is up, that would be the time to listen to Authenticity. Its purpose is to influence you to do what's right and be sensitive to your own conscience. Just don't let it fool you into becoming emotionally prickly or a martyr in your relationships.

You can also engage your 10-Year-Old in times of play, love, and intimacy. People of your type often enjoy "good vs. evil" stories (like *Star Wars*) and enjoy ethical debates. You can also use Authenticity to show sympathy for loved ones and be an emotional rock in times of distress.

The INTJ 3-Year-Old Is Sensation (Se)

Sensation is designed to get inside your body and be present in the moment. The preferred function of many athletes and performers, Sensation taps into how the body is an instrument for movement, reading body language and seeking high-adrenaline experiences. It's a here-and-now function, and rests into whatever can be verified by its senses.

As a 3-Year-Old process, Sensation for the INTJ is the part of them that whispers from the shadows. Normally quite capable of ignoring or even forgetting about the here-and-now, suddenly an INTJ will have a desire for the deeply sensual, aroused from their mind to remember that the present moment also exists and there's a whole world of activity that needs attention.

There are three ways an INTJ experiences the grip, the moments when the Driver process is stressed out, needs a break, and gives the 3-Year-Old function control of the car. This is most likely to happen when the INTJ's body may be betraying them with chronic illness.

Short-term grip. When the Driver doesn't allow itself to check out, even when stressed and exhausted, there's a strong pull toward indulgences. 3-Year-Olds rarely know when to say no to a package of cookies, and the Sensation 3-Year-Old is no different. Overeating, overdrinking, and sexual addiction are all signs of the Sensation function trying to keep things going without understanding limits. Hiding candy bars in the desk at work is a little thing to provide a burst of sugar needed to get through the day. Drinking after work helps the INTJ unwind, and three glasses of wine isn't really that bad… or so Sensation would rationalize. These are moments when "You Can't Even," and a boost of indulgence feels like the least of your worries. This behavior ignores the fact that Sensation actually would prefer to honor the body, and rest and relaxation is almost always what it's truly seeking.

Long-term grip. Here, the INTJ experiences a quiet but insistent image consciousness. They are unsure of how they're being perceived, though they're aware that all people are being judged by shallow criteria. They might be dealing with the fear that others see them as less than they are, causing them to frequently showcase their intelligence, spend too much money on flashy status symbols, or undergo over-exercising or militant dieting to look the right part.

It's difficult to shake either of these strategies since the first two can feel impossible to control, and the last is perceived by society as simply staying fit and healthy. In either case, too much attention is going to the 3-Year-Old and robbing the Driver of its opportunities for insights and vision.

Habitual grip. Which leads us to the third experience of being in the grip: laziness. Fearing the world will never accept their Perspectives insights or give them the opportunity to showcase their talents, the INTJ will fundamentally give up and pursue pleasure. This is easily the most difficult type of grip to break free of and is almost always accompanied by some form of depression.

How to Best Use Sensation

The best way to use Sensation as a 3-Year-Old is to exercise it regularly, which will help prevent the grip from occurring. In this case, find an immersive sensory experience that is simple, easy to do, and that you won't regret later. Some examples are taking a walk while listening to music, taking a bath or a shower, or going for a swim or a run. If you choose running or another form of exercise, try to do it in an environment that isn't monotonous. For example, try trail running instead of a treadmill.

Remember, Sensation is an extraverted process, so make sure you're active and engaged in your environment. Thirty minutes should be long enough, but feel free to take as long as needed to de-stress. If you keep going back to whatever it is that's stressing you out, throw yourself even more into your activity.

Increase the intensity if necessary. Just make sure you're getting as far out of your mind and as far into your body as possible. It won't feel natural at first, but it has a huge payoff. Once your Driver has had enough of a break, you can usually come back to the situation with a whole new outlook.

Using Sensation in this way can also provide a source of aspiration, the voice that whispers in the back of your mind. Sensation as an aspiration can encourage INTJs to become present and increase their enjoyment of life by emerging from being in their heads all the time. It also helps them attend to their bodies. Health and wellness or certain athletics like martial arts can be common career paths for many people of this type.

Reflection

The ways Sensation can grip an INTJ are:

_____

_____

_____

The ways I find myself being in the grip are (include behaviors and situations):

_____

_____

_____

I'm going to control the process by:

_____

_____

_____

My Sensation 3-Year-Old inspires me/is my aspiration in these ways:

_____

_____

_____

CHAPTER 11

INFJ Personality Type

INFJs are very sensitive to other people. Their ability to shift perspectives combined with a natural talent for understanding emotions can appear (and feel) like clairvoyance.

While both xNFJ types have a natural interest in human dynamics, the INFJ type seeks to understand each individual as they are in relation to others and the world. From childhood, there is a deep interest in why people experience things as they do, what needs are going unmet, how that impacts behavior, and what a person's subtle tells indicate. The deeper an INFJ digs, the more they can't help but sympathize, sometimes even in the face of egregious behavior. A quote that sums up the INFJ ethos may be, "If you truly and completely understand another human being, the only emotional response you can have is compassion."

But when INFJs can't escape their own empathetic and empathic nature, it can spell trouble. Troubled souls can unconsciously notice this quality in the INFJ, and it's not uncommon for complete strangers to start spilling their problems, sensing the INFJ's attunement to their needs and energies.

When people's challenges seem endless and their emotions blasting, the INFJ can become completely overwhelmed. Self-care is crucial, but if they aren't getting their own needs met, the INFJ can default to a number of unhealthy strategies: shutting out the world, turning cold like stone, or demanding self-perfection to avoid any negative feedback.

INFJ CAR MODEL OVERVIEW

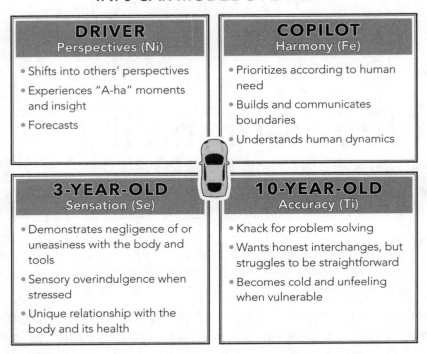

DRIVER
Perspectives (Ni)

- Shifts into others' perspectives
- Experiences "A-ha" moments and insight
- Forecasts

COPILOT
Harmony (Fe)

- Prioritizes according to human need
- Builds and communicates boundaries
- Understands human dynamics

3-YEAR-OLD
Sensation (Se)

- Demonstrates negligence of or uneasiness with the body and tools
- Sensory overindulgence when stressed
- Unique relationship with the body and its health

10-YEAR-OLD
Accuracy (Ti)

- Knack for problem solving
- Wants honest interchanges, but struggles to be straightforward
- Becomes cold and unfeeling when vulnerable

The INFJ Driver Is Perspectives (Ni)

It's important to remember that the Driver process is a talent, but that doesn't mean every INFJ will have the same skill level or use it in a healthy way. Developing Perspectives as a healthy process is crucial to becoming an amazing INFJ.

The Perspectives Driver is the least-represented mental process in the population, and so often considered the most misunderstood. When it's fully developed, Perspectives helps the INFJ see the world from another person's point of view, receive deep insight, and manage conflicts.

Perspectives of Others

Since the Perspectives Driver watches its own mind form patterns, it builds the skill of detaching from its own perspective. In this detached space, it becomes easy to jump into the perspective of others.

Being able to see things from another person's worldview helps the INFJ explain why others do the things they do. Perspectives Drivers realize the simple truth that all actions, regardless of how confusing or distasteful they are to others, make sense to the person who committed them. It ceases to be a matter of explaining the behavior and becomes a matter of explaining how it made sense to the individual.

As an INFJ, getting inside other people's minds means recognizing not only how their experiences have shaped them, but the conclusions they've come to about those experiences. This can include their beliefs, paradigms, and strategies of behavior.

Everyone has a bag of tricks life has taught them, and sometimes that includes strategies that are harmful to themselves and others. That is, "hurting people hurt others." INFJs can recognize when people are in pain, and when they lash out because of it. The key for an INFJ is not to get lost thinking about how trauma shapes the mind, but rather to focus on how it can be healed. Patterns of the mind are plastic, not static. As natural seers into the mind and its relationship to self and others, the INFJ has a talent for developing tools and strategies for shifting paradigms, especially as they relate to emotional and healing work.

This doesn't mean that all INFJs must be therapists or counselors. However, there is a strong pull for INFJs toward helping people find their path. And oftentimes, the INFJ will find the healing they need for themselves from pointing others toward a better way.

Exercise

Think of a heinous action or controversial person that you can't see yourself ever condoning. Instead of jumping to condemn the action, take a moment to really get inside the head of the person who performed the action. How did their action make complete sense to them at the time? Can you understand it so well you could defend it to another person? Don't focus on the act itself, but on the mind of the person who committed it.

Now that you are in a Perspectives frame of mind, fill out the following journal prompt. If you cannot think of anything immediately, feel free to ruminate on the question. It may guide you to some uncomfortable places, and that's okay. Developing your Perspectives process means getting outside your comfort zone. It also means applying this same generosity of spirit to yourself.

Reflection

What patterns are inside of me (beliefs, perspectives, strategies of behavior) that I've been avoiding looking at?

_____

_____

_____

Being kind to myself, I'm going to address these patterns by:

_____

_____

_____

Deep Insight

This type of pattern recognition is best done unconsciously, allowing the mind to wander wherever it needs to go. INFJs may find themselves getting their best ideas when they first wake up, or even while they dream. Attempting to direct these thoughts may actually interrupt the process. An insight in process can feel like a bloodhound on the scent, and it needs freedom to explore whatever is the next lead. The mind can offer up buried insights, if one is quiet enough to hear them.

Create a gentle, quiet space for one full hour. Turn off all sensory stimulation, turn off lights, and deaden any noise. Ensure no one will interrupt you during this time. Consider your favorite quote. (For example, Carl Sagan said, "We are a way for the universe to know itself." Rumi said, "The wound is the place where the Light enters you.") Set a timer. When one hour is up, immediately write down where your mind took you.

Reflection

My most recent insight from one hour of quiet time is:

_____

_____

_____

_____

Conflict Management

Watching how one's own mind works can give clues as to how other people's minds are working. Take a word like *loyalty* or *love*. If we believe everyone defines *love* the same way, we're going to find ourselves in trouble when someone we're in a relationship with behaves in a way that doesn't match our own definition of *love*. These misunderstandings happen all the time. Because you have Perspectives as a strength, however, you catch these misunderstandings. It's not uncommon for people of your type to watch an argument between two people and say, "Wait a minute—you guys are using the same word to mean two totally different things." Or, "You guys are using two different words to mean the same thing. You actually agree."

Exercise

Listen to a conversation as a third-person observer. Using discretion, at certain points in the conversation—when one of the speakers uses a word with an ambiguous meaning—ask them to clarify what they mean by that word. Ask the listener if that's the same meaning they took from it. Practice guessing the difference in meaning between the listener and the speaker.

Reflection

Name five ways people disagree on the definition of the word *love*.

_____

_____

_____

_____

_____

Setting Up the Right Conditions

The enemy of Perspectives is distraction. Perspectives is a delicate process, and requires as much sensory deprivation as you can afford to give it. Because this is your Driver, this is also the flow state, and if the process is not used often enough, the INFJ will eventually run out of juice and become depressed.

So, set up your conditions to access this mental process as much as possible. Find a quiet room in the house or office where you can go inside your mind and let it watch as connections form. This is when you are most creative, and how you solve your major problems.

Also, make sure you set up your office or work area facing the room, with your back to the wall. This is because distractions are jarring to the Perspectives process, and if your back is to the room, you end up dedicating a piece of mental real estate to making sure those distractions can't sneak up on you. The more distractions you can see coming, the less mental real estate you have to dedicate, and the more high-quality thinking you can get done.

UNDEVELOPED PERSPECTIVES (Ni)	DEVELOPED PERSPECTIVES (Ni)
Avoid:	Work Toward:
• Overreliance on baseless conclusions. • Fearing vulnerability. • Paranoia and assumptions that information will be used with ill intent.	• Influencing others with persuasive wording. • Plenty of alone time. • Future pacing and prediction.

Reflection

The talents Perspectives can give me are:

_____

_____

_____

The ways I usually use Perspectives are:

_____

_____

_____

I'm going to develop Perspectives more by:

_____

_____

_____

List three activities that put you into flow:

_____

_____

_____

The INFJ Copilot Is Harmony (Fe)

Without an extraverted judging process, the INFJ is not complete. The patterns and insights that emerge may be uncalibrated and filled with bias. The INFJ will wonder, "Does this worldview, thought, or insight actually work in the outside world? Or is it an insular position that only works in limited contexts?" Without an answer, the INFJ will become paranoid of encroaching thoughts and stuck in their ways, losing insight in favor of feeling invulnerable to others. An extraverted judging process also empowers the INFJ to have a true impact in the world by moving beyond simple theorizing to building proof of concept. As opposed to sitting on the sidelines of life, they can become a proactive and empowered player.

It's important to remember that, like the Driver, the Copilot process is a talent. But that doesn't mean every INFJ will have the same skill level or use it in a healthy way. Developing Harmony as a healthy process is crucial to becoming an amazing INFJ.

It can be difficult to actively develop an extraverted function when one is an Introvert. It won't be as natural as working on Perspectives, so discipline and an eye on the rich rewards Harmony brings will be key.

Identify and Meet Needs

Fluctuating emotions are often the first sign that a person has unmet needs. An INFJ may be so tuned in and sensitive to emotions that they find it easy to help people feel safe, loved, and stable. This can be as simple as hosting a party and making it look effortless, to being a shoulder for a grieving friend to cry on, to helping friends with complicated relationship issues. People who have developed their Harmony process become so skilled at this, they often become the go-to person in a time of crisis. Learning to be available to help meet people's needs also helps the INFJ become extremely industrious and have lots of unexpected talents and skills in a variety of areas.

It's equally important for an INFJ to make sure they're getting their own needs met. They can't run on fumes all the time, and they can't be of help to others if they're perpetually exhausted. It's best to express unmet needs out loud. Similarly, it's good to avoid behavior like walking away when unhappy, being silently disapproving, or crying alone. When an INFJ is comfortable expressing their own emotions, they become a role model for others who need to express themselves, and they are better able to help others meet their needs.

Exercise

Ask yourself, "What need is going unmet for me?" It could be alone time, better eating habits, more sleep, a conversation with a friend, a night out, or just some pampering. Once you identify it, ask yourself the easiest and fastest way to get that need met.

Reflection

Name your top three needs that frequently go unmet.

_____

_____

_____

Now, look at your schedule. What are you prioritizing that gets in the way of those needs being met? If it's people you care about, like your spouse, children, family, and friends, just remember that you can't get to their needs if you're running on fumes. Journal 3 to 5 ideas that you can begin implementing to fit those needs into your weekly schedule.

_____

_____

_____

_____

_____

Build Healthy Boundaries

Harmony is the process that is used to create and maintain unspoken social contracts. Contracts are designed for us to know each other's expectations and honor them (as long as they are agreed upon). If you, as an INFJ, don't know your boundaries, Harmony will encourage you to spend time with people and experience both acceptable and unacceptable behavior. Once you know your boundaries, Harmony helps you create contracts around them.

That means you'll have to communicate them to the people in your life, making sure they fully understand and agree to your boundaries. In a moment where you feel taken advantage of or thrown under a bus, ask yourself which of your boundaries has been broken, and if it was you or the other person that broke it.

— *Reflection* —

Follow the journal prompt below to become clearer about your boundaries. Feel free to repeat this journal prompt multiple times until you feel confident and authentic about the boundaries you've discovered and set. Once you've done so, share them with the three people whom you feel closest to. If they are uncomfortable with your new boundaries, ask if it's because the boundaries are unreasonable, or because they will change the relationship. Be sensitive to resistance to change while staying firm with your requirements.

Remember: Boundary setting is a skill. It might be bumpy at first, but over time and with small successes, your boundaries will become a part of your identity.

Name three (or more) things you would like to see more of in your life:

_____

_____

_____

Name three (or more) behaviors you will never allow in your life again:

_____

_____

_____

I would like to strengthen the boundaries in these areas of my life:

_____

_____

_____

I can improve the boundaries in each area of my life by:

_____

_____

_____

If someone crosses a boundary, my plan is to say:

_____

_____

———————

Understand Social Contracts

Understanding unspoken social contracts means being able to know what's expected of yourself and others. This comes from a lifelong study of what offends other people versus what makes them feel comfortable.

This type of understanding is a major advantage in new circumstances and when first meeting people. You're very rarely going to say the wrong thing or alienate others. In fact, people of your type are often popular in group settings because you can help keep the conversation going without offending anyone or leaving anyone out.

Make it your aim to meet many new people. The more people you meet, the more opportunities you have to understand the cultures they come from. What was their family's culture? What area of the country or world are they from? Do misunderstandings of culture get in the way of creating Harmony? How can your increased understanding of other people and their family or country help you to keep relationships between people in social settings congenial and happy?

Reflection

The way I feel about meeting new people is:

_____

_____

If I experience any hesitancy to meet new people, what do I suspect is going on for me?

_____

_____

_____

I will meet one new person this week. Afterward, I will record the conversation and what I learned from it here:

_____

_____

_____

Copilot Growth

Harmony is the highest leverage point for growth in your personality. It encourages you as an INFJ to proactively set boundaries for yourself and others, leading to an ultimately happier atmosphere. To encourage Harmony, ask yourself:

- Am I truly giving back, or just seeking approval?

- What is the kindest thing I can do in this situation?

- How can I be available to meet other people's needs without compromising my own?

- Does it make sense for me to put aside my desires for this relationship?

It's easy for an INFJ to get lost in seeking the approval of others. Being vulnerable and speaking up is difficult. But if relationships are never built on intimacy and understanding, you will always feel like something is missing.

Growing Harmony can be a challenge for you as an INFJ. But setting boundaries in the outside world will help you meet your needs. Harmony encourages you to seek and foster healthy relationships with other people. Hiding isn't an option when there are delightful connections to be made. It also encourages you to establish healthy boundaries so that you no longer stand behind an impenetrable wall, but rather a gate that can be opened or closed.

Try these strategies to improve your boundary-setting skills:

- Say "No" to every request for one full day. It doesn't matter how easy the request is; just say no as practice for setting boundaries.

- Every day, aim to set aside some "me time."

- Pay attention to crazymakers—those people who step on your boundaries. Practice standing up for yourself when they come into your world and demand attention.

Reflection

The talents Harmony can give me are:

_____

_____

_____

The ways I usually use Harmony are:

_____

_____

_____

I'm going to develop Harmony more by:

_____

_____

_____

List three ways you can start growing your Harmony process today:

_____

_____

_____

The INFJ 10-Year-Old Is Accuracy (Ti)

Accuracy is designed to help a person look inside their own mind and spot incongruities and inconsistencies in their thinking. Illustratively, it sees the mind as being written in computer code and is always on the lookout for "bad code." This may be information and knowledge implanted by other people, or even by younger versions of the self, that are no longer worthy and should be removed. As a 10-Year-Old function, Accuracy for the INFJ is that younger version of the self, and thus is less adept at spotting the bad code.

Sometimes it's a real pleasure to see things in technical terms. It allows the INFJ some breathing room from the flood of emotions swirling around. Accuracy allows the data collected by Perspectives and Harmony—why people do what they do, how they respond to each other—to be organized into a scientific framework. And it's nice to have some way to organize the insights Perspectives comes up with, since the intuitive function has no real mechanism for capturing and tagging those insights.

As an introverted function, Accuracy allows the INFJ to access a judging process while staying inside their own minds. This can be okay at times, but if the INFJ gets used to relying upon Accuracy to help form their conclusions they can rationalize skipping development of their extraverted judging process of Harmony. And that's when the trouble starts. For INFJs, this usually manifests by their being uncharacteristically critical, especially of another person's argument.

Accuracy is, in a large part, about breaking information down and seeing how it doesn't line up. People who have it as a strength are usually pretty good at it. They're not looking for how someone is wrong, but rather for how the information itself could be more consistent. But an INFJ is wired to be at their best when understanding the implications things have on other people's feelings and emotions.

If the INFJ 10-Year-Old gets to have the final call without consulting the Copilot, it's going to sort intricate information at a 10-Year-Old level. 10-Year-Old Accuracy will look for other people to be wrong and criticize their thinking. Especially when the INFJ is feeling threatened by another person's information, they'll end up discrediting that person's argument so as to not have to listen to it anymore.

Another way Accuracy can manifest itself as a 10-Year-Old is by being unnecessarily perfectionistic. While perfectionism can manifest in many situations, it is usually a strategy to avoid other people's disapproval.

The Driver/10-Year-Old Loop

There are three ways an INFJ experiences the loop, the echo chamber–like relationship between the Driver and 10-Year-Old functions. The way to get out of a loop is the same in all cases: focus on developing the Harmony process.

Short-term loop. This may only last for a few moments up to a few days. Its intent is to protect the INFJ from information that could be distressing at that moment. Usually, this is a reaction to feeling overwhelmed by emotions absorbed from another person or people. It's marked by uncharacteristic coldness and harsh criticism toward the person (or people) that caused the distress. The logic behind this reaction is to discredit others to protect the self: "I don't have to care about the feelings of an unworthy person, so I'll figure out all the ways this person is unworthy."

Have you ever been in an argument and used grammatical or logical technicality against your opponent to "prove" they didn't know what they're talking about? For example, "Anyone who would use a double negative is obviously an idiot, and not worth my time." This behavior is the result of not having strong enough boundaries, lacking good strategies for dealing with overload, or not having a solid self-care regimen.

Long-term loop. This is a loop of hiding away from society: living inside books and research, shutting out other people's emotional baggage, and creating a bubble of invulnerability. While this loop doesn't make the INFJ feel bad about themselves, as the first loop may do, it's more difficult to break away from. The INFJ's entire world becomes molded around self-protection, and it usually results in loneliness. The only way to escape is to overcome the fear of being vulnerable.

Habitual loop. This is possibly the most challenging loop to overcome: perfectionism. The more perfect an INFJ is, the less they can be called out on any undesirable behaviors. Or, at least, if the outer world confronts them, they have an airtight defense of having done everything by the book, exactly as expected, and without flaw. The world often rewards perfectionism more than it punishes it, so the INFJ may receive mostly positive feedback for being oh-so-good. This reinforces the perfectionistic loop, and makes it nearly impossible to break.

Perfectionism is rife with challenges, however. Growth is stunted when the INFJ is unwilling to accept and forgive themselves for faults. Additionally, perfectionists make everyone around them uncomfortable. For example, have you ever known someone so obsessed with keeping their house perfect, they put plastic over all of the furniture? Was visiting a comfortable experience?

The ways Perspectives and Accuracy can loop in an INFJ are:

_____

_____

_____

The ways I find myself looping are (include behaviors and situations):

_____

_____

_____

_____

I'm going to work on breaking my loop(s) by:

_____

_____

_____

How to Best Use Accuracy

If you find yourself getting overly critical, or hyper-focused on details and perfectionism, this is a bad use of the Accuracy function. Tap into the Harmony function and ask yourself, "Yes, but what's best for everyone? What will get everyone's needs met, as well as my own?" If your behavior ends up pushing people away or not taking their feelings into consideration, it's time to reevaluate what's important to you.

That said, if you've carefully considered how best to meet other people's needs (as well as your own), and your gut is telling you that you need to spend some time breaking down the facts of the matter, that would be the time to listen to Accuracy. Just don't let it fool you into emotionally disconnecting as a protective, defensive strategy.

You can also engage your 10-Year-Old in times of play, love, and intimacy. People of your type often enjoy puzzles and other purely analytic games.

You can use the same mental process to get inside the heads of the people you love in order to truly understand how they think and see the world. Sharing important truths with loved ones—whether they're truths about your own boundaries, the missteps others may be taking, or even your philosophical views in general—helps them trust and rest into your honesty. It prevents you from appearing fake. The key is to ensure the information has first been vetted by Harmony as an act of caring and love for both yourself and the other individual. This quality is extremely appreciated by people that love you.

The INFJ 3-Year-Old Is Sensation (Se)

Sensation is designed to get inside your body and be present in the moment. The preferred function of many athletes and performers, Sensation taps into how the body is an instrument for movement, reading body language and seeking high-adrenaline experiences. It's a here-and-now function, and rests into whatever can be verified by its senses.

As a 3-Year-Old process, Sensation is a part of the INFJ that whispers from the shadows. Normally quite capable of ignoring or even forgetting about the here-and-now, suddenly an INFJ will have a desire for the deeply sensual, realizing that the present moment also exists and there's a whole world of activity that needs attention.

There are three ways an INFJ experiences the grip, the moments when the Driver process is stressed out, needs a break, and gives the 3-Year-Old function control of the car. This is most likely to happen when the INFJ's body may be betraying them with chronic illness.

Short-term grip. When the Driver doesn't allow itself to check out even when stressed and exhausted, there's a strong pull toward indulgences. 3-Year-Olds rarely know when to say no to a package of cookies, and the Sensation 3-Year-Old is no different. Overeating, overdrinking, and sexual addiction are all signs of the Sensation function trying to keep things going without understanding limits. Hiding candy bars in the desk at work is a little thing to provide a burst of sugar needed to get through the day. Drinking after work helps the INFJ unwind, and three glasses of wine isn't really that bad... or so Sensation would rationalize. These are moments when "You Can't Even," and a boost of indulgence feels like the least of your worries. This behavior ignores the fact that Sensation actually would prefer to honor the body, and rest and relaxation is almost always what it's truly seeking.

Long-term grip. Here, the INFJ is uncertain about how to integrate the needs of the body, resulting in either neglecting the body or giving it too much attention. You might be dealing with health issues that you can't shake, or you possibly feel the need to over-exercise or engage in militant dieting, since who knows when the body will betray you?

It's difficult to shake either of these strategies since the first one can feel impossible to control, and the second can be misinterpreted as true health and fitness. In either case, too much attention is going to the 3-Year-Old and robbing the Driver of its opportunities for insights and vision.

Habitual grip. When caught in this tight grip, the INFJ ignores any uncomfortable messages coming from the Perspectives Driver. You may unconsciously "dumb yourself down" to avoid the implications of your own intuition, fearing you may be more insightful than the people in your life, or even see holes in the logic of your belief system. This is easily the most difficult type of grip to remove yourself from, since the avoiding Driver is almost always accompanied by some form of depression.

How to Best Use Sensation

The best way to use Sensation as a 3-Year-Old is to exercise it regularly, which will help prevent the grip from occurring. In this case, find an immersive sensory experience that is simple, easy to do, and that you won't regret later. Some examples are taking a walk while listening to music, taking a bath or a shower, or going for a swim or a run. If you choose running or another form of exercise, try to do it in an environment that isn't monotonous. For example, try trail running instead of a treadmill.

Remember, Sensation is an extraverted process, so make sure you're active and engaged in your environment. Thirty minutes should be long enough, but feel free to take as long as needed to de-stress. If you keep going back to whatever it is that's stressing you out, throw yourself even more into your activity.

Increase the intensity if necessary. Just make sure you're getting as far out of your mind and as far into your body as possible. It won't feel natural at first, but it has a huge payoff. Once your Driver has had enough of a break, you can usually come back to the situation with a whole new outlook.

Using Sensation in this way can also provide a source of aspiration, the voice that whispers in the back of your mind. Sensation as an aspiration can encourage INFJs to become present and increase their enjoyment of life by emerging from being in their heads all the time. It also helps them attend to their bodies. Health and wellness or certain athletics like martial arts can be common career paths for many people of this type.

Reflection

The ways Sensation can grip an INFJ are:

_____

_____

_____

The ways I find myself being in the grip are (include behaviors and situations):

_____

_____

_____

I'm going to control the process by:

_____

_____

_____

My Sensation 3-Year-Old inspires me/is my aspiration in these ways:

_____

_____

_____

CHAPTER 12

ISTJ Personality Type

ISTJs are reliable, steady, and supportive. Focused on procedure and structure, they help us track our world and keep things moving.

ISTJs help us maintain life by creating accountability and templates that we can rely upon. Whether they are teachers, engineers, managers, or police chiefs, ISTJs often show up with high levels of competency and professionalism.

Because ISTJs are masterful at developing procedures, they can often become annoyed with people who seem to waste energy on reinventing the wheel, or who don't follow the rules. This can lead to discomfort in situations that don't have an established hierarchy or guideline. If they focus too much on precedent, ISTJs may become stubborn against all things new, and even suspicious or hyper-critical.

If the ISTJ can stay focused on results and not just procedure, options open up for newer ways of solving real-world challenges. The best ISTJs lean into what works, even when there's no precedent; find solutions that fall outside the norm; and add to the stability they desire to create.

DRIVER	COPILOT
Memory (Si)	**Effectiveness (Te)**
• Reliable, careful, and honors tradition • Upholds old traditions, and creates new ones • Is resilient through difficulty, with a strong sense of duty	• Evaluates in terms of resource management (time, energy, currency) • Naturally thinks in, and sets up, streamlined systems • Has instinct for leadership
3-YEAR-OLD	**10-YEAR-OLD**
Exploration (Ne)	**Authenticity (Fi)**
• Suspicious of new experiences • Becomes anxious or catastrophizes in stressful situations • Has a sense of adventure and optimism for the future	• In touch with personal values • Struggles with feelings of vulnerability • Can get stuck in an emotion, like pride

The ISTJ Driver Is Memory (Si)

It's important to remember that the Driver process is a talent, but that doesn't mean every ISTJ will have the same skill level or use it in a healthy way. Developing Memory as a healthy process is crucial to becoming an amazing ISTJ. While this cognitive function is most commonly used as a strength, it is influenced by its unique experiences and can be rather quirky. When using the Memory Driver, an ISTJ can learn to be reliable, be careful, and honor procedure; uphold old traditions and create new ones; and be resilient through and accepting of situations that cannot be changed.

Be Reliable and Careful

For people who use Memory as a Driver, living in an unpredictable or unstable environment carries a huge penalty. To avoid this kind of environment, people of your type are amazing at maintaining procedures and processes to minimize instability. If no procedure exists, Memory is compelled to find one.

Memory users recognize the need for care and caution. There is no reason to make repeated mistakes if a process is established to track them. It can be a simple aphorism to pass helpful knowledge from one generation to the next, such as "Measure twice, cut once." There are important reasons we have standards. While it might sound fun to "reinvent the wheel," actual car wheels would be incredibly difficult to shop for if there weren't an established standard and series of regulations on their size and fit to most vehicles.

It's important for an ISTJ to avoid becoming passive or getting used to chaos they could otherwise prevent or avoid. This talent extends to a much broader scale, and it could be argued that the very infrastructure of society—the rules and procedures that keep us going—are maintained and managed primarily by people who have the Memory process as a skill.

Exercise

Identify areas in your life that are unsafe or in violation of established standards, particularly things that (if left by themselves) could become a problem in the future. Look to a trusted organization, community, or family culture to gauge what the standard is and how you can correct it. If you're unsure, consult experts for guidance on how to correct the issue.

Reflection

What areas of my life am I letting turn into chaos? Is there a procedure I can implement to reestablish sanity?

_____

_____

_____

_____

Being kind to myself, I'm going to address this chaos by:

_____

_____

_____

_____

Holds Relationship with Tradition

Memory users recognize how much each individual is influenced by their experiences. They also understand the importance of ensuring that most of those memories are positive. It is a pleasure to create wonderful memories that can be replayed and enjoyed forever. For this reason, it's common for Memory users to enjoy holidays, family gatherings, and other times when loved ones get together for momentous occasions.

They're also very touched when other people take the time to create a wonderful experience for them, and anniversaries are not to be missed. The first restaurant an ISTJ and their spouse go to isn't just another restaurant; it's a symbol of an important event, and going back to the same restaurant for anniversaries completes the experience. Once a shared memory has been repeated often enough, it becomes tradition, something upon which to anchor the relationship.

Traditions can also be used for healing. Trauma that is difficult to shake from the ISTJ's memory may require a healing tradition. For example, when a loved one dies, it may become an annual tradition to gather with others to talk about them, remember them, and pay tribute by living life fully in their honor.

The more sophisticated Memory gets, the more it's open to adopting new traditions. This is important to remember, as Memory in its infancy may be fearful of the unfamiliar. Changing one's traditions—including beliefs and paradigms—may feel disloyal to parents and other trusted authorities. But as it matures, Memory becomes a more adaptable function. It incorporates new experiences into its identity, learning to become whatever is appropriate to the context.

Consider ways you can pass on the traditions of your family to the next generation. Is there a tradition you inherited that can be taught to your children, nieces, or nephews? Do they understand the importance of it, and will they contribute to passing it on after you're gone? How can you make the tradition more enjoyable in a way that will leave a lasting impression, help mold their experience, and help them want to carry the torch?

—————— *Reflection* ——————

The tradition that has had the biggest impact on me is:

_____

_____

_____

_____

_____

Show Resilience, Acceptance, and Duty

Acceptance is not passive, nor is it complacent. It's a recognition of what cannot be changed, and a coming to terms with how those things impact one's life.

It's not easy to accept things as they are, but Memory has the greatest natural talent for it, and therefore, Memory users demonstrate great resilience during trying situations. True acceptance includes letting go of judgment and blame (including of oneself) and instead addressing situations with tolerance and forgiveness. Memory meets unfair situations with fairness, and finds peace within.

Memory users naturally understand the passage of time. They register change almost immediately and know how people are formed by their experiences. They get that we are who we are because of our past. Truly traumatic experiences can break people past their limits, but time can heal even brokenness.

As it is said, "time heals all wounds," even if it takes decades, and we can be stronger people for it.

For the ISTJ, acceptance and resiliency are coupled with a strong sense of duty. They are able to work through difficult situations while staying true to their commitments, without fanfare. When an ISTJ is working through acceptance, they will very rarely announce it to others, preferring to quietly and internally walk through the process.

It's important to remember that acceptance is not submitting to unhealthy situations. It's not needlessly putting up with physical pain, a bad relationship, or a toxic context. Predicaments that can be changed should be changed. Acceptance is not endurance; it's the opposite. It is ending the suffering that accompanies resisting reality, but it does not involve seeking out a painful reality.

Exercise

Practice self-acceptance. When you notice that you are judging or rating yourself, look for a time in your past that may have prompted the thought. Did this criticism originally come from a parent? Is this self-criticism from a time you believed you failed at something? If you are much older than you were at the origin of the thought, is there wisdom you have now that changes how you experience the inciting event? Did you do the best you could at the time? What connections do you now see that you missed then? Can you forgive your younger self? Does your younger self need forgiveness at all, or just a little understanding? Focus on letting go of the pain and the belief that caused the judgment.

Reflection

What's your biggest regret? What have you done to make amends with yourself or forgive yourself?

_____

_____

_____

_____

_____

_____

_____

Setting Up the Right Conditions

The enemy of Memory is instability. If life becomes too erratic, chaotic, or unpredictable, Memory has difficulty doing what it does best: establishing order and keeping everyone safe.

As your Driver, this is your flow state, and if you're not using this process enough, you'll eventually run out of juice and become depressed. Set up your conditions to access this mental process often. Keep life simple and manageable. And if life is throwing too many new or overwhelming things at you, make sure you have plenty of time for yourself to post-process these moments.

Journaling or otherwise recording events will help you review the details and figure out what's meaningful for you. Reaching out to others to talk about how shared life experiences impacted them can help you clarify your own thoughts and recall different aspects of your memories. Give yourself full permission to have different takeaways than others.

UNDEVELOPED MEMORY (Si)	DEVELOPED MEMORY (Si)
Avoid: • Getting used to chaos • Fearing the unfamiliar • Enduring bad situations that can be changed	Work Toward: • Implementing procedures and standards • Creating new traditions along with upholding the old • Developing acceptance of what can't be changed

Reflection

The talents Memory can give me are:

_____

_____

_____

The ways I usually use Memory are:

_____

_____

_____

I'm going to develop Memory more by:

_____

_____

_____

List three activities that put you into flow:

_____

_____

_____

The ISTJ Copilot Is Effectiveness (Te)

Without an extraverted judging process, the ISTJ is not complete. Standards and traditions need to be vetted to ensure they're still relevant and serving people. Without checking in to ensure that the systems still work and are sustainable, the ISTJ may get stuck in a rut, unable to determine if their life is on track or if they're simply existing from day to day. Rigidity may enter, along with fear of the unknown.

An extraverted judging process empowers the ISTJ to be flexible, build proof of concept, and not simply make assumptions based on past results. As opposed to sitting on the sidelines of life, they can become a proactive and empowered player.

It's important to remember that, like the Driver, the Copilot process is a talent. But that doesn't mean every ISTJ will have the same skill level or use it in a healthy way. Developing Effectiveness as a healthy process is crucial to becoming an amazing ISTJ.

It can be difficult to actively develop an extraverted function when one is an Introvert. It won't be as natural as working on Memory, so discipline and an eye on the rich rewards Effectiveness brings will be key.

Resource Management

Time, energy, money—everything that is built requires resources to build it. When it comes to determining which resources to use, the Effectiveness Copilot has a natural interest in return on investment (ROI). Is a certain resource worth the effort? To answer that question, Effectiveness also pays special attention to stress tests, which help determine if something can hold up in the long run.

Ultimately, ISTJs use Effectiveness for sustainability. The least amount of effort for the most amount of return is great, but if it's going to break down quickly and require more effort in the long run, it's not truly worth it. Thinking on a large scale helps inform whether or not something will pass the test of time.

Get good at determining the value of human or emotional factors. Time is often overlooked in ROI, as are things like emotional expense. When determining if something is worth effort, use monetary gain as only one consideration. Take into account enjoyment of process, learning, and quality of product. The standard ROI algorithm is ROI = (Gain − Cost) / Cost. Feel free to create your own algorithm to incorporate more factors.

Reflection

Name three soft factors you tend to either waste (or overprotect) that may be interrupting your ROI:

_____

_____

_____

Journal one area of your life where you would like to improve your ROI. Using the algorithm above (or one you have created), state an actionable plan that will help you get more out of the resource you're putting into it:

_____

_____

_____

_____

_____

Streamlined Systems

If Effectiveness could be expressed in a single quote, it might be, "Freedom is defined as a system that runs so well, you no longer have to think about it."

Effectiveness, like Harmony, is about attempting to create an environment where people get their needs met. But unlike Harmony, the needs of Effectiveness aren't emotional, they're logistical. Systems help groups stay in a flow without participants getting in each other's way. Automobile freeway systems are a great example of how streamlining keeps us all moving forward without having to really think about it. Once these systems are in place, even bigger goals can be attained since accomplishments build upon themselves.

Exercise

The next time you perform a task, document the process with a goal of streamlining the task. Consider that there are two types of processes: critical and optional. Which steps are necessary to the task, and which can be cut? Which resources (time, money, energy) are necessary? Can you afford to pare the resources down for outcome? Once you have a step-by-step procedure, consult with others who have accomplished this same task and discover if there was anything you missed.

Reflection

Name three resources you need to manage better:

_____

_____

_____

Now, look at your schedule. What are you prioritizing that compromises the proper management of those resources? Record three to five ideas on how to recoup those resources into your weekly schedule.

_____

_____

_____

_____

Building Necessary Skills

Effectiveness Copilots can shut off personal feelings in order to get things done. In fact, it may be argued that this is the core competency of Effectiveness. Daily tasks aren't always pleasant, nor is skill building outside one's area of expertise. ISTJs sometimes struggle with socializing, emotional intelligence, romantic partnerships, and interest in mundane chores. While it's easy to forget the need for these things on a day-to-day basis, eventually they can pile up. And at times, it's only obvious that these skills are underdeveloped when an opportunity for their use has already slipped by.

When an ISTJ builds a strong relationship with their Effectiveness Copilot, they'll bite the bullet and focus on proficiency in areas that are necessary for life. Anything unnecessary can be delegated, as long as the resources have been built to hire them out or hand them off. But for anything that can't be delegated—cultivating friendships, finding love, maintaining physical health, performing household responsibilities—the ISTJ can lean on Effectiveness to help them put their head down, muscle through, and make it happen, all the while building a sustainable system to keep the benefits of the hard work going.

Exercise

Identify one area of your life where you care about improving but have been procrastinating. It could be getting into better physical shape, improving your diet, finding a spouse, doing public speaking, finding a better job, etc…. Make a list of why this is something you want, and identify what has been holding you back. Ask yourself how much more rewarding your life would be if you just started working toward it, even if it isn't optimal or ideal in the beginning. Paint a picture of what your life would look like if you were to succeed. Write this visualization out and put it on your refrigerator.

Reflection

Name one area of your life you would like to improve:

_____

_____

_____

Name three activities you can begin immediately that would address this improvement:

_____

_____

_____

At the beginning of each day, write down what you are going to do that day to improve this area of your life by 5 percent:

_____

_____

_____

_____

At the end of each day, write down what you did to improve this area of your life by 5 percent:

_____

_____

_____

_____

Copilot Growth

Effectiveness is the highest leverage point for growth in your personality. It allows you as an ISTJ to make decisions that will help you build something real by asking "What works? What can I do today that will improve each area of my life by 5 percent?"

Growing your Effectiveness can be a challenge for you as an ISTJ. It can feel like a threat to your ideas to have them vetted in the real world. It's easy to spend a lot of time thinking and ruminating on how the world should be set up, but without testing your ideas and thoughts, they may be more rhetoric than reality. Embrace the Effectiveness mental process, as it gives you the opportunity to put your ideas into action.

Effectiveness also encourages an ISTJ to avoid becoming rigid and implacable. Fear of the unknown coupled with pride can make an ISTJ reject better ways of doing things, including building a life of happiness. If you want to choose happiness over being right, you will need to get out of your comfort zone.

Effectiveness encourages you to make something happen, like launching a project or building something. As an ISTJ, your mind is already wired to make things happen. Don't ignore the natural talent that you possess; develop it into a skill. You will bring the best version of yourself to the world when you get outside your head and create something in the outer world. Don't hesitate to act; jump into your creative process to make the most of Effectiveness. For example, create rapid prototypes of products or services you've been pondering, or practice leadership skills by working on projects with other people.

Reflection

The talents Effectiveness can give me are:

_____

_____

_____

The ways I usually use Effectiveness are:

_____

_____

_____

I'm going to develop Effectiveness more by:

_____

_____

_____

List three ways you can start growing your Effectiveness process today:

_____

_____

_____

The ISTJ 10-Year-Old Is Authenticity (Fi)

Authenticity is fascinated by the subjective human experience, which in its most simple form translates into *identity*. "Who am I?" "What am I feeling right now?" "What has meaning for me?" "What do I believe is right and true in the world and what does that say about me?" Sorting through these complicated questions is a big task, especially when an individual realizes the answers are ever changing. As Authenticity matures, it accepts that more mature versions of oneself must replace younger versions.

As a 10-Year-Old process, Authenticity may struggle with the need to change, feeling that changing who they are makes them flaky or disingenuous. ISTJs may be unaware that their inflexibility is more rooted in stubbornness than it is about staying true to self.

ISTJs can use Authenticity to see contradictions within people and understand how complicated people really are. While realizing that most people need much better tools, such as training, education, purpose, and competence, they also have an awareness that people are usually doing the best they can with what they have. Authenticity also gives ISTJs an appreciation of aesthetics. The heart yearns for beauty, as long as that beauty is clean-lined and multipurpose.

As an introverted function, Authenticity allows the ISTJ to access a judging process while avoiding the outer world. This can be okay at times, but if the ISTJ gets used to relying upon Authenticity to help form conclusions, they can rationalize skipping development of their extraverted judging Copilot, Effectiveness. And that's when the trouble starts. This usually manifests as ISTJs shutting down and digging in their heels, especially if they feel hurt.

Authenticity is, in a large part, about introspection and consulting your personal feelings on a matter. People who have it as a strength are usually pretty good at it, and they usually look at the bigger implications of how things affect both themselves and others. But as an ISTJ, you're wired to be at your best when looking at situation objectively, not subjectively. This means that if you're in a defensive place and feeling threatened by information, you'll end up forging a wall between yourself and anything you don't want to listen to. You'll take things personally, misinterpret intent, and become intractable.

Another way Authenticity can manifest itself as a 10-Year-Old is by staying in emotional comfort zones, including ones that don't serve the ISTJ. An example would be avoiding relationships to prevent getting hurt, but rationalizing it as good resource management.

You may tell yourself you don't have the time and energy to develop new relationships and so you avoid getting close to people, when really it's the fear that an unknown person, if they worm their way into your heart, may have the ability to hurt you.

The Driver/10-Year-Old Loop

There are three ways an ISTJ experiences the loop, the echo chamber–like relationship between the Driver and 10-Year-Old functions. The way to get out of a loop is the same in all cases: focus on developing the Effectiveness process and let the 10-Year-Old serve the Copilot.

Short-term loop. This may only last for a few moments up to a few days. Its intent is to protect the ISTJ from information that could be emotionally distressing in the moment. If someone respected or close to them hurts their feelings, they can use the loop to build a fortress of pride. Instead of its usual role of understanding, Memory holds onto a grudge, and 10-Year-Old Authenticity supports the animosity by believing the offender was either deliberately malicious or capriciously careless. Either way, pride won't allow the ISTJ to crack in front of the culprit, even if that person happens to be a lover or trusted friend. Difficult conversations—the ones that would help smooth the situation over—are avoided, and the ISTJ licks their wounds in private.

Long-term loop. This is a loop of hiding from responsibility. This is usually in contexts when life requires something from the ISTJ that feels bigger or more demanding than it "should be," causing the ISTJ to become overwhelmed. This loop is marked by avoidance and a belief that they shouldn't have to do anything they don't feel like doing. They'll know when they're ready, they'll claim; don't push them. A little pride may show up here, too. If pushed too hard, the result can be a feeling of disdain. Avoiding responsibilities doesn't make them go away; it exacerbates them. What seems overwhelming at first can become a serious problem later in life. At its worst, it can turn into panic.

Habitual loop. This is possibly the most challenging loop to overcome: rigidity. This loop of rigidity encourages the ISTJ to stick with the familiar, digging their heels in and rejecting anything that challenges their worldview.

The biggest challenge with rigidity is that there's no incremental, measurable way to determine if a new concept or person is valid. Authenticity has become their metric: New information is judged by how it makes the ISTJ feel. Even when feedback tells them this person or situation is perfectly acceptable, the ISTJ may reject them to avoid dealing with uncomfortable feelings within, such as prejudices and misconceptions.

Reflection

The ways Memory and Authenticity can loop in an ISTJ are:

_____

_____

_____

The ways I find myself looping are (include behaviors and situations):

_____

_____

_____

I'm going to work on breaking my loop(s) by:

_____

_____

_____

How to Best Use Authenticity

If you find yourself getting overly sensitive, ignoring your tasks, or setting unrealistic expectations for yourself, this is a bad use of the Authenticity function. Tap into Effectiveness and ask yourself, "Yes, but what really works in this situation? Are these feelings getting in the way of me accomplishing my goals?"

That said, when you've carefully scrutinized what's objective and rational and your heart is still telling you something is up, that would be the time to listen to Authenticity. Its purpose is to influence you to do what's right and be sensitive to your own conscience. Just don't let it fool you into becoming emotionally prickly or a martyr in your relationships.

You can also engage your 10-Year-Old in times of play, love, and intimacy. People of your type often enjoy "good vs. evil" stories (like *Star Wars*) and enjoy ethical debates. You can also use Authenticity to show sympathy for loved ones and be an emotional rock in times of distress.

The ISTJ 3-Year-Old Is Exploration (Ne)

Exploration encourages new experiences and helps people see a bigger, interconnected world. The preferred function for entrepreneurs and adventurers, Exploration helps people imagine and champion a better world...as long as they are willing to take chances and make big changes. It's an optimistic and imaginative function, activating intuition to spot opportunities.

As a 3-Year-Old function, Exploration for the ISTJ is the part of them that whispers from the shadows. Normally capable of sticking to the same routines and patterns day in and day out, suddenly the ISTJ will have be craving something new, unique, and adventurous.

There are three ways an ISTJ experiences the grip, the moments when the Driver process is stressed out, needs a break, and gives the 3-Year-Old function control of the car. This is most likely when the ISTJ suddenly sours on some aspect of their life or is haunted by a traumatic memory not fully processed.

Short-term grip. This surfaces when the usual solutions can't solve the current problem. After repeated attempts to find a familiar explanation for a new challenge, the ISTJ may become so frustrated that they try a quick fix, sometimes with consequences that cause even more damage. Impulsively quitting a job, spending money they can't afford, leaving town without a plan, starting or ending a relationship… the bigger and more impulsive the decision, the more likely the long-term consequences will be ugly.

Long-term grip. The ISTJ may become addicted to owning new things (at least, things new to them) and find their house overwhelmed with growing collections and clutter. If pressed to get rid of the clutter they've become emotionally attached to, the normally careful and detailed ISTJ may start losing facts and dates and find themselves in a mental fog.

Habitual grip. Unable to fully shut down the voice of Exploration but poor at interpreting its patterns, the ISTJ may become a catastrophizer. They'll fear that every new situation will end in calamity, that each new person is suspect. Anxiety over impending doom will cast a shadow over the ISTJ's life, twisting Exploration from an optimistic function into perpetual pessimism. As the ISTJ becomes increasingly closed off, they'll become bitter about the missed opportunities they denied themselves. This is the most difficult grip to disrupt. It wasn't built on proof or reason, so no proof or reason can counter it.

How to Best Use Exploration

The best way to use Exploration as a 3-Year-Old is to exercise it regularly, which will help prevent the grip from occurring. In this case, give yourself the novelty you crave. Start a DIY (do-it-yourself) project at home, or consider painting a wall a different color. Plan a trip to somewhere you've never been, or eat at a restaurant you've been meaning to try. Do something that brings out your inner craftsperson.

The goal is to give yourself a break from the familiar. Remind yourself that life doesn't have to be so predictable. Keep it simple, active, and safe—this isn't the time to make big decisions, it's a time to get playful. Once your Driver has had enough of a break, you can usually come back to the situation with a whole new outlook.

Using Exploration in this way can also provide a source of aspiration, the voice that whispers in the back of your mind. Exploration as an aspiration can encourage ISTJs to become creative and adventurous, knowing that if things aren't working, they can always be changed and improved through a little experimentation. It helps the ISTJ become open to new ideas and situations, letting them release fear of the unknown and rigidity of belief.

Reflection

The ways Exploration can grip an ISTJ are:

_____

_____

_____

The ways I find myself being in the Grip are (include behaviors and situations):

_____

_____

_____

I'm going to control the process by:

_____

_____

_____

My Exploration 3-Year-Old inspires me/is my aspiration in these ways:

_____

_____

_____

———————————————

CHAPTER 13

ISFJ Personality Type

ISFJs are great at accepting people and situations. They understand that our unique experiences over time shape us into the people we are.

With a natural ability to understand individual human needs, ISFJs craft a caring, socially supportive, and special world for those they love by creating routines and traditions. They are the reliable friend, parent, boss, or child who allows other people to feel rested and secure in their space.

Because they focus on stability and tradition, ISFJs may become overwhelmed if too much social change occurs too quickly. If this is left unchecked, it can develop into full-fledged fear, causing them to retreat into what is comfortable or become defensively critical.

If an ISFJ can open their heart and develop ways to increase connection with others, they will see their natural talents meeting the needs of others even beyond their immediate social groups. This, combined with principled love, allows the ISFJ to extend the care and support they naturally give to the world at large.

ISFJ CAR MODEL OVERVIEW

DRIVER Memory (Si)	COPILOT Harmony (Fe)
• Reliable, careful, and honors tradition • Upholds old traditions, and creates new ones • Is resilient through difficulty, with a strong sense of duty	• Prioritizes according to human need • Builds and communicates boundaries • Understands human dynamics

3-YEAR-OLD Exploration (Ne)	10-YEAR-OLD Accuracy (Ti)
• Suspicious of new experiences • Becomes anxious or catastrophizes in stressful situations • Has a sense of adventure and optimism for the future	• Knack for problem solving • Wants honest interchanges but struggles to be straightforward • Becomes cold and unfeeling when vulnerable

The ISFJ Driver Is Memory (Si)

It's important to remember that the Driver process is a talent, but that doesn't mean every ISFJ will have the same skill level or use it in a healthy way. Developing Memory as a healthy process is crucial to becoming an amazing ISFJ. While this cognitive function is most commonly used as a strength, it is influenced by its unique experiences and can be rather quirky. When using the Memory Driver, an ISFJ can learn to be reliable, be careful, and honor procedure; uphold old traditions and create new ones; and be resilient through and accepting of situations that cannot be changed.

Be Reliable and Careful

For people who use Memory as a Driver, living in an unpredictable or unstable environment carries a huge penalty. To avoid this kind of environment, people of your type are amazing at maintaining procedures and processes to minimize instability. If no procedure exists, Memory is compelled to find one.

Memory users recognize the need for care and caution. There is no reason to make repeated mistakes if a process is established to track them. It can be a simple aphorism to pass helpful knowledge from one generation to the next, such as "Measure twice, cut once." There are important reasons we have standards. While it might sound fun to "reinvent the wheel," actual car wheels would be incredibly difficult to shop for if there weren't an established standard and series of regulations on their size and fit to most vehicles.

It's important for an ISFJ to avoid becoming passive or getting used to chaos they could otherwise prevent or avoid. This talent extends to a much broader scale, and it could be argued that the very infrastructure of society—the rules and procedures that keep us going—are maintained and managed primarily by people who have the Memory process as a skill.

Exercise

Identify areas in your life that are unsafe or in violation of established standards, particularly things that (if left by themselves) could become a problem in the future. Look to a trusted organization, community, or family culture to gauge what the standard is and how you can correct it. If you're unsure, consult experts for guidance on how to correct the issue.

What areas of my life am I letting turn into chaos? Is there a procedure I can implement to reestablish sanity?

_____

_____

_____

_____

Being kind to myself, I'm going to address this chaos by:

_____

_____

_____

_____

Holds Relationship with Tradition

Memory users recognize how much each individual is influenced by their experiences. They also understand the importance of ensuring that most of those memories are positive. It is a pleasure to create wonderful memories that can be replayed and enjoyed forever. For this reason, it's common for Memory users to enjoy holidays, family gatherings, and other times when loved ones get together for momentous occasions. They may stay up all night Christmas Eve to make sure Christmas morning is everything their family hoped it would be.

They're also very touched when other people take the time to create a wonderful experience for them, and anniversaries are not to be missed. The first restaurant an ISFJ and their spouse go to isn't just another restaurant; it's a symbol of an important event, and going back to the same restaurant for anniversaries completes the experience. Once a shared memory has been repeated often enough, it becomes tradition, something upon which to anchor the relationship.

Traditions can also be used for healing. Trauma that is difficult to shake from the ISFJ's memory may require a healing tradition. For example, when a loved one dies, it may become an annual tradition to gather with others to talk about them, remember them, and pay tribute by living life fully in their honor.

The more sophisticated Memory gets, the more it's open to adopting new traditions. This is important to remember, as Memory in its infancy may be fearful of the unfamiliar. Changing one's traditions—including beliefs and paradigms—may feel disloyal to parents and other trusted authorities. But as it matures, Memory becomes a more adaptable function. It incorporates new experiences into its identity, learning to become whatever is appropriate to the context.

Exercise

Consider ways you can pass on the traditions of your family to the next generation. Is there a tradition you inherited that can be taught to your children, nieces, or nephews? Do they understand the importance of it, and will they contribute to passing it on after you're gone? How can you make the tradition more enjoyable in a way that will leave a lasting impression, help mold their experience, and help them want to carry the torch?

Reflection

The tradition that has had the biggest impact on me is:

_____

_____

_____

_____

_____

Show Resilience and Acceptance

Acceptance is not passive, nor is it complacent. It's a recognition of what cannot be changed, and a coming to terms with how those things impact one's life.

It's not easy to accept things as they are, but Memory has the greatest natural talent for it, and therefore, Memory users demonstrate great resilience during trying situations. True acceptance includes letting go of judgment and blame (including of oneself) and instead addressing situations with tolerance and forgiveness. Memory meets unfair situations with fairness, and finds peace within.

Memory users naturally understand the passage of time. They register change almost immediately and know how people are formed by their experiences. They get that we are who we are because of our past. Truly traumatic experiences can break people past their limits, but time can heal even brokenness. As it is said, "time heals all wounds," even if it takes decades, and we can be stronger people for it. They trek through their healing without fanfare. When an ISFJ is working through acceptance, they will very rarely announce it to others, preferring to quietly and internally walk through the process. It's not uncommon for outsiders to worry about ISFJs going through hard times, only to later remark on their seemingly superhuman resilience.

It's important to remember that acceptance is not submitting to unhealthy situations. It's not needlessly putting up with physical pain, a bad relationship, or a toxic context. Predicaments that can be changed should be changed. Acceptance is not endurance; it's the opposite. It is ending the suffering that accompanies resisting reality, but it does not involve seeking out a painful reality.

Exercise

Practice self-acceptance. When you notice that you are judging or rating yourself, look for a time in your past that may have prompted the thought. Did this criticism originally come from a parent? Is this self-criticism from a time you believed you failed at something? If you are much older than you were at the origin of the thought, is there wisdom you have now that changes how you experience the inciting event? Did you do the best you could at the time? What connections do you now see that you missed then?

Can you forgive your younger self? Does your younger self need forgiveness at all, or just a little understanding? Focus on letting go of the pain and the belief that caused the judgment.

Reflection

What's your biggest regret? What have you done to make amends with yourself or forgive yourself?

_____

_____

_____

_____

_____

_____

_____

Setting Up the Right Conditions

The enemy of Memory is instability. If life becomes too erratic, chaotic, or unpredictable, Memory has difficulty doing what it does best: establishing order and keeping everyone safe.

As your Driver, this is your flow state, and if you're not using this process enough, you'll eventually run out of juice and become depressed. Set up your conditions to access this mental process often. Keep life simple and manageable. And if life is throwing too many new or overwhelming things at you, make sure you have plenty of time for yourself to post-process these moments.

Journaling or otherwise recording events will help you review the details and figure out what's meaningful for you. Reaching out to others to talk about how shared life experiences impacted them can help you clarify your own thoughts and recall different aspects of your memories. Give yourself full permission to have different takeaways than others.

UNDEVELOPED MEMORY (Si)	DEVELOPED MEMORY (Si)
Avoid: • Getting used to chaos • Fearing the unfamiliar • Enduring bad situations that can be changed	Work Toward: • Implementing procedures and standards • Creating new traditions along with upholding the old • Developing acceptance of what can't be changed

Reflection

The talents Memory can give me are:

_____

_____

_____

The ways I usually use Memory are:

_____

_____

_____

I'm going to develop Memory more by:

_____

_____

_____

List three activities that put you into flow:

_____

_____

_____

The ISFJ Copilot Is Harmony (Fe)

Without an extraverted judging process, the ISFJ is not complete. Standards and traditions need to be vetted to ensure they're still relevant and serving people. Without checking in to ensure that the systems still work and are sustainable, the ISFJ may get stuck in a rut, unable to determine if their life is on track or if they're simply existing from day to day. They may become rigid and afraid of the unknown.

An extraverted judging process empowers the ISFJ to be flexible, build proof of concept, and not simply make assumptions based on past results. As opposed to sitting on the sidelines of life, they can become a proactive and empowered player.

It's important to remember that, like the Driver, the Copilot process is a talent. But that doesn't mean every ISFJ will have the same skill level or use it in a healthy way. Developing Harmony as a healthy process is crucial to becoming an amazing ISFJ.

It can be difficult to actively develop an extraverted function when one is an Introvert. It won't be as natural as working on Memory, so discipline and an eye on the rich rewards Harmony brings will be key.

Identify and Meet Needs

Fluctuating emotions are often the first sign that a person has unmet needs. An ISFJ may be so tuned in and sensitive to emotions that they find it easy to help people feel safe, loved, and stable. This can be as simple as hosting a party and making it look effortless, to being a shoulder for a grieving friend to cry on, to helping friends with complicated relationship issues. People who have developed their Harmony process become so skilled at this, they often become the go-to person in a time of crisis. Learning to be available to help meet people's needs helps the ISFJ become extremely industrious and have lots of unexpected talents and skills in a variety of areas.

It's equally important for an ISFJ to make sure they're getting their own needs met. They can't run on fumes all the time, and they can't be of help to others if they're perpetually exhausted. It's best to express unmet needs out loud. Similarly, it's good to avoid behavior like walking away when unhappy, being silently disapproving, or crying alone. When an ISFJ is comfortable expressing their own emotions, they become a role model for others who need to express themselves, and they are better able to help others meet their needs.

Exercise

Ask yourself, "What need is going unmet for me?" It could be alone time, better eating habits, more sleep, a conversation with a friend, a night out, or just some pampering. Once you identify it, ask yourself the easiest and fastest way to get that need met.

Reflection

Name your top three needs that frequently go unmet.

_____

_____

_____

Now, look at your schedule. What are you prioritizing that gets in the way of those needs being met? If it's people you care about, like your spouse, children, family, and friends, just remember that you can't get to their needs if you're running on fumes. Journal 3 to 5 ideas that you can begin implementing to fit those needs into your weekly schedule.

_____

_____

_____

_____

Build Healthy Boundaries

Harmony is the process that is used to create and maintain unspoken social contracts. Contracts are designed for us to know each other's expectations and honor them (as long as they are agreed upon). If you, as an ISFJ, don't know your boundaries, Harmony will encourage you to spend time with people and experience both acceptable and unacceptable behavior. Once you know your boundaries, Harmony helps you create contracts around them.

That means you'll have to communicate them to the people in your life, making sure they fully understand and agree to your boundaries. In a moment where you feel taken advantage of or thrown under a bus, ask yourself which of your boundaries has been broken, and if it was you or the other person that broke it.

Reflection

Follow the journal prompt below to become clearer about your boundaries. Feel free to repeat this journal prompt multiple times until you feel confident and authentic about the boundaries you've discovered and set. Once you've done so, share them with the three people who you feel closest to. If they are uncomfortable with your new boundaries, ask if it's because the boundaries are unreasonable, or because they will change the relationship. Be sensitive to resistance to change while staying firm with your requirements.

Remember: Boundary setting is a skill. It might be bumpy at first, but over time and with small successes, your boundaries will become a part of your identity.

Name three (or more) things you would like to see more of in your life:

1. _____

2. _____

3. _____

Name three (or more) behaviors you will never allow in your life again:

1. _____

2. _____

3. _____

I would like to strengthen the boundaries in these areas of my life:

_____

_____

_____

_____

I can improve the boundaries in each area of my life by:

_____

_____

_____

_____

If someone crosses a boundary, my plan is to say:

_____

_____

_____

_____

Understand Social Contracts

Understanding unspoken social contracts means being able to know what's expected of yourself and others. This comes from a lifelong study of what offends other people versus what makes them feel comfortable.

This type of understanding is a major advantage in new circumstances and when first meeting people. You're very rarely going to say the wrong thing or alienate others. In fact, people of your type are often popular in group settings because you can help keep the conversation going without offending anyone or leaving anyone out.

Most importantly, tapping into the spectrum of social contracts reminds an ISFJ that people have different values and needs. This opens them up to a bigger, broader world. Creating relationships with a variety of people reminds the ISFJ that everyone has had a unique experience and may come with fresh ideas and relevant perspectives.

Exercise

Make it your aim to meet many new people. The more people you meet, the more opportunities you have to understand the cultures they come from. What was their family's culture? What area of the country or world are they from? Do misunderstandings of culture get in the way of creating Harmony? How can your increased understanding of other people and their family or country help you to keep relationships between people in social settings congenial and happy?

Reflection

The way I feel about meeting new people is: _____

If I experience any hesitancy about meeting new people, what do I suspect is going on for me?

_____

_____

_____

I will meet one new person this week. Afterward, I will record the conversation and what I learned from it here:

_____

_____

_____

Copilot Growth

Harmony is the highest leverage point for growth in your personality. It encourages you as an ISFJ to proactively set boundaries for yourself and others, leading to an ultimately happier atmosphere. To encourage Harmony, ask yourself:

- Am I truly giving back, or just seeking approval?

- What is the kindest thing I can do in this situation?

- How can I be available to meet other people's needs without compromising my own?

- Does it make sense for me to put aside my desires for this relationship?

It's easy for an ISFJ to get lost in seeking the approval of others. Being vulnerable and speaking up can feel threatening. But if relationships are never built on intimacy and understanding, you will always feel like something is missing. Developing Harmony will encourage the ISFJ to break the cycle of perfectionism and approval seeking. The Harmonious ISFJ will focus on the comfort of others, not their mistakes and shortcomings.

Growing Harmony can be a challenge for you as an ISFJ. But setting boundaries in the outside world will help you meet your needs. Harmony encourages you to seek and foster healthy relationships with other people. Hiding isn't an option when there are delightful connections to be made. It also encourages you to establish healthy boundaries so that you no longer stand behind an impenetrable wall, but rather a gate that can be opened or closed.

Try these strategies to improve boundary-setting:

- Say "No" to every request for one full day. It doesn't matter how easy the request is; just say no as practice for setting boundaries.

- Every day, aim to set aside some "me time."

- Pay attention to crazymakers—those people who step on your boundaries. Practice standing up for yourself when they come into your world and demand attention.

Reflection

The talents Harmony can give me are:

_____

_____

_____

The ways I usually use Harmony are:

_____

_____

_____

I'm going to develop Harmony more by:

_____

_____

_____

List three ways you can start growing your Harmony process today:

_____

_____

_____

The ISFJ 10-Year-Old Is Accuracy (Ti)

Accuracy is designed to help a person look inside their own mind and spot incongruities and inconsistencies in their thinking. Illustratively, it sees the mind as being written in computer code and is always on the lookout for "bad code." This may be information and knowledge implanted by other people, or even by younger versions of the self, that are no longer worthy and should be removed. As a 10-Year-Old function, Accuracy for the ISFJ is that younger version of the self, and thus is less adept at spotting the bad code.

Sometimes it's a real pleasure to see things in technical terms. It allows the ISFJ some breathing room from the flood of emotions swirling around. Accuracy allows the data collected by Memory and Harmony—why people do what they do, how they respond to each other—to be organized into a scientific framework. And it's nice to have some way to organize the Memory function's observations since the sensory function has no real mechanism for capturing and tagging those insights.

As an introverted function, Accuracy allows the ISFJ to access a judging process while staying inside their own minds. This can be okay at times, but if the ISFJ gets used to relying upon Accuracy to help form their conclusions they can rationalize skipping development of their extraverted judging process of Harmony. And that's when the trouble starts. For ISFJs, this usually manifests by their being uncharacteristically critical, especially of other people's behavior.

Accuracy is, in a large part, about breaking information down and seeing how it doesn't line up. People who have it as a strength are usually pretty good at it. They're not looking for how someone is wrong, but rather for how the information itself could be more consistent. But an ISFJ is wired to be at their best when understanding the effects things have on other people's feelings and emotions.

If the ISFJ 10-Year-Old gets to have the final call without consulting the Copilot, it's going to sort intricate information at a 10-Year-Old level. 10-Year-Old Accuracy will look for other people to be wrong and criticize their thinking. Especially when the ISFJ is feeling threatened by untraditional or unfamiliar habits, they'll end up discrediting the new worldview.

Another way Accuracy can manifest itself as a 10-Year-Old is by being unnecessarily perfectionistic. While perfectionism can manifest in many situations, it is usually a strategy to avoid other people's disapproval.

The Driver/10-Year-Old Loop

There are three ways an ISFJ experiences the loop, the echo chamber–like relationship between the Driver and 10-Year-Old functions. The way to get out of a loop is the same in all cases: focus on developing the Harmony process.

Short-term loop. This may only last for a few moments up to a few days. Its intent is to protect the ISFJ from information that could be distressing at that moment. Usually, this is a reaction to feeling overwhelmed by unfamiliar perspectives or ideals. It's marked by uncharacteristic coldness and harsh criticism toward the person (or people) that caused the distress. The logic behind this reaction is to discredit others to protect the self: "I don't have to care about the feelings of an unworthy person, so I'll figure out all the ways this person is unworthy."

Have you ever been in an argument and used a grammatical or logical technicality against your opponent to "prove" they didn't know what they're talking about? For example, "Anyone who would use a double negative is obviously an idiot, and not worth my time." This behavior is the result of not having strong enough boundaries, lacking good strategies for dealing with overload, or not having a solid self-care regimen.

Long-term loop. This strategy entails hiding away from society: living inside books and research, shutting out other people's emotional baggage, and creating a bubble of invulnerability. While this loop doesn't make the ISFJ feel bad about themselves, as the first loop may do, it's more difficult to break away from. The ISFJ's entire world becomes molded around self-protection, and it usually results in loneliness. The only way to escape is to overcome the fear of being vulnerable.

Habitual loop. This is possibly the most challenging loop to overcome: perfectionism. The more perfect an ISFJ is, the less they can be called out on any undesirable behaviors. Or, at least, if the outer world confronts them, they have an airtight defense of having done everything by the book, exactly as expected, and without flaw. The world often rewards perfectionism more than it punishes it, so the ISFJ may receive mostly positive feedback for being oh-so-good. This reinforces the perfectionistic loop, and makes it nearly impossible to break.

Perfectionism is rife with challenges, however. Growth is stunted when the ISFJ is unwilling to accept and forgive themselves for faults. Additionally, perfectionists make everyone around them uncomfortable. For example, have you ever known someone so obsessed with keeping their house so perfect, they put plastic over all of the furniture? Was visiting a comfortable experience?

As a Harmony person, an ISFJ should want to make their guests as comfortable as possible. But when stuck in the perfectionist loop, they stop considering how their home will make their guests feel and start hyper-focusing on the details. They inadvertently create an inhospitable environment.

Reflection

The ways Memory and Accuracy can loop in an ISFJ are:

_____

_____

_____

The ways I find myself looping are (include behaviors and situations):

_____

_____

_____

I'm going to work on breaking my loop(s) by:

_____

_____

_____

How to Best Use Accuracy

If you find yourself getting overly critical, or hyper-focused on details and perfectionism, this is a bad use of the Accuracy function. Tap into the

Harmony function and ask yourself, "Yes, but what's best for everyone? What will get everyone's needs met, as well as my own?" If your behavior ends up pushing people away or not taking their feelings into consideration, it's time to reevaluate what's important to you.

That said, if you've carefully considered how best to meet other people's needs (as well as your own), and your gut is telling you that you need to spend some time breaking down the facts of the matter, that would be the time to listen to Accuracy. Just don't let it fool you into emotionally disconnecting as a protective, defensive strategy.

You can also engage your 10-Year-Old in times of play, love, and intimacy. People of your type often enjoy puzzles and other purely analytic games.

You can use the same mental process to get inside the heads of the people you love in order to truly understand how they think and see the world. Sharing important truths with loved ones—whether they're truths about your own boundaries, the missteps others may be taking, or even your philosophical views in general—helps them trust and rest into your honesty. It prevents you from appearing fake. The key is to ensure the information has first been vetted by Harmony as an act of caring and love for both yourself and the other individual. This quality is extremely appreciated by people that love you.

The ISFJ 3-Year-Old Is Exploration (Ne)

Exploration encourages new experiences and helps people see a bigger, interconnected world. The preferred function for entrepreneurs and adventurers, Exploration helps people imagine and champion a better world...as long as they are willing to take chances and make big changes. It's an optimistic and imaginative function, activating intuition to spot opportunities.

As a 3-Year-Old function, Exploration for the ISFJ is the part of them that whispers from the shadows. Normally capable of sticking to the same routines and patterns day in and day out, suddenly the ISFJ will have be craving something new, unique, and adventurous.

There are three ways an ISFJ experiences the grip, the moments when the Driver process is stressed out, needs a break, and gives the 3-Year-Old function control of the car. This is most likely when the ISFJ suddenly sours on some aspect of their life or is haunted by a traumatic memory not fully processed.

Short-term grip. This surfaces when the usual solutions can't solve the current problem. After repeated attempts to find a familiar explanation for a new challenge, the ISFJ may become so frustrated that they try a quick fix, sometimes with consequences that cause even more damage. Impulsively quitting a job, spending money they can't afford, leaving town without a plan, starting or ending a relationship… the bigger and more impulsive the decision, the more likely the long-term consequences will be ugly.

Long-term grip. The ISFJ may become addicted to owning new things (at least, things new to them) and find their house overwhelmed with growing collections and clutter. If pressed to get rid of the clutter they've become emotionally attached to, the normally careful and detailed ISFJ may start losing facts and dates and find themselves in a mental fog.

Habitual grip. Unable to fully shut down the voice of Exploration but poor at interpreting its patterns, the ISFJ may become a catastrophizer. They'll fear that every new situation will end in calamity, that each new person is suspect. Anxiety over impending doom will cast a shadow over the ISFJ's life, twisting Exploration from an optimistic function into perpetual pessimism. As the ISFJ becomes increasingly closed off, they'll become bitter about the missed opportunities they denied themselves. This is the most difficult grip to disrupt. It wasn't built on proof or reason, so no proof or reason can counter it.

How to Best Use Exploration

The best way to use Exploration as a 3-Year-Old is to exercise it regularly, which will help prevent the grip from occurring. In this case, give yourself the novelty you crave. Start a DIY (do-it-yourself) project at home, or consider painting a wall a different color. Plan a trip to somewhere you've never been, or eat at a restaurant you've been meaning to try. Do something that brings out your inner craftsperson.

The goal is to give yourself a break from the familiar and from the record playing in your mind. Remind yourself that life doesn't have to be so predictable. Keep it simple, active, and safe—this isn't the time to make big decisions, it's a time to get playful. Once your Driver has had enough of a break, you can usually come back to the situation with a whole new outlook.

Using Exploration in this way can also provide a source of aspiration, the voice that whispers in the back of your mind. Exploration as an aspiration can encourage ISFJs to become creative and adventurous, knowing that if things aren't working, they can always be changed and improved through a little experimentation. It helps the ISFJ become open to new ideas and situations, letting them release fear of the unknown and rigidity of belief.

Reflection

The ways Exploration can grip an ISFJ are:

_____

_____

_____

The ways I find myself being in the grip are (include behaviors and situations):

_____

_____

_____

I'm going to control the process by:

_____

_____

_____

My Exploration 3-Year-Old inspires me/is my aspiration in these ways:

_____

_____

_____

CHAPTER 14

INTP Personality Type

There is a thought leader living inside every INTP. For this thought leader to affect the world, the INTP must build the skills of persuasion, influence, and connection in the midst of raw data collection.

INTPs have the capacity to manage immense amounts of information and data. It is common for INTPs to claim they know nothing about a subject until they know everything about it. They can also turn that data and information into knowledge and wisdom. This comes from gaining reference experiences and testing theoretical information in the real world. INTPs move toward thought leadership, but only when they are willing to prove themselves wrong instead of finding ways in which they are always right.

INTPs have a deep, sometimes unconscious, yearning to connect with others. If a connection remains aloof even after an INTP's best attempts have been made, they can become jaded by people and their "silly social games." It can be a challenge for the INTP to avoid cynicism. But when the INTP prioritizes exploring life over defending their conclusions, they develop a cheerfulness that attracts others and leads to the connections they secretly crave.

DRIVER Accuracy (Ti)	**COPILOT** Exploration (Ne)
• Prunes out logical inconsistencies and incongruities • Practices integrity and radical honesty • Focus and skill mastery	• Innovates • Recognizes patterns in behaviors and processes • Sees between the lines and makes connections
3-YEAR-OLD Harmony (Fe)	**10-YEAR-OLD** Memory (Si)
• Uncertain of how to maintain connections and reputation • Emotional outbursts when stressed • Desires to meet society's needs	• Remembers the past and how it shaped the present • Appreciates routines, though has difficulty sticking to them • Somewhat suspicious of new routines; prefers creature comforts and what is known

The INTP Driver Is Accuracy (Ti)

It's important to remember that the Accuracy process is a talent, and that means not every INTP will have the same skill level or use it in a healthy way. Developing Accuracy as a healthy process is crucial to becoming an amazing INTP. Accuracy gives the INTP the ability to prune out logical inconsistencies and incongruities, as well as integrity, radical honesty, focus, and mastery.

Prune Out Logical Inconsistencies and Incongruities

People with a strong Accuracy process often have no problem slicing through emotionally difficult circumstances in order to see the situation as presented.

Accuracy users have the ability to spot logical fallacies and biases. That said, it's far easier to see other people's biases than our own. The more an INTP develops Accuracy, the more the function will enable an INTP to spot their own biases and dissonance.

Accuracy is a subjective function. This means the Accuracy user asks, "What makes sense to *me*?" When the function is in its infancy, it can rationalize nearly anything. Over time, as the process develops and matures, Accuracy users begin spotting incongruities not only in what others are saying, but in their own thinking. Like a programmer working through lines of code, an Accuracy user's first job is to clean up corrupt script within their own mind.

This can be challenging. Once a mental code is discovered to be faulty, it can seem like the mind is being ripped apart in an effort to dismantle the flawed idea. This may manifest as an existential crisis, and can be as emotionally impactful as the death of a loved one. But the more you build the skill of Accuracy, the more survivable the surgical removal of faulty code becomes. Eventually, the rewards of clean thinking are felt, and removing cognitive dissonance and bias becomes part of your identity as an INTP.

Reflection

What if there were no right answers, only better questions? If you were able to craft your own ideas from scratch, what would they be? Do you fear losing your competency if you lose your thoughts? Can you ever truly lose who you are, or are you constantly changing, anyway?

At its best, Accuracy learns to say, "I don't know," without being disturbed by uncertainty. Reflect on the following questions:

What thought or belief have I not been looking at too carefully? If I looked at it critically, would it survive an honest analysis? Do I fear letting it go? What else would I have to look at critically if I let this one go?

_____

_____

_____

Being kind to myself, I'm going to address this belief by:

_____

_____

_____

Integrity and Radical Honesty

Well-developed Accuracy allows you to express truths no matter how hurtful they can be. While truth can hurt, it doesn't have to be unkind or cruel. In fact, Accuracy users intend to be kind when speaking harsh truths, and are usually appreciative when others do them the service of being honest. Accuracy users would much rather know the truth now than be deluded and taken off guard later.

Young Accuracy users can feel like they're always on the wrong side of the conversation. It's not uncommon for INTPs to get the feedback that they're always saying the wrong thing or being offensive. The world has a push-pull relationship with the idea of truth, and INTPs can sometimes find themselves grasping at how to say something.

As the Accuracy skill matures, however, INTPs become less concerned with forcing truth on others and develop a skill in sharing truths in context. For example, the proverbial question, "Do I look fat in this dress?" may appear to be a trap, but to the developed Accuracy user, this is a simple question to answer: either the individual is thin and no dress will make them appear fat, or they are fat and no dress will make them appear thin. If the person is, in reality, asking about how flattering the dress is, then yes, there are some dresses that are more and less flattering to the body. The keen Accuracy user would love to know if that is the actual question, and they would likely ask for clarification. Because if it is, they would wonder, why doesn't the person just ask it that way?

While candor can be disconcerting at first, most people are relieved to hear people give unbiased thoughts. On this front, Accuracy is the watchman that makes sure we don't drift too far into collective dissonance just to keep up social pretenses. But it also ensures that the INTP doesn't drift too far into their own pretenses, and so it helps the INTP develop a strong appreciation for integrity and duty. Doing the right thing is logically consistent, even when it's uncomfortable or unpleasant. Of course, if an INTP hasn't first been honest with themselves, then their views can instead be antisocial opinions, which are rarely welcome.

Exercise

Observe how often you lie to other people. According to a study done by the University of Massachusetts at Amherst, 60 percent of people tell an average of two to three lies in a ten-minute conversation.

For example, when people ask how you're doing, do you answer honestly? Do you feign interest in conversations that are boring to you? Do you hide the truth to avoid hurt feelings? While you watch yourself lie in conversation, don't judge or justify yourself by saying, "I have to lie in this situation because...." Just observe.

Now that you've watched the different ways you tend to lie, turn this inward. Watch how often you lie to yourself. Keep a finger on the pulse of your cognitive dissonance.

Reflection

How could I be more honest with others and myself? Am I willing to speak the truth even if it's hurtful? Do others find me condescending when I do this? How can I learn to speak complete truths?

_____

_____

_____

_____

_____

Focus and Mastery

Accuracy offers an amazing ability to focus, which is represented in a huge variety of ways. It's seen in the best athletes, philosophers, and mechanics. When they break down ideas, machines, or systems, they have to keep track of all the moving parts. It's not easy to do, and it requires them to develop focus. People who use Accuracy keep track of data by creating frameworks. With a framework in place, they can zoom in and focus all of their attention on one thing, thereby mastering it.

A basketball player using Accuracy can spend endless hours practicing 3-point shots, ever so slightly altering the angle of their wrist until they can shoot a perfect 3-point shot each time. This same talent starts with noticing incongruities of thoughts as a child. The same process takes place in the mind and on the court: When something doesn't line up, keep working until it lines up perfectly. Philosophers and scientists often use Accuracy when breaking down ideas and beliefs.

It's important to discipline the mind to focus on mastering practical skills, not simply pleasurable activities. It's easy to focus on things that are fun and engaging, but INTPs make a true difference when they can use their skill to focus on mundane or "boring" activities. Using focus and skill mastery to improve yourself and fulfill duties creates a rewarding life.

Exercise

When we focus our eyes, we zero in on a single object and allow everything else to become fuzzy around it. That object becomes very clear and sharp, and if we focus long enough, we'll begin to see the object in detail. All of the object's parts become obvious.

Do this with your mind. Work on a problem while allowing everything outside the problem to become fuzzy. This could anything from trying to master a musical refrain or working out a complex mathematical problem. As you spend more time focusing your attention, you will start to see its parts, such as the notes in the refrain or the formulas of the math problem.

How can I discipline my mind to be 5 percent more focused today?

_____

_____

_____

Setting Up the Right Conditions

The enemy of Accuracy is relationship overload. Accuracy users require concentrated, focused time. If an INTP is responsible for meeting other people's needs or is frequently interrupted, they will lose focus and mental stamina.

As your INTP Driver, Accuracy is your flow state, and if you're not using this process enough, you'll eventually run out of energy and may become depressed. Set up your daily conditions to access this mental process often. For example, if you find yourself getting overwhelmed with the demands of others or with domestic responsibilities, find time in your day for just yourself and your research. Learning complex systems—whether they're conceptual or mechanical—may not be taxing for your mind, but they are demanding of your full attention.

Developing your Driver process may seem unneeded, since it's natural for you to regularly use it. But there's a difference between using the Accuracy process and developing it.

When Accuracy is young, it over-relies on its own logic. It can assume others aren't as knowledgeable, smart, or thoughtful. Young Accuracy disregards others' experiences and observations, assuming the human experience is without merit unless it has been supported by hard science or data. Blind to the impact they have on others, INTPs can appear harsh and callous when delivering information they think others should already know. On the other hand, Accuracy users can zoom into a subject and miss relevant pieces of information, assuming they already have everything worked out.

INTPs must recognize that other people can be the source of knowledge and wisdom. There is much to learn from another's experience. An INTP can expand their own reason by learning from a broader world.

UNDEVELOPED ACCURACY (Ti)	DEVELOPED ACCURACY (Ti)
Avoid:	Work Toward:
• Rationalizing biases	• Pruning biases and dissonance
• Unkind opinions justified as truths	• Articulating complete truths
• Focusing on indulgent skills	• Mastering skills to fulfill duties

Reflection

The talents Accuracy can give me are:

_____

_____

_____

The ways I usually use Accuracy are:

_____

_____

_____

I'm going to develop Accuracy more by:

_____

_____

_____

List three activities that put you into flow:

_____

_____

_____

The INTP Copilot Is Exploration (Ne)

Without an extraverted perceiving process, the INTP is not complete. Without access to feedback from the world and noticing how other people experience reality, the INTP's convictions and beliefs will be insular and self-serving. Broadening their territory to include people of many walks of life, receiving dissenting views, and allowing themselves to fail encourages the INTP to loosen their attachment to identity while pursuing a better version of themselves.

An extraverted perceiving process also empowers the INTP to learn different forms of communication and persuasion. They can, over time, become powerful change agents, as opposed to silenced idealists who hope the world will change for them.

It's important to remember that, like the Driver, the Copilot process is a talent. But that doesn't mean every INTP will have the same skill level or use it in a healthy way. Developing Exploration as a healthy process is crucial to becoming an amazing INTP.

It can be difficult to actively develop an extraverted function as an Introvert. It won't be as natural as working on Accuracy, so discipline and a focus on the rich rewards Exploration brings will be key.

Pattern Recognition

Exploration, as an intuitive process, uses advanced pattern recognition to see connections other people miss. It wants to know what's going on behind the curtain, what it can't directly access. As it gets more sophisticated, Exploration's predictive powers improve, and the Exploration user eventually becomes adept at not only seeing what others miss, but imagining what could exist. Whiteboard sessions, or meetings where ideas are shared and built upon with other creative minds, are contexts where this ability truly shines. Feeding off the energy of other people's suggestions, Exploration will come up with truly novel and unique ideas that transform the mundane into the extraordinary.

Remember, this ability is a skill that must be honed. It's easy to assume that one's ability to recognize patterns is infallible, and without proper development, this can become a justification for declaring that one is right without further explanation.

But pattern recognition gets better over time only if the Exploration user lets themselves experience the world at large. Reading and researching are part of the process, but they are not a complete expression of Exploration. It is an extraverted function. Theories have to be acted upon to get real-world feedback, and if the theory was wrong, it has to be revised.

Exploration benefits from testing and iterating. When the Exploration user finds that they are wrong, they view it as an opportunity for expanding their understanding, learning even greater possibilities, and transforming this amazing talent into real opportunities. Instead of getting defensive when they learn their original idea was wrong, the INTP can say a mental "thanks!" to the universe for giving them the gift of calibration.

Exercise

Get good at pattern recognition by making quick predictions about how a mystery movie will end. Mystery movies follow a limited set of plot twists. Use your Exploration process to not only predict an individual movie's ending, but to identify the types of plot twists movie scripts use.

Reflection

Name three times your pattern recognition was confirmed to be accurate:

_____

_____

_____

Name three times your pattern recognition was confirmed to be wrong:

_____

_____

_____

The next time I'm wrong, I'm going to learn to enjoy the process by:

_____

_____

_____

Excitement, Fuel, and Optimism

The Exploration function burns a lot of fuel, so it must also generate a lot fuel. According to Dario Nardi, author of *Neuroscience of Personality*, Extraverted Intuition is the cognitive function that takes the longest to get into a flow state but, once there, it's the most difficult to slow down.

INTPs are wired to have energy to burn when they tap into the Exploration function. They ride on the feeling of optimism and being fully engaged. There are so many things the world has to offer, so many possibilities for improvement. The sheer brightness of it all can be contagious.

There can be challenges, of course. Possibility thinking can be seen as threatening to some people, and those who use Exploration may feel they have to fight to represent it. Fortunately, Exploration is unfazed by negative feedback. Its job isn't to accept defeat but to see all the different ways to make something happen.

The greatest gift INTPs can give themselves is permission to continue using Exploration in the face of opposition. Part of Exploration's genius is finding new ways to present itself. If one style doesn't work, it will modify its strategy to become what the situation needs it to be. This is why Exploration users are often highly charismatic.

Exercise

Practice starting your day with active Exploration. That means actually doing something in the outer world, not just reading something new online. An example could be getting lost on the way to or from work each day. Go to work for 21 days straight without taking the same route twice. This will force you to find creative solutions and observe connections you didn't focus on in the past.

Name the most exciting thing in your life right now:

_____

_____

_____

Name something that always gives you joy, just by thinking about it. How can you include this in your life every single day? Be creative with how you can introduce this activity daily:

_____

_____

———————————————

Leaving Comfort Zones

Exploration loves novelty and blazing new trails. It faces six-foot-tall grass holding a machete, screaming, "tigers be damned!" Getting fully into this function means being willing to leave comfort zones, physically, psychologically, and emotionally.

This can be truly difficult for INTPs. As natural Introverts, much about the outer world can seem threatening. But it can also be difficult to explore inner terrain that seems threatening. Each person has their own beliefs and ideas inside them that they get attached to and may be unwilling to reevaluate. There are also parts of everyone's egos that don't want to be questioned, even though they must be. This requires INTPs to work hard to get around all of those tricky defensive strategies they've formed, both consciously and unconsciously.

Conveniently, as comfort zones are expanded, anxiety and fear of the unknown turn into the excitement of what could be. All growth happens outside of comfort zones, and the feeling of growing can become a healthy addiction. INTPs know they've fully developed this function when growth becomes the new normal.

Exercise

Practice getting out of your comfort zone by seeking out new situations you would not normally pursue. If there's a question of doing something that feels right to you, but may include some hassle or an "unsafe" element, practice taking the risk instead of playing it safe. It's common for people of your type, once they get past the scary part of a new experience, to say "Was that it?" Most of your growth happens by being adventurous and letting go of the belief that you must live the way others want you to live.

Reflection

Today, I will get outside of my comfort zone by:

_____

_____

_____

I will make this a daily practice by:

_____

_____

_____

Copilot Growth

Exploration is one of the highest leverage points for growth in your personality. It allows an INTP to test theories and beliefs in real-life situations. Are they congruent? Do they play out, or do they only hold up in theory? Is there a piece of awareness you're missing? Here are some ways that an INTP can phrase questions using their Exploration process:

- What's a creative solution to this problem?

- What am I seeing that no one else seems to be addressing?

- Where's the most exotic place I could travel?

As an INTP, your Exploration process can help you reconcile what's true to you and what's true for the outside world. As you increase your understanding, instead of being seen by others as implacable and unable to accept being wrong, you will become a source of wisdom and creative thought.

To become a thought leader, you'll need to get outside yourself and experience the world for what it is, not what you wish it was. Only then can you discover what beliefs and paradigm shifts are leverage points for society. You may discover a radically new way of experiencing a new point of view, leading to an awesome new innovation.

Exploration reminds the INTP of their natural thirst for life. Comfort will never nourish the inner adventurer, the one that thirsts to make a difference in the world. Instead of burying the feeling of a wasted life, Exploration will help the INTP focus on that voice and answer it with an insistence that this life will not be squandered. It will help the INTP suck the marrow out of life.

You can experiment with the world around you and learn to hone your Exploration by:

- Exploring a new part of town, with no agenda

- Trying a new food each time you go out

- Flirting or bantering with someone, without thinking about what you'll say

- Joining an improv class

As an INTP, you will bring the best version of yourself to the world when you get outside your comfort zone and explore every aspect of life. Developing Exploration makes you inspirational.

Reflection

The talents Exploration can give me are:

_____

_____

_____

The ways I usually use Exploration are:

_____

_____

_____

I'm going to develop Exploration more by:

_____

_____

_____

List three ways you can start growing your Exploration process today:

_____

_____

_____

The INTP 10-Year-Old Is Memory (Si)

Memory is designed to seek reliability. As a perceiving function, it instinctively asks, how can I know this to be true? Have I seen this before? Have experts spoken on this? What has already been established? A desire for reliability encourages Memory to seek the safety in all things, whether tangible or intangible.

The INTP can use the Memory function as a connection point to the past, reminding them of how the present world came to be. Memory gives the INTP a sense of continuity, countering their idealism around timelines. Memory can also augment creative solutions by knowing what has already been suggested, what has and hasn't worked, and what is well-covered territory. It helps develop routines, and can solidify an INTP's sense of duty. However, as a 10-Year-Old function, Memory can throttle creative thinking and opportunity spotting.

As an introverted function, Memory allows the INTP to access a perceiving process while staying inside their own mind. This can be okay at times, but if the INTP gets used to relying on Memory to support their judgments, they can rationalize skipping development of their Copilot, Exploration. And that's when the trouble starts. For INTPs, this usually manifests by staying in a physical, emotional, or intellectual comfort zone.

Memory is, in a large part, about seeking reliability. It craves the safe bet. People who have Memory as a strength are usually pretty good at it, and they use this function to maintain precedent, stabilize systems, and continue traditions that work. But you're an INTP, meaning you're at your best when looking for the possibilities and what could be, not when dwelling on the past or present.

If your 10-Year-Old gets to have the final call without consulting the Copilot of Exploration, it's going to see the world like a child would. Children aren't thinking in terms of carrying on time-honored traditions and maintaining precedent. When in the midst of seeking reliability, they're usually scared and looking for whatever is familiar to keep them safe.

Memory can manifest as a 10-Year-Old by claiming expertise on a topic without fully testing the information. "I read somewhere that...." can be turned into a statement of authority, even when there are more possibilities (even esoteric ones) to be discovered. However it shows up, the motive is to protect Accuracy's conclusions and, ultimately, the INTP's competency.

The Driver/10-Year-Old Loop

There are three ways an INTP experiences the loop, the echo chamber–like relationship between the Driver and 10-Year-Old functions. The way to get out of a loop is the same in all cases: focus on developing the Exploration process.

Short-term loop. This may only last for a few moments up to a few days. Being proven wrong can feel truly awful for an INTP, as if their competency has been called into question. Many INTPs can even sense when this is approaching, and will instinctively shut off their ability to take in new information. They may begin by arguing their position, but if they sense that the other person has better points, they may retreat inside their minds or physically leave the situation. Alternatively, some INTPs take over the conversation, becoming a know-it-all and drowning out the new information. Either way, the normal input and output of conversation is interrupted.

Long-term loop. When stuck in this loop, the INTP sticks to comfort zones. They are reluctant to leave the house, preferring to stay home to play video games, do endless research on a new topic, rewatch favorite movies, and generally surround themselves with well-worn creature comforts. They may leave the house to go to work, go to the store, run necessary errands, or visit family and long-term friends. But new friends are never made, and new experiences are only had when they're forced. The INTP finds themselves repeating the same sort of day over and over, ignoring the sense they are wasting their life.

Habitual loop. This is possibly the most challenging loop to overcome. The INTP checks out of life, unquestionably believing that all of life is pain, and they must do whatever they have to do to survive until the ride is over. They might have a job, but one they hate and put no effort into improving. Or they're jobless and live off of the kindness of other people, sleeping on couches without much attempt to exchange value. They see no beauty left in life. They only offer the bare minimum, which means avoiding human connection even when it's craved. The INTP isn't willing to take any chances, isn't willing to be brave. The story is that they've already tried and failed, been rejected and experienced too much pain. Their entire life reflects this loop.

Reflection

The ways Accuracy and Memory can loop in an INTP are:

_____

_____

_____

The ways I find myself looping are (include behaviors and situations):

_____

_____

_____

I'm going to work on breaking my loop(s) by:

_____

_____

_____

How to Best Use Memory

If you find yourself shutting yourself off from outer-world feedback, becoming passive, or hiding away from the world, this is a bad use of the Memory function. Tap into the Exploration function and ask yourself, "Who would I be if I became the best version of myself?" And, maybe a little easier, "What mischief can I get into today?"

That said, if you've been taking life by the horns and exploring your heart out, and your gut is telling you that you may need to dig in some roots or reestablish your connection with who you are, that would be the time to listen to Memory. Just don't let it fool you into stagnating.

You can also engage your 10-Year-Old in times of play, love, and intimacy. People of your type can absorb an impressive amount of information. When an INTP is at their best, they use Memory to kindle a sense of responsibility and duty, implementing routines in their life. Many INTPs enjoy plunging into the history of their favorite topics, understanding their full etymology. There's nothing wrong with playing video games, rereading favorite books, or rewatching favorite movies. Use these activities as relaxation, not as a way of life. And share your favorites with friends, reliving the experience to make it feel like the first time.

The INTP 3-Year-Old Is Harmony (Fe)

Harmony is designed to connect with other people, get needs met, and understand interpersonal dynamics. The preferred function of both nurturers and culture creators, Harmony users spend a lifetime asking how to meet the needs of the collective and keep everyone's morale up. Data can be important, but not at the expense of causing conflict and hurting people.

As a 3-Year-Old process, Harmony is the part of the INTP that whispers from the shadows. Normally quite capable of ignoring societal expectations and people's feelings, suddenly an INTP will feel the need to connect with other people, emotionally express themselves, and receive positive feedback—especially respect—from others.

There are three ways an INTP experiences the grip, the moments when the Driver process is stressed out and needs a break, and the 3-Year-Old function takes over the wheel of the car. This is most likely when the INTP gets rejected or receives harsh criticism for sharing their thoughts.

Short-term grip. This is generally manifested as an explosion of emotion. Usually unfamiliar with emotional expression, the INTP will experience a temper tantrum, often lashing out with blame at others. Without the skill developed to reign the emotion in, usually it has to be fully expressed and worked through before the INTP calms down enough to reflect.

Long-term grip. While Harmony is plugged in to social dynamics, its 3-Year-Old form focuses on one of the most self-centered elements: personal status. The INTP may get into the habit of bragging, constantly showcasing their brilliance and perpetually bringing the conversation back around to them.

Unable to rest into their own self-esteem, the INTP will use the childlike version of Harmony to implore others to give them approval.

Habitual grip. This shows up as codependent or otherwise unhealthy relationships. Connection is difficult for INTPs to create, which is why they tend to be loyal to the people they love. But in this version of the grip, they fear that they cannot replicate connection. The INTP may think that no one else will ever love them, so stay in an unhealthy relationship for far too long. They may show up either as the victim or as the perpetrator of abuse, or as both. Efforts toward getting healthy will be seen as threats: Any change to the relationship, including an improvement, may destroy it.

How to Best Use Harmony

The best way to use Harmony as a 3-Year-Old is to exercise it regularly, which will help prevent the grip from occurring. In this case, connect with a friend or family member through physical touch (hugging) or through shared emotional experience. Watch something funny together. If you can't be in each other's presence, give them a call and let them know you missed them and wanted to reconnect. Remind yourself that there are people who love you as you are.

Remember, Harmony is an extraverted process, so make sure you're active and engage with other people. Thirty minutes should be long enough, but feel free to take as long as needed to de-stress. If you're still not feeling settled, invite someone to go to the movies, or play a board or video game together. If you're in a romantic relationship, cuddles are your best friend.

The goal is to give yourself a break from having to rationalize everything. Make sure you're getting as far out of your head and as far into connections as possible. It won't feel natural at first, but it has a huge payoff. Once your Driver has had enough of a break, you can usually come back to the situation with a whole new outlook.

Using Harmony in this way can also provide a source of aspiration. It can encourage INTPs to be contributors and thought leaders. People of your type have literally changed how we see reality, and when an INTP understands the power within, they can be the calibrator of entire societies.

Reflection

The ways Harmony can grip an INTP are:

_____

_____

_____

The ways I find myself being in the Grip are (include behaviors and situations):

_____

_____

_____

I'm going to control the process by:

_____

_____

_____

My Harmony 3-Year-Old inspires me/is my aspiration in these ways:

_____

_____

_____

CHAPTER 15

INFP Personality Type

There may be no type that understands Carl Rogers' quote, "What is most personal is most universal," more than the INFP.

From a young age, INFPs are wired to be deeply in touch with their emotions, constantly scanning and observing their responses to situations. They recognize that everyone is the hero of their own story, and they can get into flow by listening to the experiences of other people, understanding more about themselves in the process.

Everything is subjective for INFPs. Because most systems strip away personal feelings and subjective expression to favor accomplishment, it becomes difficult for INFPs to create effective, productive systems in their lives. INFPs often find themselves dreaming big without taking the practical steps to make them a reality.

INFPs crave deep validation of their authentic emotions. They often feel unable to fully express their nuanced feelings in the outside world. This can lead to feelings of loneliness or distance from those they desperately want to commune with.

When an INFP can clarify what they truly value, they can focus on their goals and become motivated. They can then become an unstoppable force in the world.

DRIVER Authenticity (Fi)	**COPILOT** Exploration (Ne)
• Lives by core values and ethics • Has inner alignment and conviction • Sympathy, art, and emotional aikido	• Innovates • Recognizes patterns in behaviors and processes • Sees between the lines and makes connections
3-YEAR-OLD Effectiveness (Te)	**10-YEAR-OLD** Memory (Si)
• Difficulty setting up efficient systems • Uses controlling or aggressive tactics when feeling pressure • Inner ambition to make big things happen	• Remembers the past and how it shaped the present • Appreciates routines, though has difficulty sticking to them • Somewhat suspicious of new routines; prefers creature comforts and what is known

The INFP Driver Is Authenticity (Fi)

It's important to remember that the Driver process is a talent, but that doesn't mean every INFP will have the same skill level or use it in a healthy way. Developing Authenticity as a healthy process is crucial to becoming an amazing INFP. It will give you core values and ethics, inner alignment and conviction, and sympathy, art, and emotional aikido.

Core Values and Ethics

Being aware of one's emotional responses at all times creates an ethical complication. A person may feel one way in one situation but completely different in a seemingly identical situation. They must learn to judge the

context of their reactions: Are their responses fully subjective, or are they based on certain principles that can be used to guide future behaviors?

What is a truly ethical action? When one feels the full emotional force of all behaviors, they ask this question frequently to create a personal list of what's ethical and what isn't. Since the majority of behaviors fall on a spectrum, INFPs are pretty laid back about most actions people take. A person may be insensitive or obtuse, but unless they offend one of the INFP's core values or true principles, the behavior is likely to be forgotten or even go unnoticed.

Once a core value has been upset, however, the Authenticity process will immediately register the offending action as unacceptable, and the INFP will have to figure out how to deal with the offense. At this point, they may become uncharacteristically impassioned, outraged, and aggressive.

This is why it is incredibly important to know one's core values and revise them frequently. It's important for an Authenticity user to not simply default to whatever feels good in the moment, or get locked into values formed at a less sophisticated age. When one's core values are set in youth and not reviewed, a person can show up as self-absorbed, indulgent, and fixated on their own experience. A truly healthy Authenticity function will draft a set of values that are both meaningful and adaptable. Just like people change and grow, one's core values should change and grow with them. As an INFP gets to know themselves better over time, their core values will be a natural emergent of greater self-knowledge.

Exercise

Core values are guiding principles. In all situations, core values determine right or wrong and let you know if you're on the right path. Take a sheet of paper and write down all behaviors you believe are either right or wrong, regardless of the situation. Give yourself plenty of time to do this exercise: hours, days, even weeks. Feel free to revisit this list on a regular basis and refine it as you learn more about yourself.

My top five core values are ... because...:

_____

_____

_____

_____

_____

Five core values that I have reevaluated and adapted over the years are:

_____

_____

_____

_____

Inner Alignment and Conviction

Everyone has experienced inner conflict, but the Authenticity Driver function knows that being of two minds is just the tip of the iceberg. Focused on being true to themselves, INFPs know there isn't just one self; rather, there's a legion of voices inside, all vying for attention. It's difficult to know what to do when listening intently to all those voices, each with their own agenda.

The task of Authenticity is to listen closely to what each part of the individual is saying and prioritize based on what's true, what's right, and what will get needs or desires met.

If the burden of Authenticity is to listen to one's inner council, the responsibility of Authenticity is to lead those voices into alignment. Or, if they can't be in full chorus, Authenticity must determine which parts should have the stage at any given time.

The easiest decisions are ones that present no inner conflict, which could be said to align with convictions. The moments when all inner voices are in full agreement are beautiful moments and produce such momentum that the INFP can feel unstoppable. It's difficult for Authenticity users to feel motivated when they feel uncertain, but once certainty is on the table, the INFP becomes an unstoppable force capable of extraordinary feats.

Managing the inner council of voices and ideas is a skill that must be built, similar to managing groups of people. It's imperative for an INFP to learn to prioritize their needs and desires based on core values and a code of ethics, not simply what feels good in the moment.

It's important for INFPs to develop a healthy relationship with conviction. When Authenticity is young, it focuses on the good feelings of being right. In fact, it can get addicted to the feeling of righteousness. This addiction leads to a synthetic conviction, where the INFP will choose only the voice that wants desperately to be right while shutting out both internal and external dissent. This behavior is invariably followed by wracking self-doubt.

Self-confidence comes from seeking out dissenting voices and sitting with them, asking difficult questions, and considering what the answers mean for the INFP's identity. If some of those voices are unhealthy and have ill intent, it becomes the INFP's responsibility to heal that part of themselves, or even allow the toxic parts of themselves to die. It's a painful process that can feel like literal death to Authenticity users, but it is a crucial aspect of self-management and self-leadership.

Exercise

Think of a decision you've been ruminating on, maybe even putting off. Listen for any internal conflict. Imagine yourself in a council room where each voice comes up with a compelling argument. Allow them plenty of time to get through their concerns, considerations, and valid points. After each voice has stated their case, pull out your list of core values. Ask yourself which arguments are most in alignment with your core values, and why some of the voices may be counter to your values. If this is a values-based decision, why are some of the voices representing a solution that runs counter to your values? Are these less mature or unhealed parts of yourself? What would persuade them to stay consistent with your values? Alternatively, is it a decision that isn't values based? Is more information needed and are the voices stumped? Do you need to learn more and revisit the council later?

Reflection

What parts of yourself have you been avoiding listening to? Is it because they aren't saying things of value, or because what they have to say represents changes for which you may not feel ready?

_____

_____

_____

_____

Being kind to myself, I'm going to address these parts by:

_____

_____

_____

_____

Sympathy, Art, and Emotional Aikido

So much of the human experience is impossible to express using verbal language. Despite that, all of us have a need to understand each other and to be understood. When Authenticity is in its infancy, a person can be quite self-absorbed. Without sharpening the function, an INFP will stay fixated on their own experience, unable to surface long enough to feel sympathy with others.

Over time and with development, Authenticity users recognize that other people's experiences are incredibly real to them, and so they offer their compassion and sympathy. People with Authenticity Drivers know that to understand a person's inner workings is to demonstrate their emotions and motivations back to them, showing that all people share these things in common and can also experience them on a deeply personal level. The most powerful medium through which humans accomplish this task is art and self-expression.

Throughout history, Authenticity users have found themselves unable to convey their own subjective emotional experience in conversation, which has driven them to become artists. They have become great at replicating an aspect of humanity in a single, time-bound piece of art: painting, song, poem, statue, choreographed dance, performance, or even their lifestyle. The foundation of art is the expression of universal human experiences, honoring that it will be personalized by the receiver.

Authenticity uses art to perform emotional aikido (page 73), transforming one person's energy into a shared experience. It's difficult to deny the poignancy of a shared experience, or to judge it harshly. Authenticity encourages onlookers to see themselves and the world with sympathy.

Exercise

Communicate an emotion to a friend without using words. You may use hand gestures, facial expressions, drawings, noises, and sounds. Ask your friend if they understood the emotion you were trying to share, and if they were able to replicate the emotion within themselves by linking it to their own experience.

Reflection

How can I use my chosen art form to help me better understand others and myself?

_____

_____

_____

_____

If you do not currently have an art form, what is style of art you've always been attracted to? What is the lowest barrier of entry to begin engaging in this art form?

_____

_____

Setting Up the Right Conditions

The enemy of Authenticity is logistical overload and a one-size-fits-all system. Authenticity users need to honor their own individuality and tailor situations to what feels right; too much conformity will crush their spirits. They also require freedom from too many demands or items on a to-do list, which smother the more gentle but important voices inside. The key is to keep life simple. INFPs should find careers and opportunities whose core values and constituents match their core values.

INFPs should also actively pursue self-expression. If you are an artist, make sure you set aside plenty of time to engage in your art of choice. If you don't see yourself as an artist, is there a form of art you've always been interested in but haven't given yourself permission to try? Even if you've never been attracted to art, identify your favorite way of expressing yourself. It could be conversations with intimate friends, an audio diary, or a standard written journal. Exploring your inner terrain is crucial, and if you don't get enough time to do it, you will become dysthymic and eventually depressed.

UNDEVELOPED AUTHENTICITY (Fi)	DEVELOPED AUTHENTICITY (Fi)
Avoid:	Work Toward:
• Rigid values	• Meaningful and adaptable values
• Addiction to righteousness	• Conviction based on inner alignment
• Self-absorption	• Sympathy and self-expression

The talents Authenticity can give me are:

_____

_____

_____

The ways I usually use Authenticity are:

_____

_____

_____

I'm going to develop Authenticity more by:

_____

_____

_____

List three activities that put you into flow:

_____

_____

_____

The INFP Copilot Is Exploration (Ne)

Without an extraverted perceiving process, the INFP is not complete. Without access to feedback from the world and noticing how other people experience reality, the INFP's convictions and beliefs will be insular and self-serving. Broadening their territory to include people of many walks of life, receiving dissenting views, and allowing themselves to fail encourage the INFP to loosen their attachment to identity while pursuing a better version of themselves.

An extraverted perceiving process also empowers the INFP to learn different forms of communication and persuasion. They can, over time, become powerful change agents, as opposed to silenced idealists who hope the world will change for them.

It's important to remember that, like the Driver, the Copilot process is a talent. But that doesn't mean every INFP will have the same skill level or use it in a healthy way. Developing Exploration as a healthy process is crucial to becoming an amazing INFP.

It can be difficult to actively develop an extraverted function as an Introvert. It won't be as natural as working on Authenticity, so discipline and a focus on the rich rewards Exploration brings will be key.

Pattern Recognition

Exploration, as an intuitive process, uses advanced pattern recognition to see connections other people miss. It wants to know what's going on behind the curtain, what it can't directly access. As it gets more sophisticated, Exploration's predictive powers improve, and the Exploration user eventually becomes adept at not only seeing what others miss, but imagining what could exist. Whiteboard sessions, or meetings where ideas are shared and built upon with other creative minds, are contexts where this ability truly shines. Feeding off the energy of other people's suggestions, Exploration will come up with truly novel and unique ideas that transform the mundane into the extraordinary.

Remember, this ability is a skill that must be honed. It's easy to assume that one's ability to recognize patterns is infallible, and without proper development, this can become a justification for declaring one is right without further explanation.

But pattern recognition gets better over time only if the Exploration user lets themselves experience the world at large. Reading and researching are part of the process, but they are not a complete expression of Exploration. It is an extraverted function. Theories have to be acted upon to get real-world feedback, and if the theory was wrong, it has to be revised.

Exploration benefits from testing and iterating. When the Exploration user finds that they are wrong, they view it as an opportunity for expanding their understanding, learning even greater possibilities, and transforming this amazing talent into real opportunities. Instead of getting defensive when they learn their original idea was wrong, the INFP can say a mental "thanks!" to the universe for giving them the gift of calibration.

Exercise

Get good at pattern recognition by making quick predictions about how a mystery movie will end. Mystery movies follow a limited set of plot twists. Use your Exploration process to not only predict an individual movie's ending, but to identify the types of plot twists movie scripts use.

Reflection

Name three times your pattern recognition was confirmed to be accurate:

_____

_____

_____

Name three times your pattern recognition was confirmed to be wrong:

_____

_____

_____

The next time I'm wrong, I'm going to learn to enjoy the process by:

_____

_____

_____

_____

Excitement, Fuel, and Optimism

The Exploration function burns a lot of fuel, so it must also generate a lot fuel. According to Dario Nardi, author of *Neuroscience of Personality*, Extraverted Intuition is the cognitive function that takes the longest to get into a flow state but, once there, it's the most difficult to slow down.

INFPs are wired to have energy to burn when they tap into the Exploration function. They ride on the feeling of optimism and being fully engaged. There are so many things the world has to offer, so many possibilities for improvement. The sheer brightness of it all can be contagious.

There can be challenges, of course. Possibility thinking can be seen as threatening to some people, and those who use Exploration may feel they have to fight to represent it. Fortunately, Exploration is unfazed by negative feedback. Its job isn't to accept defeat but to see all the different ways to make something happen.

The greatest gift INFPs can give themselves is permission to continue using Exploration in the face of opposition. Part of Exploration's genius is finding new ways to present itself. If one style doesn't work, it will modify its strategy to become what the situation needs it to be. This is why Exploration users are often highly charismatic.

Exercise

Practice starting your day with active Exploration. That means actually doing something in the outer world, not just reading something new online. An example could be getting lost on the way to or from work each day. Go to work for 21 days straight without taking the same route twice. This will force you to find creative solutions and observe connections you didn't focus on in the past.

Reflection

Name the most exciting thing in your life right now:

_____

_____

_____

Name something that always gives you joy, just by thinking about it. How can you include this in your life every single day? Be creative with how you can introduce this activity daily:

_____

_____

Leaving Comfort Zones

Exploration loves novelty and blazing new trails. It faces six-foot-tall grass holding a machete, screaming, "tigers be damned!" Getting fully into this function means being willing to leave comfort zones, physically, psychologically, and emotionally.

This can be truly difficult for INFPs. As natural Introverts, much about the outer world can seem threatening. But it can also be difficult to explore inner terrain that seems threatening. Each person has their own beliefs and ideas inside them that they get attached to and may be unwilling to reevaluate. There are also parts of everyone's egos that don't want to be questioned, even though they must be. This requires INFPs to work hard to get around all of those tricky defensive strategies they've formed, both consciously and unconsciously.

Conveniently, as comfort zones are expanded, anxiety and fear of the unknown turn into the excitement of what could be. All growth happens outside of comfort zones, and the feeling of growing can become a healthy addiction. INFPs know they've fully developed this function when uncertainty becomes the new comfort zone.

Exercise

Practice getting out of your comfort zone by seeking out new situations you would not normally pursue. If there's a question of doing something that feels right to you, but may include some hassle or an "unsafe" element, practice taking the risk instead of playing it safe. It's common for people of your type, once they get past the scary part of a new experience, to say "Was that it?" Most of your growth happens by being adventurous and letting go of the belief that you must live the way others want you to live.

Reflection

Today, I will get outside of my comfort zone by:

_____

_____

_____

I will make this a daily practice by:

_____

_____

_____

Copilot Growth

Exploration is one of the highest leverage points for growth in your personality. It allows an INFP to test convictions and core values in real-life situations. Are they authentic? Do you have unrealistic expectations for the outer world, or is there a piece of awareness you're missing? Here are some ways that an INFP can phrase questions using their Exploration process:

- What's a creative solution to this problem?

- What am I seeing that no one else seems to be addressing?

- Where's the most exotic place I could travel?

As an INFP, your Exploration process can help you reconcile what feels right to you with what feels right to others. Don't ignore this advantage of increasing your awareness of the outside world. As you increase your understanding, instead of being seen by others as having your head in the clouds, you will be seen as inspirational.

Exploration reminds the INFP of their natural thirst for life. Comfort will never nourish the inner adventurer, the one that thirsts to make a difference in the world. Instead of burying the feeling of a wasted life, Exploration will help the INFP focus on that voice and answer it with a promise that this life will not be squandered. It will help the INFP suck the marrow out of life.

To stay focused on doing the right things, you'll need to get outside yourself and experience the world for what it is, not what you wish it was. Only then can you discover what really matters to you on a core level. You can experiment with the world around you and learn to hone your Exploration by:

- Exploring a new part of town, with no agenda

- Trying a new food each time you go out

- Flirting or bantering with someone, without thinking about what you'll say

- Joining an improv class

As an INFP, you will bring the best version of yourself to the world when you get outside your comfort zone and explore every aspect of life. Developing Exploration makes you inspirational.

Reflection

The talents Exploration can give me are:

_____

_____

_____

The ways I usually use Exploration are:

_____

_____

_____

I'm going to develop Exploration more by:

_____

_____

_____

List three ways you can start growing your Exploration process today:

_____

_____

_____

———————————————

The INFP 10-Year-Old Is Memory (Si)

Memory is designed to seek reliability. As a perceiving function, it instinctively asks, how can I know this to be true? Have I seen this before? Have experts spoken on this? What has already been established? A desire for reliability encourages Memory to seek the safety in all things, whether tangible or intangible.

The INFP can use the Memory function as a connection point to the past, reminding them of how the present world came to be. Memory gives the INFP a sense of continuity, countering their idealism around timelines. Memory can also augment creative solutions by knowing what has already been suggested, what has and hasn't worked, and what is well-covered territory. It helps develop routines and gives INFPs a sense of groundedness: two positive characteristics to have when on a mission. However, as a

10-Year-Old function, Memory can throttle creative thinking and opportunity spotting.

As an introverted function, Memory allows the INFP to access a perceiving process while staying inside their own mind. This can be okay at times, but if the INFP gets used to relying on Memory to support their judgments, they can rationalize skipping development of their Copilot, Exploration. And that's when the trouble starts. For INFPs, this usually manifests by staying in a physical, emotional, or intellectual comfort zone.

Memory is, in a large part, about seeking reliability. It craves the safe bet. People who have Memory as a strength are usually pretty good at it, and they use this function to maintain precedent, stabilize systems, and continue traditions that work. But you're an INFP, meaning you're at your best when looking for the possibilities and what could be, not when dwelling on the past or present.

If your 10-Year-Old gets to have the final call without consulting the Copilot of Exploration, it's going to see the world like a child would. Children aren't thinking in terms of carrying on time-honored traditions and maintaining precedent. When in the midst of seeking reliability, they're usually scared and looking for whatever is familiar to keep them safe.

Memory can manifest as a 10-Year-Old by claiming expertise of a topic without fully testing the information. "I read somewhere that..." can be turned into a statement of authority, even when there are more possibilities (even esoteric ones) to be discovered.

However it shows up, the motive is to protect Authenticity's conclusions and, ultimately, the INFP's very identity.

The Driver/10-Year-Old Loop

There are three ways an INFP experiences the loop, the echo chamber–like relationship between the Driver and 10-Year-Old functions. The way to get out of a loop is the same in all cases: focus on developing the Exploration process.

Short-term loop. This may only last for a few moments up to a few days. Being proven wrong can feel truly awful for an INFP, as if their competency has been called into question. Many INFPs can even sense when it's approaching, and will instinctively shut off their ability to take in new information. They may begin by arguing their position, but if they sense that the other person has better points, they may retreat inside their minds or physically leave the situation. Alternatively, some INFPs take over the conversation, becoming a know-it-all and drowning out the new information. Either way, the normal input and output of conversation is interrupted.

Long-term loop. When stuck in this loop, the INFP sticks to comfort zones. They are reluctant to leave the house, preferring to stay home to play video games, do endless research on a new topic, rewatch favorite movies, and generally surround themselves with well-worn creature comforts. They may leave the house to go to work, go to the store, run necessary errands, or visit family and long-term friends. But new friends are never made, and new experiences are only had when they're forced. The INFP finds themselves repeating the same sort of day over and over, ignoring the sense they are wasting their life.

Habitual loop. Possibly the most challenging loop to overcome, the INFP can develop a lifestyle of deference. INFPs often pride themselves on being genuinely nice people, but niceness can become a lifelong defense strategy. Nice people are never challenged; in fact, when they are challenged, others often rush to their defense.

In this most insidious type of loop, the INFP will never show their true nature to anyone but instead keep it buried only for themselves to see. While appearing sweet and demure, they are actually unwilling to have any element of themselves confronted. They play it safe in all ways, passively allowing the world to dictate their experience. "Where does everyone want to go for dinner?" They don't care; they're just along for the ride. The strategy uses almost childlike body language and ways of speaking to encourage others to handle their challenges for them.

Reflection

The ways Authenticity and Memory can loop in an INFP are:

_____

_____

_____

The ways I find myself looping are (include behaviors and situations):

_____

_____

_____

I'm going to work on breaking my loop(s) by:

_____

_____

_____

How to Best Use Memory

If you find yourself shutting yourself off from outer-world feedback, becoming passive, or hiding away from the world, this is a bad use of the Memory function. Tap into the Exploration function and ask yourself, "Who would I be if I became the best version of myself?" And, maybe a little easier, "What mischief can I get into today?"

That said, if you've been taking life by the horns and exploring your heart out, and your gut is telling you that you may need to dig in some roots or reestablish your connection with who you are, that would be the time to listen to Memory. Just don't let it fool you into stagnating.

You can also engage your 10-Year-Old in times of play, love, and intimacy. People of your type can absorb an impressive amount of information. When an INFP is at their best, they use Memory to kindle a sense of responsibility and duty, implementing routines in their life. Many INFPs enjoy plunging into the history of their favorite topics, understanding their full etymology. There's nothing wrong with playing video games, rereading favorite books, or rewatching favorite movies. Use these activities as relaxation, not as a way of life. And share your favorites with friends, reliving the experience to make it feel like the first time.

The INFP 3-Year-Old Is Effectiveness (Te)

Effectiveness is designed to measure results, accomplish goals, and make projects happen. The preferred function of many executives and politicians, Effectiveness spends a lifetime asking about return on investment (ROI) and looking for ways to create autonomous systems. Personal feelings are an interruption that must be accounted for, but eliminated if at all possible.

As a 3-Year-Old process, Effectiveness is a part of the INFP that whispers from the shadows. Normally quite capable of ignoring systems and to-do lists, suddenly an INFP will be flooded by ambition to get things done.

There are three ways an INFP experiences the grip, the moments when the Driver process is stressed out and needs a break, and the 3-Year-Old function takes over the wheel of the car. This is most likely when the INFP's emotions overwhelm them and they feel like they need to do something right away.

Short-term grip. This happens when the INFP is overwhelmed by emotion and the conviction that something isn't right. Unsure how to express this conviction to others, the INFP will blow up, certain that there's a wrong that must be righted. They'll express offense, indignation, and anger. This is when the INFP will become uncharacteristically aggressive, sometimes even violent in words or action, surprising themselves after they've hit a cool-down period.

Long-term grip. When there's a nagging feeling the INFP is trying to get away from, they choose distraction as an outlet. It can be working all the time, hyper-focusing on a major project, or trying to make something happen—especially if that thing isn't healthy. For example, an INFP in an unhappy marriage may turn to an unrequited relationship as a "project." The desire isn't to cheat on their spouse; the desire is to distract themselves with scheming and strategizing. Knowing the relationship will remain unrequited makes it feel safe. More often, this grip shows up as workaholism.

Habitual grip. A gripped INFP may use manipulative behavior. The INFP will exploit their emotional aikido to seed stress, anxiety, or other negative emotions in other people, hoping to force them to act on the INFP's behalf. Unable to inspire others to stay motivated with healthy convictions, the INFP lacks the ability to meet their own needs and must continue to manipulate others.

How to Best Use Effectiveness

The best way to use Effectiveness as a 3-Year-Old is to exercise it regularly, which will help prevent the grip from occurring. In this case, find a simple set of tasks to accomplish that you won't regret later. Some examples are clearing out your email inbox, cleaning out your car, or playing construction or strategy video games, such as Sim City or Civilization.

Remember, Effectiveness is an extraverted process, so make sure you're active and engaged in your environment. Thirty minutes should be long enough, but feel free to take as long as needed to de-stress. If you keep going back to whatever it is that's stressing you out, throw yourself even more into your activity.

The goal is to give yourself a break from introspection. Make sure you're getting as far out of your emotions and as far into a task as possible. It won't feel natural at first, but it has a huge payoff. Once your driver has had enough of a break, you can usually come back to the situation with a whole new outlook.

Using Effectiveness in this way can also provide a source of aspiration. It can encourage INFPs to accomplish big-game goals, sometimes even idealistically big. And that's part of its magic: When you shoot for the moon, even if you miss, you'll still land among the stars.

Reflection

The ways Effectiveness can grip an INFP are:

_____

_____

_____

The ways I find myself being in the grip are (include behaviors and situations):

_____

_____

_____

I'm going to control the process by:

_____

_____

_____

My Effectiveness 3-Year-Old inspires me/is my aspiration in these ways:

_____

_____

_____

CHAPTER 16

ISTP Personality Type

ISTPs are amazing at mastering and applying real-world skills. Whether it's mechanics, athletics, art, or performance, the ISTP has high levels of precision and competency in their chosen field. They become masters at manipulating their bodies and tools for desired results.

ISTPs can often shut down feedback from the outer world if it makes them feel incompetent. If this continues to develop into a chronic habit, they can dip into various degrees of rebellion against the society that they believe punishes them for focusing on precision over others' feelings.

When the ISTP moves away from protecting their identity and instead focuses on what's happening in the moment, their self-esteem and self-reliance increases. When calibrating to actual events and situations instead of speculations, ISTPs can feel and become even more competent and can create the healthy relationships they secretly crave.

ISTP CAR MODEL OVERVIEW

DRIVER Accuracy (Ti)	COPILOT Sensation (Se)
• Prunes out logical inconsistencies and incongruities • Practices integrity and radical honesty • Focus and skill mastery	• Simplifies problems and takes action • Is realistic and objective • Stays present in a situation
3-YEAR-OLD Harmony (Fe)	10-YEAR-OLD Perspectives (Ni)
• Uncertain of how to maintain connections and reputation • Emotional outbursts when stressed • Desires to meet society's needs	• Plans for a better future • Desires insight but may misinterpret meaning • Becomes paranoid and anxious when feeling threatened

The ISTP Driver Is Accuracy (Ti)

It's important to remember that the Accuracy process is a talent, and that means not every ISTP will have the same skill level or use it in a healthy way. Developing Accuracy as a healthy process is crucial to becoming an amazing ISTP. Accuracy gives the ISTP the ability to prune out logical inconsistencies and incongruities, as well as integrity, radical honesty, focus, and mastery.

Prune Out Logical Inconsistencies and Incongruities

People with a strong Accuracy process often have no problem slicing through emotionally difficult circumstances in order to see the situation as presented. Accuracy users have the ability to spot logical fallacies and biases. That said, it's far easier to see other people's biases than our own. The more an ISTP develops Accuracy, the more the function will enable an ISTP to spot their own biases and dissonance.

Accuracy is a subjective function. This means the Accuracy user asks, "What makes sense to *me*?" When the function is in its infancy, it can rationalize nearly anything. Over time, as the process develops and matures, Accuracy users begin spotting incongruities not only in what others are saying, but also in their own thinking. Like a programmer working through lines of code, an Accuracy user's first job is to clean up corrupt script within their own mind.

This can be challenging. Once a mental code is discovered to be faulty, it can seem like the mind is being ripped apart in an effort to dismantle the flawed idea. This may manifest as an existential crisis, and can be as emotionally impactful as the death of a loved one. But the more you build the skill of Accuracy, the more survivable the surgical removal of faulty code becomes. Eventually, the rewards of clean thinking are felt, and removing cognitive dissonance and bias becomes part of your identity as an ISTP.

Reflection

What if there were no right answers, only better questions? If you were able to craft your own ideas from scratch, what would they be? Do you fear losing your competency if you lose your thoughts? Can you ever truly lose who you are, or are you constantly changing, anyway?

At its best, Accuracy learns to say, "I don't know," without being disturbed by uncertainty. Reflect on the following questions:

What thought or belief have I not been looking at too carefully? If I looked at it critically, would it survive an honest analysis? Do I fear letting it go? What else would I have to look at critically if I let this one go?

_____

_____

_____

Being kind to myself, I'm going to address this belief by:

_____

_____

_____

Integrity and Radical Honesty

Well-developed Accuracy allows you to express truths no matter how hurtful they can be. While truth can hurt, it doesn't have to be unkind or cruel. In fact, Accuracy users intend to be kind when speaking harsh truths, and are usually appreciative when others do them the service of being honest. Accuracy users would much rather know the truth now than be deluded and taken off guard later.

Young Accuracy users can feel like they're always on the wrong side of the conversation. It's not uncommon for ISTPs to get the feedback that they're always saying the wrong thing or being offensive. The world has a push-pull relationship with the idea of truth, and ISTPs can sometimes find themselves grasping at how to say something.

As the Accuracy skill matures, however, ISTPs become less concerned with forcing truth on others and develop a skill in sharing truths in context. For example, the proverbial question, "Do I look fat in this dress?" may appear to be a trap, but to a developed Accuracy user, this is a simple question to answer: Either the individual is thin and no dress will make them appear fat, or they are fat and no dress will make them appear thin. If the person is, in reality, asking about how flattering the dress is, then yes, there are some dresses that are more and less flattering to the body. The keen Accuracy user would love to know if that is the actual question, and they would likely ask for clarification. Because if it is, they would wonder, why doesn't the person just ask it that way?

While candor can be disconcerting at first, most people are relieved to hear people give unbiased thoughts. On this front, Accuracy is the watchman that makes sure we don't drift too far into collective dissonance just to keep up social pretenses. But it also ensures that the ISTP doesn't drift too far into their own pretenses, and so it helps the ISTP develop a strong appreciation for integrity and duty. Doing the right thing is logically consistent, even when it's uncomfortable or unpleasant. Of course, if an ISTP hasn't first been honest with themselves, then their views can instead be antisocial opinions, which are rarely welcome.

Exercise

Observe how often you lie to other people. According to a study done by the University of Massachusetts at Amherst, 60 percent of people tell an average of two to three lies in a ten-minute conversation.

For example, when people ask how you're doing, do you answer honestly? Do you feign interest in conversations that are boring to you? Do you hide the truth to avoid hurt feelings? While you watch yourself lie in conversation, don't judge or justify yourself by saying, "I have to lie in this situation because...." Just observe.

Now that you've watched the different ways you tend to lie, turn this inward. Watch how often you lie to yourself. Keep a finger on the pulse of your cognitive dissonance.

Reflection

How could I be more honest with others and myself? Am I willing to speak the truth even if it's hurtful? Do others find me condescending when I do this? How can I learn to speak complete truths?

_____

_____

_____

_____

_____

Focus and Mastery

Accuracy offers an amazing ability to focus, which is represented in a huge variety of ways. It's seen in the best athletes, philosophers, and mechanics. When they break down ideas, machines, or systems, they have to keep track of all the moving parts. It's not easy to do, and it requires them to develop focus. People who use Accuracy keep track of data by creating frameworks. With a framework in place, they can zoom in and focus all of their attention on one thing, thereby mastering it.

A basketball player using Accuracy can spend endless hours practicing 3-point shots, ever so slightly altering the angle of their wrist until they can shoot a perfect 3-point shot each time. This same talent starts with noticing incongruities of thoughts as a child. The same process takes places in the mind and on the court: When something doesn't line up, keep working until it lines up perfectly. Philosophers and scientists often use Accuracy when breaking down ideas and beliefs.

It's important to discipline the mind to focus on mastering practical skills, not simply pleasurable activities. It's easy to focus on things that are fun and engaging, but ISTPs make a true difference when they can use their skill to focus on mundane or "boring" activities. Using focus and skill mastery to improve yourself and fulfill duties creates a rewarding life.

Exercise

When we focus our eyes, we zero in on a single object and allow everything else to become fuzzy around it. That object becomes very clear and sharp, and if we focus long enough, we'll begin to see the object in detail. All of the object's parts become obvious.

Do this with your mind. Work on a problem while allowing everything outside the problem to become fuzzy. This could anything from trying to master a musical refrain to working out a complex mathematical problem. As you spend more time focusing your attention, you will start to see its parts, such as the notes in the refrain or the formulas of the math problem.

How can I discipline my mind to be 5 percent more focused today?

_____

_____

_____

Setting Up the Right Conditions

The enemy of Accuracy is relationship overload. Accuracy users require concentrated, focused time. If an ISTP is responsible for meeting other people's needs or is frequently interrupted, they will lose focus and mental stamina.

As your ISTP Driver, Accuracy is your flow state, and if you're not using this process enough, you'll eventually run out of energy and may become depressed. Set up your daily conditions to access this mental process often. For example, if you find yourself getting overwhelmed with the demands of others or with domestic responsibilities, find time in your day for just yourself and your research. Learning complex systems—whether they're conceptual or mechanical—may not be taxing for your mind, but they are demanding of your full attention.

Developing your Driver process may seem unneeded, since it's natural for you to regularly use it. But there's a difference between using the Accuracy process and developing it.

When Accuracy is young, it over-relies on its own logic. It can assume others aren't as knowledgeable, smart, or thoughtful. Young Accuracy disregards others' experiences and observations, assuming the human experience is without merit unless it has been supported by hard science or data. Blind to the impact they have on others, ISTPs can appear harsh and callous when delivering information they think others should already know. On the other hand, Accuracy users can zoom into a subject and can miss relevant pieces of information, assuming they already have everything worked out.

ISTPs must recognize that other people can be the source of knowledge and wisdom. There is much to learn from another's experience. An ISTP can expand their own reason by learning from a broader world.

UNDEVELOPED ACCURACY (Ti)	DEVELOPED ACCURACY (Ti)
Avoid:	Work Toward:
• Rationalizing biases	• Pruning biases and dissonance
• Unkind opinions justified as truths	• Articulating complete truths
• Focusing on indulgent skills	• Mastering skills to fulfill duties

Reflection

The talents Accuracy can give me are:

_____

_____

_____

The ways I usually use Accuracy are:

_____

_____

_____

I'm going to develop Accuracy more by:

_____

_____

_____

List three activities that put you into flow:

_____

_____

_____

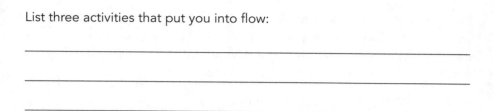

The ISTP Copilot Is Sensation (Se)

Without an extraverted perceiving process, the ISTP is not complete. Without getting realistic feedback about how the world actually works, the ISTP's convictions and beliefs will be unrealistic and self-serving. Broadening their observations to include people of many walks of life, receiving dissenting views, and allowing themselves to fail encourage ISTPs to loosen their attachment to identity while pursuing a better version of themselves.

An extraverted perceiving process also empowers the ISTP to become less isolated by learning different forms of communication and persuasion. Over time, they can become skilled agents of expression as opposed to silenced idealists, hoping the world will change for them.

It's important to remember that, like the Driver, the Copilot process is a talent. But that doesn't mean every ISTP will have the same skill level or use it in a healthy way. Developing Sensation as a healthy process is crucial to becoming an amazing ISTP.

It can be difficult to actively develop an extraverted function as an Introvert. It won't be as natural as working on Accuracy, so discipline and a focus on the rich rewards Sensation brings will be key.

Simplify Problems and Take Action

Healthy Sensation users don't have a problem with overanalyzing; instead, they reduce situations down to their fundamentals and address them head-on. They take action immediately, happy to have something on which to expend their energy. In this way, Sensation Copilots handle problems quickly without letting them stack up. While there are complexities in life that must be addressed as such, ISTPs know that much of life is a matter of simply showing up and carving a direct path.

When an ISTP fully develops the Sensation function, they are better able to manage daily tasks and challenges, as opposed to avoiding them or letting them spiral out of control. Sensation can also help an ISTP communicate artistically. Though they often struggle with verbal communication, movement can become a powerful form of expression, including dance, performance, painting, music, and other platforms. Sensation helps the ISTP build confidence, though hesitating to act slows down skill development and, ultimately, the power of their art.

Exercise

Turn your cell phone's voicemail off for a week, only allowing yourself to take calls as they come. This lets you remove a "to-do" item from your list (calling people back) in favor of handling business in the moment.

Reflection

Name three tasks you've been avoiding that you could take care of immediately:

_____

_____

_____

Name a skill (like playing a musical instrument) that you've been dreaming about starting but have been putting off:

_____

Make a commitment to yourself to finish these tasks and then begin building that skill by this date: _____

Objectivity

There are few things as disruptive to a fantasy as cold, hard reality. "Seeing is believing," as it's often said, and the Sensation process is always scanning for facts can be directly experienced. This creates pragmatism, as well as a relationship with what's physically possible and what is not.

The idea of imposed physical limitations reminds ISTPs that people have a shared objective reality, and that there is a place for impersonal rules. The ISTP must think carefully about which rules to question and which rules to adopt. The more realistic they become, the more powerful their impact will be, should they take up a cause.

Exercise

How often do you ask that exceptions be made for you? Monthly? Weekly? Daily? Think about the last time you asked for a rule to be bent in your favor. Spend ten minutes considering:

* Why the rule existed in the first place.

* What the implications were for other people in the situation.

* Was it okay to ask for the rule to be broken in your favor? Why, or why not?

Reflection

Name your most important value or conviction. How realistic is it? Would you maintain it, even if given evidence to contradict it?

_____

_____

_____

Stay Present

All people betray what's going on inside of themselves with "tells," unique actions that flag their internal condition. When the Sensation function is present in the moment, other people's tells are obvious. These tells are crucial for ISTPs. When they can observe the impact they're having on other people, the ISTP can calibrate whether or not they're being congruent with their own values.

It's easy to sit on the sidelines and judge other people for hypocrisy. It's much more difficult to stay congruent with difficult truths when in the game. Getting real-time feedback is like a checks-and-balances system that ensures integrity. If the logic doesn't add up, it may be time to reevaluate it.

Staying present in a situation also brings out the ISTP's playful side. If the ISTP becomes anxious for what's coming next, Sensation grounds them into reality and the joy of the moment. It's important to remember the adage: "Don't let your future rob you of your today."

Exercise

Find a partner. Have a conversation with them where you get to talk but they can only use nonverbal cues. Find out how far into the conversation you can get and still be accurate about what they're trying to communicate to you.

Reflection

I am going to live more in the present moment by:

_____

_____

_____

Copilot Growth

Sensation is one of the highest leverage points for growth in your personality. It allows you to test your convictions and core values in real-life situations.

Are your values authentic? Do you have unrealistic expectations for the outer world? Is there a piece of awareness you're missing?

Here are some ways that an ISTP can phrase questions to help grow their Sensation process:

- What's the situation trying to tell me?

- How can I get into action right now?

- What's a realistic expectation?

- How can I make each moment more fun and playful?

As an ISTP, your Sensation process can help you reconcile what's true to you and what's true for the outside world. As you increase your understanding, instead of being seen by others as self-serving, you will be seen as inspirational.

To stay focused on doing the right things, you'll need to get outside yourself and experience the world for what it is, not what you wish it was. Only then can you discover what really matters to you on a core level.

As an ISTP, your Sensation process can help you refine what's right for you. Don't ignore this advantage of increasing your awareness of the outside world. You can do this by asking questions about what things are, and by getting more involved with your body and your senses to help you see life practically. You can learn to hone your Sensation process by:

- Crossing things off your to-do list.

- Picking up that new skill you've been wanting to learn.

- Trying a new form of artistic expression.

- Being spontaneous and having fun!

- Joining an acting class.

As an ISTP you will bring the best version of yourself to the world when you get outside your comfort zone and engage in every aspect of life. Developing Sensation makes you inspirational.

The talents Sensation can give me are:

_____

_____

_____

The ways I usually use Sensation are:

_____

_____

_____

I'm going to develop Sensation more by:

_____

_____

_____

List three ways you can start growing your Sensation process today:

_____

_____

_____

The ISTP 10-Year-Old Is Perspectives (Ni)

Perspectives is designed to seek meaning and look toward the future. It can help people resonate with other viewpoints and not overvalue their own experiences. It future-paces, predicts outcomes, plays with abstraction, and pushes the boundaries of what can be known. It sees what cannot be seen.

ISTPs can use the Perspectives function as a way to seek meaning in their lives. Perspectives can give them insight into how other people are thinking, adding an extra layer of sympathy for the plights of others. Perspectives can also help them access a more esoteric interpretation of reality, from which comes an almost magical style of art. It helps them dream big and set a purpose-filled trajectory for their life. However, Perspectives can also cause self-sabotaging mental patterns.

As an introverted function, Perspectives allows the ISTP to access a perceiving process while staying inside their own mind. This can be okay at times, but if the ISTP gets used to relying on Perspectives to support their judgments, they can rationalize skipping development of their Sensation Copilot. And that's when the trouble starts. For ISTPs, this usually manifests as assuming they already know something, even if they have an insufficient amount of evidence or information.

Perspectives is, in a large part, about seeing what can't be seen. It speculates and makes leaps of intuition. People who have Perspectives as a strength are usually pretty good at it, and they use this function to create a vision for the future. But you're an ISTP and are wired to be at your best when seeing reality for what it is, not when making baseless assumptions.

If your 10-Year-Old gets to have the final call without consulting the Sensation Copilot, it's going to see the world like a child would. Children aren't great at pattern recognition, and without high self-confidence, speculating on what other people are thinking of them or what the future holds can produce anxiety.

Perspectives can manifest as a 10-Year-Old by taking in far too little information yet still having hubris when drawing conclusions. A gut feeling can substitute for actual experience. There may be suspicion of people who have better insight.

However it shows up, the motive is to protect Accuracy's conclusions and, ultimately, the ISTP's very identity.

The Driver/10-Year-Old Loop

There are three ways an ISTP experiences the loop, the echo chamber–like relationship between the Driver and 10-Year-Old functions. The way to get out of a loop is the same in all cases: focus on developing the Sensation process.

Short-term loop. This may only last for a few moments up to a few days. Being proven wrong can feel truly awful for an ISTP, as if their competency has been called into question. Many ISTPs can even sense when it's approaching, and will instinctively shut off their ability to take in new information. Perspectives users usually observe information and then form a pattern from what they've learned. But when Perspectives is used defensively in a loop, the ISTP will form a pattern and then shoehorn information to match it. They can even believe they've seen or experienced something they haven't, forcing their senses to confirm their intuition.

Long-term loop. Anxiety is the fear of what hasn't yet happened, and an ISTP unwilling to face even subtle fears will become increasingly anxious until they cannot cope with their life or future. If the anxiety has attached to a person, group of people, or entity, the ISTP may become paranoid. Real, more mundane fears that could be addressed are replaced by talk of agendas and conspiracy theories, which the ISTP believes are beyond their ability to influence.

Habitual loop. Without having a way to observe their impact in the world or get feedback on their value, an ISTP will go to great lengths to avoid the horrible feeling of being without value. Perspectives users interpret meaning, but when the ISTP exploits Perspectives in a loop, they will construct a simple narrative or fantasy when they need some sort of relief. ISTPs may tell themselves they're iconoclasts, but in reality, they do not question tradition or follow a new path. They may become antisocial, feeling no one could ever understand them. Often, they'll create a villain, someone or something to pass all the blame for life onto. The broken-down ISTP will not attempt to improve their situation. Instead, they'll shut down as much feedback from the world as possible. In this way, they take no personal responsibility and avoid facing life realistically.

Reflection

The ways Accuracy and Perspectives can loop in an ISTP are:

_____

_____

_____

The ways I find myself looping are (include behaviors and situations):

_____

_____

_____

I'm going to work on breaking my loop(s) by:

_____

_____

_____

How to Best Use Perspectives

If you find yourself shutting yourself off from outer-world feedback, becoming paranoid, or shying away from responsibility, this is a bad use of the Perspectives function. Tap into the Sensation function and ask yourself, "Life is so short—do I want to spend it feeling negative emotions?"

That said, if you feel inspired to live a life of purpose, make plans to play a bigger game in life, or have compassionate insights into other people's experiences, that would be the time to listen to Perspectives. Just don't let it fool you into becoming paranoid.

You can also engage your 10-Year-Old in times of play, love, and intimacy. People of your type often enjoy outwitting other people in games, sharing the latest technology, and learning psychology. You can also use this process to become better at reading and interpreting the body language of friends and family members to get clues about what's going on with them.

The ISTP 3-Year-Old Is Harmony (Fe)

Harmony is designed to connect with other people, get needs met, and understand interpersonal dynamics. The preferred function of both nurturers and culture creators, Harmony users spend a lifetime asking how to meet the needs of the collective and keep everyone's morale up. Data can be important, but not at the expense of causing conflict and hurting people.

As a 3-Year-Old process, Harmony is the part of the ISTP that whispers from the shadows. Normally quite capable of ignoring societal expectations and people's feelings, suddenly an ISTP will feel the need to connect with other people, emotionally express themselves, and receive positive feedback—especially respect—from others.

There are three ways an ISTP experiences the grip, the moments when the Driver process is stressed out and needs a break, and the 3-Year-Old function takes over the wheel of the car. This is most likely when the ISTP gets rejected or receives harsh criticism for sharing their thoughts.

Short-term grip. This is generally manifested as an explosion of emotion. Usually unfamiliar with emotional expression, the ISTP will experience a temper tantrum, often lashing out with blame at others. Without the skill developed to reign the emotion in, usually it has to be fully expressed and worked through before the ISTP calms down enough to reflect.

Long-term grip. While Harmony is plugged in to social dynamics, its 3-Year-Old form focuses on one of the most self-centered elements: personal status. The ISTP may get into the habit of bragging, constantly showcasing their brilliance and perpetually bringing the conversation back around to themselves. Unable to rest into their own self-esteem, the ISTP will use the childlike version of Harmony to implore others to give them approval.

Habitual grip. This grip shows up as codependent or otherwise unhealthy relationships. Connection is difficult for ISTPs to create, which is why they tend to be loyal to the people they love. But in this version of the grip, they fear that they cannot replicate connection. The ISTP may think that no one else will ever love them, so stay in an unhealthy relationship for far too long. They may show up either as the victim or as the perpetrator of abuse, or as both. Efforts toward getting healthy will be seen as threats: Any change to the relationship, including an improvement, may destroy it.

How to Best Use Harmony

The best way to use Harmony as a 3-Year-Old is to exercise it regularly, which will help prevent the grip from occurring. In this case, connect with a friend or family member through physical touch (hugging) or through shared emotional experience. Watch something funny together. If you can't be in each other's presence, give them a call and let them know you missed them and wanted to reconnect. Remind yourself that there are people who love you as you are.

Remember, Harmony is an extraverted process, so make sure you're active and engage with other people. Thirty minutes should be long enough, but feel free to take as long as needed to de-stress. If you're still not feeling settled, invite someone to go to the movies, or play a board or video game together. If you're in a romantic relationship, cuddles are your best friend.

The goal is to give yourself a break from having to rationalize everything. Make sure you're getting as far out of your head and as far into connections as possible. It won't feel natural at first, but it has a huge payoff. Once your Driver has had enough of a break, you can usually come back to the situation with a whole new outlook.

Using Harmony in this way can also provide a source of aspiration. It can encourage ISTPs to be contributors and thought leaders. People of your type have literally changed how we see reality, and when an ISTP understands the power within, they can be the calibrator of entire societies.

Reflection

The ways Harmony can grip an ISTP are:

_____

_____

_____

The ways I find myself being in the grip are (include behaviors and situations):

_____

_____

_____

I'm going to control the process by:

_____

_____

_____

My Harmony 3-Year-Old inspires me/is my aspiration in these ways:

_____

_____

_____

CHAPTER 17

ISFP Personality Type

There is an inner artist living in the heart of every ISFP. It is easy for the ISFP to use art, performance, dance, or other forms of expression to share their inner truth with others. They may even choose a spiritual mission or social cause to communicate their values. They are masterful at embodying deeply personal emotions and experiences, and they help others find and express their own.

When an ISFP attempts to rationalize or explain inner truths, they can become frustrated when others don't readily understand. This can lead to their projecting ill intent on a listener that doesn't understand them. Because they feel emotions so deeply and in such a nuanced way, explanatory language seems insufficient. If they feel too isolated with their intense emotions, they can become grumpy and withdrawn. At their worst, they can go down the road of self-harm.

A healthy ISFP has figured out strategies to communicate emotions through their preferred art form. By taking up poetry, painting, dance, music, missions, causes, or performances, ISFPs can find an outlet for the deep, and sometimes overwhelming, emotions they face every day.

ISFP CAR MODEL OVERVIEW

DRIVER — Authenticity (Fi)	COPILOT — Sensation (Se)
• Lives by core values and ethics • Has inner alignment and conviction • Sympathy, art, and emotional aikido	• Simplifies problems and takes action • Is realistic and objective • Stays present in a situation
3-YEAR-OLD — Effectiveness (Te)	**10-YEAR-OLD** — Perspectives (Ni)
• Difficulty setting up efficient systems • Uses controlling or aggressive tactics when feeling pressure • Inner ambition to make big things happen	• Plans for a better future • Desires insight but may misinterpret meaning • Becomes paranoid and anxious when feeling threatened

The ISFP Driver Is Authenticity (Fi)

It's important to remember that the Driver process is a talent, but that doesn't mean every ISFP will have the same skill level or use it in a healthy way. Developing Authenticity as a healthy process is crucial to becoming an amazing ISFP. It will give you core values and ethics, inner alignment and conviction, and sympathy, art, and emotional aikido.

Core Values and Ethics

Being aware of one's emotional responses at all times creates an ethical complication. A person may feel one way in one situation but completely different in a seemingly identical situation. They must learn to judge the

context of their reactions: Are their responses fully subjective, or are they based on certain principles that can be used to guide future behaviors?

What is a truly ethical action? When one feels the full emotional force of all behaviors, they can't help but frequently ask this question and create a growing but deeply personal list of what's okay and what's not. Since the majority of behaviors fall on a spectrum, ISFPs are pretty laid back about most actions people take. A person may be insensitive or obtuse, but unless they offend one of the ISFP's core values or true principles, the behavior is likely to be forgotten or even go unnoticed.

Once a core value has been upset, however, the Authenticity process will immediately register the offending action as unacceptable, and the ISFP will have to figure out how to deal with the offense. At this point, they may become uncharacteristically impassioned, outraged, and aggressive.

This is why it is incredibly important to know one's core values and revise them frequently. It's important for an Authenticity user to not simply default to whatever feels good in the moment, or get locked into values formed at a less sophisticated age. When one's core values are set in youth and not reviewed, a person can show up as self-absorbed, indulgent, and fixated on their own experience. A truly healthy Authenticity function will draft a set of values that are both meaningful and adaptable. Just like people change and grow, one's core values should change and grow with them. As an ISFP gets to know themselves better over time, their core values will be a natural emergent of greater self-knowledge.

Exercise

Core values are guiding principles. In all situations, core values determine right or wrong and let you know if you're on the right path. Take a sheet of paper and write down all behaviors you believe are either right or wrong, regardless of the situation. Give yourself plenty of time to do this exercise: hours, days, even weeks. Feel free to revisit this list on a regular basis and refine it as you learn more about yourself.

Reflection

My top five core values are ... because...:

1. _____

_____

2. _____

_____

3. _____

_____

4. _____

_____

5. _____

_____

Five core values that I have reevaluated and adapted over the years are:

1. _____

2. _____

3. _____

4. _____

5. _____

Inner Alignment and Conviction

Everyone has experienced inner conflict, but the Authenticity function knows that being of two minds is just the tip of the iceberg. Focused on being true to themselves, ISFPs know there isn't just one self; rather, there's a legion of voices inside, all vying for attention. It's difficult to know what to do when listening intently to all those voices, each with their own agenda.

The task of Authenticity is to listen closely to what each part of the individual is saying and prioritize based on what's true, what's right, and what will get needs or desires met.

If the burden of Authenticity is to listen to one's inner council, the responsibility of Authenticity is to lead those voices into alignment. Or, if they can't be in full chorus, Authenticity must determine which parts should have the stage at any given time.

The easiest decisions are ones that present no inner conflict, which could be said to align with convictions. The moments when all inner voices are in full agreement are beautiful moments and produce such momentum that the ISFP can feel unstoppable. It's difficult for Authenticity users to feel motivated when they feel uncertain, but once certainty is on the table, the ISFP becomes an unstoppable force capable of extraordinary feats.

Managing the inner council of voices and ideas is a skill that must be built, similar to managing groups of people. It's imperative for an ISFP to learn to prioritize their needs and desires based on core values and a code of ethics, not simply what feels good in the moment.

It's important for ISFPs to develop a healthy relationship with conviction. When Authenticity is young, it focuses on the good feelings of being right. In fact, it can get addicted to the feeling of righteousness. This addiction leads to a synthetic conviction, where the ISFP will choose only the voice that wants desperately to be right while shutting out both internal and external dissent. This behavior is invariably followed by wracking self-doubt.

Self-confidence comes from seeking out dissenting voices and sitting with them, asking difficult questions, and considering what the answers mean for the ISFP's identity. If some of those voices are unhealthy and have ill intent, it becomes the ISFP's responsibility to heal that part of themselves, or even allow the toxic parts of themselves to die. It's a painful process that can feel like literal death to Authenticity users, but it is a crucial aspect of self-management and self-leadership.

Exercise

Think of a decision you've been ruminating on, maybe even putting off. Listen for any internal conflict. Imagine yourself in a council room where each voice comes up with a compelling argument. Allow them plenty of time to get through their concerns, considerations, and valid points. After each voice has stated their case, pull out your list of core values. Ask yourself which arguments are most in alignment with your core values, and why some of the voices may be counter to your values. If this is a values-based decision, why are some of the voices representing a solution that runs counter to your values? Are these less mature or unhealed parts of yourself? What would persuade them to stay consistent with your values? Alternatively, is it a decision that isn't values based? Is more information needed and are the voices stumped? Do you need to learn more and revisit the council later?

— *Reflection* —

What parts of yourself have you been avoiding listening to? Is it because they aren't saying things of value, or because what they have to say represents changes for which you may not feel ready?

_____

_____

_____

Being kind to myself, I'm going to address these parts by:

_____

_____

_____

Sympathy, Art, and Emotional Aikido

So much of the human experience is impossible to express using verbal language. Despite that, all of us have a need to understand each other and to be understood. When Authenticity is in its infancy, a person can be quite self-absorbed. Without sharpening the function, an ISFP will stay fixated on their own experience, unable to surface long enough to feel sympathy with others.

Over time and with development, Authenticity users recognize that other people's experiences are incredibly real to them, and so they offer their compassion and sympathy. People with Authenticity Drivers know that to understand a person's inner workings is to demonstrate their emotions and motivations back to them, showing that all people share these things in common and can also experience them on a deeply personal level. The most powerful medium through which humans accomplish this task is art and self-expression.

Throughout history, Authenticity users have found themselves to be unable to convey their own subjective emotional experience in conversation, which has driven them to become artists. They have become great at replicating an aspect of humanity in a single, time-bound piece of art: painting, song, poem, statue, choreographed dance, performance, or even their lifestyle. The foundation of art is the expression of universal human experiences, honoring that it will be personalized by the receiver.

Authenticity uses art to perform emotional aikido (page 73), transforming one person's energy into a shared experience. It's difficult to deny the poignancy of a shared experience, or to judge it harshly. Authenticity encourages onlookers to see themselves and the world with sympathy.

Exercise

Communicate an emotion to a friend without using words. You may use hand gestures, facial expressions, drawings, noises, and sounds. Ask your friend if they understood the emotion you were trying to share, and if they were able to replicate the emotion within themselves by linking it to their own experience.

Reflection

How can I use my chosen art form to help me better understand others and myself?

_____

_____

_____

_____

If you do not currently have an art form, what is style of art you've always been attracted to? What is the lowest barrier of entry to begin engaging in this art form?

_____

_____

_____

Setting Up the Right Conditions

The enemy of Authenticity is logistical overload and a one-size-fits-all system. Authenticity users need to honor their own individuality and tailor situations to what feels right; too much conformity will crush their spirits. They also require freedom from too many demands or items on a to-do list, which smother the more gentle but important voices inside. The key is to keep life simple. ISFPs should find careers and opportunities whose core values and constituents match their core values.

ISFPs should also actively pursue self-expression. If you are an artist, make sure you set aside plenty of time to engage in your art of choice. If you don't see yourself as an artist, is there a form of art you've always been interested in but haven't given yourself permission to try? Even if you've never been attracted to art, identify your favorite way of expressing yourself. It could be conversations with intimate friends, an audio diary, or a standard written journal. Exploring your inner terrain is crucial, and if you don't get enough time to do it, you will become dysthymic and eventually depressed.

UNDEVELOPED AUTHENTICITY (Fi)	DEVELOPED AUTHENTICITY (Fi)
Avoid:	Work Toward:
• Rigid values	• Meaningful and adaptable values
• Addiction to righteousness	• Conviction based on inner alignment
• Self-absorption	• Sympathy and self-expression

Reflection

The talents Authenticity can give me are:

_____

_____

_____

The ways I usually use Authenticity are:

_____

_____

_____

I'm going to develop Authenticity more by:

_____

_____

_____

List three activities that put you into flow:

_____

_____

_____

The ISFP Copilot Is Sensation (Se)

Without an extraverted perceiving process, the ISFP is not complete. Without getting realistic feedback about how the world actually works, the ISFP's convictions and beliefs will be unrealistic and self-serving. Broadening their observations to include people from many walks of life, receiving dissenting views, and allowing themselves to fail encourage the ISFP to loosen their attachment to identity while pursuing a better version of themselves.

An extraverted perceiving process also empowers the ISFP to become less isolated by learning different forms of communication and persuasion. They can over time become skilled agents of expression as opposed to silenced idealists, hoping the world will change for them.

It's important to remember that, like the Driver, the Copilot process is a talent. But that doesn't mean every ISFP will have the same skill level or use it in a healthy way. Developing Sensation as a healthy process is crucial to becoming an amazing ISFP.

It can be difficult to actively develop an extraverted function as an Introvert. It won't be as natural as working on Authenticity, so discipline and a focus on the rich rewards Sensation brings will be key.

Simplify Problems

Healthy Sensation users don't have a problem with overanalyzing; instead, they reduce situations down to their fundamentals and address them head-on. They take action immediately, happy to have something on which to expend their energy. In this way, Sensation Copilots handle problems quickly without letting them stack up. While there are complexities in life that must be addressed as such, ISFPs know that much of life is a matter of simply showing up and carving a direct path.

When an ISFP fully develops the Sensation function, they are better able to manage daily tasks and challenges, as opposed to avoiding them or letting them spiral out of control. Sensation can also help an ISFP communicate artistically. Though they often struggle with verbal communication, movement can become a powerful form of expression, including dance, performance, painting, music, and other platforms. Sensation helps the ISFP build confidence, though hesitating to act slows down skill development and, ultimately, the power of their art.

Exercise

Turn your cell phone's voicemail off for a week, only allowing yourself to take calls as they come. This lets you remove a "to-do" item from your list (calling people back) in favor of handling business in the moment.

Reflection

Name three tasks you've been avoiding that you could take care of immediately:

_____

_____

_____

Name a skill (like playing a musical instrument) you've been dreaming about starting but have been putting off:

_____

Make a commitment with yourself to finish these tasks and then begin building that skill by this date: _____

Objectivity

There are few things as disruptive to a fantasy as cold, hard reality. "Seeing is believing," as it's often said, and the Sensation process is always scanning for facts can be directly experienced. This creates pragmatism, as well as a relationship with what's physically possible and what is not.

The idea of imposed physical limitations reminds ISFPs that people have a shared objective reality, and that there is a place for impersonal rules. The ISFP must think carefully about which rules to question and which convictions to adopt. The more realistic they become, the more powerful their impact will be, should they take up a cause.

— *Exercise* —

How often do you ask that exceptions be made for you? Monthly? Weekly? Daily? Think about the last time you asked for a rule to be bent in your favor. Spend ten minutes considering:

- Why the rule existed in the first place.

- What the implications were for other people in the situation.

- Was it okay to ask for the rule to be broken in your favor? Why, or why not?

— *Reflection* —

Name your most important value or conviction. How realistic is it? Would you maintain it, even if given evidence to contradict it?

_____

_____

_____

Stay Present

All people betray what's going on inside of themselves with "tells," unique actions that flag their internal condition. When the Sensation function is present in the moment, other people's tells are obvious. These tells are crucial for ISFPs. When they can observe the impact they're having on other people, they can calibrate to whether or not they're being congruent with their own values.

It's easy to sit on the sidelines and judge other people for hypocrisy. It's much more difficult to stay in alignment with ideals and values when in the game. Getting real-time feedback is like a checks-and-balances system that ensures congruence of values. If the values don't add up, it may be time to reevaluate them.

Staying present in a situation also brings out the ISFP's playful side. If the ISFP becomes anxious for what's coming next, Sensation grounds them into reality and the joy of the moment. It's important to remember the adage: "Don't let your future rob you of your today."

Exercise

Find a partner. Have a conversation with them where you get to talk but they can only use nonverbal cues. Find out how far into the conversation you can get and still be accurate about what they're trying to communicate to you.

Reflection

I am going to live more in the present moment by:

_____

_____

_____

Copilot Growth

Sensation is one of the highest leverage points for growth in your personality. It allows you to test your convictions and core values in real-life situations. Are your values authentic? Do you have unrealistic expectations for the outer world? Is there a piece of awareness you're missing?

Here are some ways that an ISFP can phrase questions to help grow their Sensation process:

- What's the situation trying to tell me?

- How can I get into action right now?

- What's a realistic expectation?

- How can I make each moment more fun and playful?

As an ISFP, your Sensation process can help you reconcile what's true to you and what's true for the outside world. As you increase your understanding, instead of being seen by others as having your head in the clouds, you will be seen as inspirational.

To stay focused on doing the right things, you'll need to get outside yourself and experience the world for what it is, not what you wish it was. Only then can you discover what really matters to you on a core level.

As an ISFP, your Sensation process can help you refine what's right for you. Don't ignore this advantage of increasing your awareness of the outside world. You can do this by asking questions about what things are, and by getting more involved with your body and your senses to help you see life practically. You can learn to hone your Sensation process by:

- Crossing things off your to-do list.

- Picking up that new skill you've been wanting to learn.

- Trying a new form of artistic expression.

- Being spontaneous and having fun!

- Joining an acting class.

As an ISFP, you will bring the best version of yourself to the world when you get outside your comfort zone and engage in every aspect of life. Developing Sensation makes you inspirational.

Reflection

The talents Sensation can give me are:

_____

_____

_____

The ways I usually use Sensation are:

_____

_____

_____

I'm going to develop Sensation more by:

_____

_____

_____

List three ways you can start growing your Sensation process today:

_____

_____

_____

The ISFP 10-Year-Old Is Perspectives (Ni)

Perspectives is designed to seek meaning and look toward the future. It can help people resonate with other viewpoints and not overvalue their own experiences. It future-paces, predicts outcomes, plays with abstraction, and pushes the boundaries of what can be known. It sees what cannot be seen.

The ISFP can use the Perspectives function as a way to seek meaning in their lives. Perspectives can give them insight into how other people are thinking, adding an extra layer of sympathy for the plights of others. Perspectives can also help them access a more esoteric interpretation of reality, from which comes an almost magical style of art. It helps them dream big and set a purpose-filled trajectory for their life. However, Perspectives can cause self-sabotaging mental patterns.

As an introverted function, Perspectives allows the ISFP to access a perceiving process while staying inside their own mind. This can be okay at times, but if the ISFP gets used to relying on Perspectives to support their judgments, they can rationalize skipping development of their Sensation Copilot. And that's when the trouble starts. For ISFPs, this usually manifests as assuming they already know something, even if they have an insufficient amount of evidence or information.

Perspectives is, in a large part, about seeing what can't be seen. It speculates and makes leaps of intuition. People who have Perspectives as a strength are usually pretty good at it, and they use this function to create a vision for the future. But you're an ISFP and are wired to be at your best when seeing reality for what it is, not when making baseless assumptions.

If your 10-Year-Old gets to have the final call without consulting the Copilot of Sensation, it's going to see the world like a child would. Children aren't great at pattern recognition, and without high self-confidence, speculating on what other people are thinking of them or what the future holds can produce anxiety.

Perspectives can manifest as a 10-Year-Old by taking in far too little information yet still having hubris when drawing conclusions. A gut feeling can substitute for actual experience. There may be suspicion of people who have better insight.

However it shows up, the motive is to protect Authenticity's conclusions and, ultimately, the ISFP's very identity.

The Driver/10-Year-Old Loop

There are three ways an ISFP experiences the loop, the echo chamber–like relationship between the Driver and 10-Year-Old functions. The way to get out of a loop is the same in all cases: focus on developing the Sensation process.

Short-term loop. This may only last for a few moments up to a few days. Being proven wrong can feel truly awful for an ISFP, as if their competency has been called into question. Many ISFPs can even sense when it is approaching, and will instinctively shut off their ability to take in new information. Perspectives users usually observe information and then form a pattern from what they've learned. But when Perspectives is used defensively in a loop, the ISFP will form a pattern and then shoehorn information to match it. They can even believe they've seen or experienced something they haven't, forcing their senses to confirm their intuition.

Long-term loop. Unwilling to face even subtle fears, the ISFP will become increasingly anxious until they cannot cope with their life or future. If the anxiety has attached to a person, group of people, or entity, the ISFP may become paranoid. Real, more mundane fears that could be addressed are replaced by talk of agendas and conspiracy theories, which the ISFP believes are beyond their ability to influence.

Habitual loop. Without having a way to observe their impact in the world or get feedback on their value, an ISFP will go to great lengths to avoid the horrible feeling of being without value. Perspectives users interpret meaning, but when the ISFP exploits Perspectives in a loop, they will construct a simple narrative or fantasy when they need some sort of relief. The ISFP may tell themselves they're iconoclasts, but in reality, they do not question tradition or follow a new path. They may become antisocial, feeling no one could ever understand them. Often, they'll create a villain, someone or something to pass all the blame for life onto. The broken-down ISFP will not attempt to improve their situation. Instead, they'll shut down as much feedback from the world as possible. In this way, they take no personal responsibility and avoid facing life realistically.

Reflection

The ways Authenticity and Perspectives can loop in an ISFP are:

_____

_____

_____

The ways I find myself looping are (include behaviors and situations):

_____

_____

_____

I'm going to work on breaking my loop(s) by:

_____

_____

_____

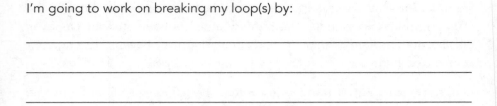

How to Best Use Perspectives

If you find yourself shutting yourself off from outer-world feedback, becoming paranoid, or shying away from responsibility, this is a bad use of the Perspectives function. Tap into the Sensation function and ask yourself, "Life is so short—do I want to spend it feeling negative emotions?"

That said, if you feel inspired to live a life of purpose, make plans to play a bigger game in life, or have compassionate insights into other people's experiences, that would be the time to listen to Perspectives. Just don't let it fool you into becoming paranoid.

You can also engage your 10-Year-Old in times of play, love, and intimacy. People of your type often enjoy outwitting other people in games, sharing the latest technology, and learning psychology. You can also use this process to become better at reading and interpreting the body language of friends and family members to get clues about what's going on with them.

The ISFP 3-Year-Old Is Effectiveness (Te)

Effectiveness is designed to measure results, accomplish goals, and make projects happen. The preferred function of many executives and politicians, Effectiveness spends a lifetime asking about return on investment (ROI) and looking for ways to create autonomous systems. Personal feelings are an interruption that must be accounted for, but eliminated if at all possible.

As a 3-Year-Old process, Effectiveness is a part of the ISFP that whispers from the shadows. Normally quite capable of ignoring systems and to-do lists, suddenly an ISFP will be flooded by ambition to get things done.

There are three ways an ISFP experiences the grip, the moments when the Driver process is stressed out and needs a break, and the 3-Year-Old function takes over the wheel of the car. This is most likely when the ISFP's emotions overwhelm them and they feel like they must do something right away.

Short-term grip. This occurs when the ISFP is overwhelmed by emotion and the conviction that something isn't right. Unsure how to express this conviction to others, the ISFP will blow up, certain that there's a wrong that must be righted. They'll express offense, indignation, and anger. This is when the ISFP will become uncharacteristically aggressive, sometimes even violent in words or action, surprising themselves after they've hit a cool-down period.

Long-term grip. When there's a nagging feeling the ISFP is trying to get away from, they choose distraction as an outlet. It can be working all the time, hyper-focusing on a major project, or trying to make something happen—especially if that thing isn't healthy. For example, an ISFP in an unhappy marriage may turn to an unrequited relationship as a "project." The desire isn't to cheat on their spouse; the desire is to distract themselves with scheming and strategizing. Knowing the relationship will remain unrequited makes it feel safe. More often, this grip shows up as workaholism.

Habitual grip. A gripped ISFP may use manipulative behavior. The ISFP will exploit their emotional aikido to seed stress, anxiety, or other negative emotions in other people, hoping to force them to act on the ISFP's behalf. Unable to inspire others to stay motivated with healthy convictions, the ISFP lacks the ability to meet their own needs and must continue to manipulate others.

How to Best Use Effectiveness

The best way to use Effectiveness as a 3-Year-Old is to exercise it regularly, which will help prevent the grip from occurring. In this case, find a simple set of tasks to accomplish that you won't regret later. Some examples are clearing out your email inbox, cleaning out your car, or playing construction or strategy video games, such as Sim City or Civilization.

Remember, Effectiveness is an extraverted process, so make sure you're active and engaged in your environment. Thirty minutes should be long enough, but feel free to take as long as needed to de-stress. If you keep going back to whatever it is that's stressing you out, throw yourself even more into your activity.

The goal is to give yourself a break from introspection. Make sure you're getting as far out of your emotions and as far into a task as possible. It won't feel natural at first, but it has a huge payoff. Once your Driver has had enough of a break, you can usually come back to the situation with a whole new outlook.

Using Effectiveness in this way can also provide a source of aspiration. It can encourage ISFPs to accomplish big-game goals, sometimes even idealistically big. And that's part of its magic: When you shoot for the moon, even if you miss, you'll still land among the stars.

Reflection

The ways Effectiveness can grip an ISFP are:

_____

_____

_____

The ways I find myself being in the grip are (include behaviors and situations):

_____

_____

_____

I'm going to control the process by:

_____

_____

_____

My Effectiveness 3-Year-Old inspires me/is my aspiration in these ways:

_____

_____

_____

CHAPTER 18

ENTJ Personality Type

ENTJs are innovators of complex systems and have the ability to build support structures for their creations. They are willing and able to create outside of templates, making big things happen in the world.

With the drive to accomplish goals combined with a willingness to challenge convention, ENTJs naturally rise to positions of influence in business, government, and industry. It is obvious to an ENTJ where to allocate resources and how to lead people in what they should be doing.

However, ENTJs can become cynical when people make bad decisions or don't do the reasonable or obvious thing. This can make it challenging for an ENTJ to sympathize with people's individual situations and struggles. In fact, ENTJs may cause trouble for others, as they are unaware of how their actions impact other people.

At the top of their game, ENTJs understand that true power is more effective than force or domination. A feeling of personal empowerment in the ENTJ makes space for other people to also express their own power. Life is not a zero-sum game. This fosters more sustainable results and better relationships in their life.

When ENTJs construct the life they want while still honoring personal relationships and ethics, they become powerful, benevolent executives over their own life, creating the results they envision in the outer world.

ENTJ CAR MODEL OVERVIEW

DRIVER
Effectiveness (Te)

- Evaluates in terms of resource management (time, energy, currency)
- Naturally thinks in and sets up streamlined systems
- Has an instinct for leadership

COPILOT
Perspectives (Ni)

- Shifts into other people's perspectives
- Has "a-ha" moments and insights
- Forecasts

3-YEAR-OLD
Authenticity (Fi)

- Resists need to be introspective
- Can become emotionally overwhelmed and lost
- Develops an artistic outlet, becomes kinder to self and others

10-YEAR-OLD
Sensation (Se)

- Enjoys sensory stimulation
- Likes being realistic about the world, but struggles to be realistic about the self
- Can get caught in image management and self-indulgence

The ENTJ Driver Is Effectiveness (Te)

It's important to remember that the Driver process is a talent, but that doesn't mean every ENTJ will have the same skill level or use it in a healthy way. Developing Effectiveness as a healthy process is crucial to becoming an amazing ENTJ.

Effectiveness, when developed and sharpened, allows you to gain a natural understanding of resource management, set up streamlined systems, and build skills that may be uncomfortable, but are necessary for life.

Resource Management

Time, energy, money—everything that is built requires resources to build it. When it comes to determining which resources to use, the Effectiveness Driver has a natural interest in return on investment (ROI). Is a certain resource worth the effort? To answer that question, Effectiveness also pays special attention to stress tests, which help determine if something can hold up in the long run.

Ultimately, ENTJs use Effectiveness for sustainability. The least amount of effort for the most amount of return is great, but if it's going to break down quickly and require more effort in the long run, it's not truly worth it. Thinking on a large scale helps inform whether or not something will pass the test of time.

When an ENTJ is managing resources, they must consider their feelings and the feelings of others. This means they must learn to manage their emotional and psychological resources. Without allotting time for the personal things in life, unexpected emotions may creep in, shutting all production down. Scheduling time out for R&R and reconnecting with family is crucial for overall maintenance.

Exercise

Get good at determining the value of human or emotional factors. Time is often overlooked in ROI, as are things like emotional expense. When determining if something is worth effort, use monetary gain as only one consideration. Take into account enjoyment of process, learning, and quality of product. The standard ROI algorithm is ROI = (Gain − Cost) / Cost. Feel free to create your own algorithm to incorporate more factors.

Name three soft factors you tend to either waste (or overprotect) that may be interrupting your ROI:

_____

_____

_____

Journal one area of your life where you would like to improve your ROI. Using the algorithm above (or one you have created), state an actionable plan that will help you get more out of the resources you're putting into it:

_____

_____

_____

_____

_____

Streamlined Systems

If Effectiveness could be expressed in a single quote, it might be, "Freedom is defined as a system that runs so well, you no longer have to think about it."

Effectiveness, like Harmony, is about attempting to create an environment where people get their needs met. But the needs of Effectiveness aren't emotional, they're logistical. Systems help groups stay in a flow without participants getting in each other's way. Automobile freeway systems are a great example of how streamlining keeps us all moving forward without having to really think about it. Once these systems are in place, even bigger goals can be attained since accomplishments build upon themselves.

When ENTJs develop patience, they no longer feel the need to force things to happen too quickly. An efficient system should be set up according to the principle of water flowing downhill. In terms of money, it flows to the cheapest effective solution to a problem. This principle should be applied to all resources, not just money. It's tempting to jump on what is expedient, but if it's not a sustainable solution, it won't be effective overall. A good system recognizes a little acceptable loss while maintaining itself for the long term.

Exercise

The next time you perform a task, document the process with a goal of streamlining the task. Consider that there are two types of processes: critical and optional. Which steps are necessary to the task, and which can be cut? Which resources (time, money, energy) are necessary? Can you afford to pare the resources down for outcome? Once you have a step-by-step procedure, consult with others who have accomplished this same task and discover if there was anything you missed.

Reflection

Name three resources you need to improve your management of:

_____

_____

_____

Now, look at your schedule. What are you prioritizing that compromises the proper management of those resources? Record three to five ideas on how to recoup those resources into your weekly schedule.

_____

_____

_____

_____

_____

Building Necessary Skills

Effectiveness Drivers can shut off personal feelings in order to get things done. In fact, it may be argued that this is the core competency of Effectiveness. Daily tasks aren't always pleasant, nor is skill building outside one's area of expertise. While completing these tasks, ENTJs may struggle to show up authentically or they may unintentionally come across as having bad intent. Expanding their emotional and social intelligence can be a struggle, especially if the ENTJ has developed just enough to get what they want.

While it's easy to marginalize one's own weaknesses, eventually their effects can pile up. And at times, it's only obvious that these skills are underdeveloped when an opportunity for their use has already slipped by.

When an ENTJ builds a strong relationship with their Effectiveness Driver, they'll bite the bullet and focus on proficiency in areas that are necessary for life. Anything unnecessary can be delegated, as long as the resources have been built to hire them out or hand them off. But for anything that can't be delegated—cultivating friendships, finding love, maintaining physical health, performing household responsibilities—the ENTJ can lean on Effectiveness to help them put their head down, muscle through, and make it happen, all the while building a sustainable system to keep the benefits of the hard work going.

Exercise

Identify one area of your life where you care about improving but have been procrastinating. It could be getting into better physical shape, improving your diet, finding a spouse, doing public speaking, finding a better job, etc…. Make a list of why this is something you want, and identify what has been holding you back. Ask yourself how much more rewarding your life would be if you just started working toward it, even if it isn't optimal or ideal in the beginning. Paint a picture of what your life would look like if you were to succeed. Write this visualization out and put it on your refrigerator.

Reflection

Name one area of your life you would like to improve:

_____

_____

_____

Name three activities you can begin immediately that would address this improvement:

_____

_____

_____

At the beginning of each day, write down what you are going to do that day to improve this area of your life by 5 percent:

_____

_____

_____

At the end of each day, write down what you did to improve this area of your life by 5 percent:

_____

_____

_____

_____

Setting Up the Right Conditions

The enemy of Effectiveness is emotional insecurity. If you're troubled, Effectiveness has difficulty doing what it does best: creating plans and making rational decisions to get the job done.

As your Driver, Effectiveness is your Flow state, and if you're not using this function enough you'll eventually run out of juice and become depressed. So, set up your conditions to access this mental process often. Keep life streamlined and manageable. And if life is throwing too many emotionally confusing things at you, make sure you schedule time to address them instead of letting them creep into all your activities.

Addressing your emotional state may feel self-indulgent, but it can also be seen as a task. Focus on actual effectiveness, not efficiency. While it may seem inefficient to give energy to introspection, if ignoring your feelings disrupts your life, then doing so robs you of your overall effectiveness. It can be as simple as reflecting on how far you've come, the lessons you've learned throughout your life, and how they influence your plans to move forward.

UNDEVELOPED EFFECTIVENESS (Te)	DEVELOPED EFFECTIVENESS (Te)
Avoid:	Work Toward:
• Emotional insecurity	• Scheduling time for the self
• Forcing outcomes	• Patiently building systems
• Marginalizing weaknesses	• Cultivating necessary skills

Reflection

The talents Effectiveness can give me are:

_____

_____

_____

The ways I usually use Effectiveness are:

_____

_____

_____

I'm going to develop Effectiveness more by:

_____

_____

_____

List three activities that put you into flow:

_____

_____

_____

The ENTJ Copilot Is Perspectives (Ni)

Without an introverted perceiving process, the ENTJ is not complete. They may demand that everyone contort themselves to serve the systems that have been put in place, forgetting that systems are there to serve people. Without checking in to ensure that individual experiences are taken into consideration, the ENTJ may become unsympathetic, rash, and presumptuous.

An introverted perceiving process reminds the ENTJ to be patient and recognize that longer timelines are always at play. It also helps them connect to their subjective experience, peer into future possibilities, speculate on outcomes, and apply this understanding to interactions with and on behalf of other people.

It's important to remember that, like the Driver, the Copilot process is a talent. But that doesn't mean every ENTJ will have the same skill level or use it in a healthy way. Developing Perspectives as a healthy process is crucial to becoming an amazing ENTJ.

It can be difficult to actively develop an introverted function when one is an Extravert. It won't be as natural as working on Effectiveness, so discipline and an eye on the rich rewards Perspectives brings will be key.

Perspectives of Others

Since the Perspectives Copilot watches its own mind form patterns, it builds the skill of detaching from its own perspective. In this detached space, it is easy to jump into the perspective of others.

Being able to see things from another person's worldview helps the ENTJ explain why others do the things they do. Perspectives Copilots realize the simple truth that all actions, regardless of how confusing or distasteful they are to others, make sense to the person who committed them. It ceases to be a matter of explaining the behavior and becomes a matter of explaining how it made sense to the individual.

As an ENTJ, getting inside other people's minds means recognizing not only how their experiences have shaped them, but the conclusions they've come to about how life works. This can include their beliefs, paradigms, and strategies of behavior.

Influencing people toward a better future, whether they have smaller or larger ambitions, means recognizing which mental patterns need to be improved upon and how to communicate in a way that impacts those patterns.

This doesn't mean that all ENTJs must be consultants or thought leaders. However, there is a strong pull for ENTJs to help organizations and structures carve a better path. Building the skills necessary for influence—writing, public speaking, creating models, and showing results-based evidence—also benefit ENTJs internally. They can shine a light on those patterns within the ENTJ that may be erroneous.

Exercise

Think of a heinous action or controversial person that you can't see yourself ever condoning. Instead of jumping to condemn the action, take a moment to really get inside the head of the person who performed the action. How did their action make complete sense to them at the time? Can you understand it so well you could defend it to another person? Don't focus on the act itself, but on the mind of the person who committed it.

Now that you are in a Perspectives frame of mind, fill out the following journal prompt. If you cannot think of anything immediately, feel free to ruminate on the question. It may guide you to some uncomfortable places, and that's okay. Developing your Perspectives process means getting outside your comfort zone. It also means applying this same generosity of spirit to yourself.

Reflection

What patterns are inside of me (beliefs, perspectives, strategies of behavior) that I've been avoiding looking at?

_____

_____

_____

Being kind to myself, I'm going to address these patterns by:

_____

_____

_____

Deep Insight

This type of pattern recognition is best done unconsciously, allowing the mind to wander wherever it needs to go. ENTJs may find themselves getting their best ideas when they first wake up, or even while they dream. Attempting to direct these thoughts may actually interrupt the process. An insight in process can feel like a bloodhound on the scent, and it needs freedom to explore whatever is the next lead. The mind can offer up buried insights, if one is quiet enough to hear them.

Exercise

Create a gentle, quiet space for one full hour. Turn off all sensory stimulation, turn off lights, and deaden any noise. Ensure no one will interrupt you during this time. Consider your favorite quote. (For example, Carl Sagan said, "We are a way for the universe to know itself." Rumi said, "The wound is the place where the Light enters you.") Set a timer. When one hour is up, immediately write down where your mind took you.

Reflection

My most recent insight from one hour of quiet time is:

_____

_____

_____

Future Perspectives

ENTJs solve problems by shifting perspectives until the solution becomes clear. Running simulations becomes second nature, watching how each possible scenario plays out over time. Using their Copilot process to do this, the ENTJ will get into a flow state by future-pacing, and will clock many pleasurable hours considering the fate of relationships, business, politics, technology, and humanity itself.

This is a far healthier exercise than its bastard cousin, conspiracy theorizing. While some conspiracies are interesting thought exercises and may even have some foundation in truth, attempting to know the malevolent forces at work doesn't really help move the needle of humanity as much as it encourages paranoia. For ENTJs to be the best version of themselves, asking what's possible for humanity is generally better than assuming humanity is doomed (and only the ENTJ can see it).

Personalize this skill by future-pacing. Theorize how an upcoming event or activity will pan out. Rehearse how you expect to behave in the situation and how others will respond to you. Continue to do this exercise with more complex situations—social encounters, romantic evenings, board meetings, etc. If you find yourself sabotaging situations in order to affirm your predictions (that is, expecting that nobody will talk to you at a party while spending the evening in a dark corner), whenever possible, future pace a positive outcome, the one you would love to experience. What are small actions that influence the trajectory of the outcome? Were they what you expected?

Reflection

Write down the five most recent predictions you made that came true.

1. _____

_____

2. _____

_____

3. _____

_____

4. _____

_____

5. _____

_____

Copilot Growth

Perspectives is the highest leverage point for growth in your personality. It helps you, as an ENTJ, make better decisions by reflecting on outcomes and personal meaning, as well as consider timelines and your impact on other people.

Here are some ways that an ENTJ can phrase questions using their Perspectives process:

- What are the long-term effects of this decision?

- What impact will this decision have on me? What about other people?

- Am I missing important details?

Perspectives encourages you to slow down, think through your plans, and have patience with the results. This process helps you to be thoughtful in actions, look at the big picture, and avoid completing tasks for their own sake. It also helps you determine which insights matter; Perspectives helps an ENTJ keep track of meaning.

It's easy for an ENTJ to get into action and cross things off their to-do list. But without slowing down enough to take their own intuition into consideration, ENTJs may find themselves dissatisfied, without meaning or meaningful relationships.

Growing your Perspectives can be a challenge for you as an ENTJ. It can feel like a threat to turn inward, facing painful scenarios and uncomfortable emotions. There's a fear that the further inward you go, the less control you will have. However, you should embrace this mental process because it gives you the opportunity to be inventive and imbue meaning into your daily flurry of activity. If you want to choose fulfillment over meaningless activity, you will need to get out of your comfort zone.

To develop your Perspectives function, start by asking, "What bigger purpose am I working toward?" Then, take these actions as you go through life:

- Spend time alone with your thoughts. Run future simulations of probabilities.

- Before settling on a thought, check to see if you've already made a similar decision. Reflect on what you learned about human nature and how things played out.

- Ask your advisors and people you respect to spin you a narrative of what they see so you can learn from it.

- Be sensitive to anyone working under you. Get feedback on their experience and consider changes that could be made in everyone's best interest.

- Slow down, lean into your intuition, be honest about which actions actually make meaning, and be thoughtful toward all the people around you.

You will bring the best version of yourself to the world when you look inward and imbue humanity into your decisions.

Reflection

The talents Perspectives can give me are:

_____

_____

_____

The ways I usually use Perspectives are:

_____

_____

_____

I'm going to develop Perspectives more by:

_____

_____

_____

List three ways you can start growing your Perspectives process today:

_____

_____

_____

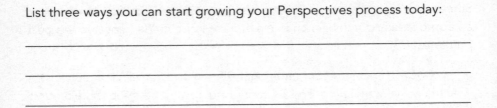

The ENTJ 10-Year-Old Is Sensation (Se)

Sensation lives in the here and now. Its purpose is to be present, realistic, and to simplify challenges so they can be acted upon. Sensation asks questions like, "What are my senses telling me?", "How are people over-complicating this?", "What can I know to be empirically true?", and "What is other people's body language telling me?" Taking reality at face value is the name of Sensation's game. As it matures, it gets better at interpreting the information given to it and knowing how to respond quickly to situations.

There's an energy that ENTJs can tap into when using Sensation. Making meaning from personal experience means getting out and experiencing, and the Sensation function encourages the ENTJ to move through the world, finding stimuli to feed into their intuition. They become more practical in their speculations about how it all works. The meaning and impact the ENTJ wants to have is fueled by the Sensation function. It also means that not everything has to be taken seriously, as Sensation is the most playful function of the eight cognitive functions. However, as a 10-Year-Old process, Sensation may struggle with knowing how to respond to feedback from other people.

As an extraverted function, Sensation allows the ENTJ to access a perceiving process while staying focused on outer-world feedback. This can be okay at times, but if the ENTJ gets used to relying upon Sensation to support their conclusions, they can rationalize skipping development of their Perspectives Copilot. And that's when the trouble starts. For ENTJs, this usually manifests as getting a shallow read on a situation or acting thoughtlessly.

Sensation is, in a large part, about getting quick impressions and then taking an appropriate action. People who have Sensation as a strength are usually pretty good at it, and they use it to test limitations. But as an ENTJ, you're wired to be at your best when looking for deeper meaning, not just at what's being presented.

If your 10-Year-Old acts without consulting the Copilot, it's going to sort intricate information at a 10-Year-Old level, and you'll find yourself justifying all sorts of bad decisions. If you're in a defensive place and feeling threatened by bad feedback, you may even go on the offensive to "destroy" the source.

Another way Sensation can manifest itself as a 10-Year-Old is by being self-indulgent with the senses. This can show up as a lack of self-discipline with food or substances, and sometimes laziness.

The Driver/10-Year-Old Loop

There are three ways an ENTJ experiences the loop, the echo chamber–like relationship between the Driver and 10-Year-Old functions. The way to get out of a loop is the same in all cases: focus on developing the Perspectives process.

Short-term loop. When stuck in an emotion and unable to get out, the ENTJ may get caught in a loop of aggressive behavior or "monkey mind" for a few moments up to a few days. In the first case, the ENTJ is reactive to the situation, upset, and unable to think things through. They may become violent and hostile, and even start to throw objects. Alternatively, when experiencing monkey mind, the ENTJ may become unsettled, restless, indecisive, and uncontrollable. They may feel an intense need to escape a situation.

Long-term loop. Compensating for insecurities, the ENTJ will focus on their image. They will see superficial markers, such as the social clubs they're able to gain access to or the cars they drive, as genuine examples of success. In the loop, the ENTJ will convince themselves that they are deep and able to see things that others miss, but in reality, they avoid introspection out of the fear that they are not enough. Superiority covers their fear of inadequacy, and the ENTJ may keep the people in their lives from meeting each other so no one has the full story.

Habitual loop. A less intense loop than the first, and far less offensive to others than the second, an ENTJ may stay in a loop of self-indulgence for an entire lifetime. Eating to mask emotions, binging on TV shows, following the path of least resistance…the ENTJ will fully embrace the monkey mind, chasing whatever is interesting to them in the moment, lacking any type of life plan, and drifting from one thing to the next. In this loop, the ENTJ hides from their real feelings and removes any meaning from their life.

Reflection

The ways Effectiveness and Sensation can loop in an ENTJ are:

_____

_____

_____

The ways I find myself looping are (include behaviors and situations):

_____

_____

_____

I'm going to work on breaking my loop(s) by:

_____

_____

_____

How to Best Use Sensation

If you find yourself getting reactive, image-conscious, or self-indulgent, this is a bad use of the Sensation function. Tap into the Perspectives function and ask yourself, "What am I trying to accomplish here? Do these actions or judgments have the long-term consequences I want?"

That said, if you've considered personal meaning and long-range conse-quences, and your mind is eager for excitement, that would be the time to listen to Sensation. Its job isn't to keep you focused on the superficial; it's meant to give you energy and be lively. Just don't let it fool you into becoming impulsive or indulgent. And if you can't back up the answers to your questions with solid results, take some time to reevaluate your actions.

You can also engage your 10-Year-Old in times of play, love, and intimacy. People of your type often enjoy experiences with friends, hosting parties, being artistic, and dressing with flair. You can use Sensation for relaxation, self-care, and getting pampered. And you can use Sensation to be honest and humble about your limitations, inspiring others with your transparency.

The ENTJ 3-Year-Old Is Authenticity (Fi)

Authenticity helps us get in touch with our emotions and value systems. The preferred function of many artists and counselors, the Authenticity process helps us recognize that each person has their own subjective experience that should be honored. Authenticity users often share the kaleidoscope of emotional experience, which can be difficult to express, through nonverbal forms of expression, and try hard to stay true to themselves.

As a 3-Year-Old function, Authenticity for the ENTJ is a part of them that whispers from the shadows. Normally capable of ignoring their emotions in favor of productivity, suddenly the ENTJ will be overwhelmed by an intense emotional experience and a desire to be understood.

There are three ways an ENTJ experiences the grip, the moments when the Driver process is stressed out, needs a break, and gives the 3-Year-Old function control of the car. This is most likely when the ENTJ avoids dealing with their emotions or offends their sense of values.

Short-term grip. This surfaces when emotions become overwhelming. Typically preferring to ignore emotions, ENTJs can get hit with an emotional tsunami when situations become too intense. Rage, despair, terror, or even a panic attack will grip the ENTJ, who may not have developed the resources to navigate their way out of such an intense emotional experience.

Long-term grip. A less intense grip, insecurity can interrupt the ENTJ's ability to confidently make decisions. It may be accompanied by self-doubt, even helplessness. Generally uncomfortable with sharing their emotions, the gripped ENTJ may feel that no one understands them, or that people would lose faith in them if their lack of self-confidence were revealed. Unable to confide in others and process their emotions, they get trapped, leading to more anxiety. The ENTJ loses the clarity that usually accompanies their decision-making. Despite their uncertainty, they may feel forced to take action, which may lead to bad consequences. This reinforces their fear of incompetence and perpetuates the cycle of insecurity.

Habitual grip. The third experience of being in the grip shows up as self-sabotage. Unable to communicate the pain within them and lacking the resources to address it, the ENTJ will project their feelings onto the outside world in a last, desperate attempt to understand their emotions. They may become passive aggressive, biting, and hurtful. This is to mirror their own feelings of being unappreciated, disrespected, and hurt. It's not uncommon for this grip to be accompanied with dysthymia, a persistent mild form of depression, though the ENTJ may not register it as depression. In this grip, the ENTJ has to monitor themselves for depression as they would a friend, by looking for the signs: low energy, trouble getting out of bed, an unhealthy relationship with food, and cheerlessness.

How to Best Use Authenticity

The best way to use Authenticity as a 3-Year-Old is to exercise it regularly, which will help prevent the grip from occurring. In this case, give yourself permission to be emotionally self-indulgent. Even though emotional expression seems time-consuming and impractical, do it anyway. Start an art project, write, make music, dance, or journal. Talk to a friend who is a good listener. Cry, laugh, emote, and express.

Give yourself a break from being productive and instead, be fully in your experience. If 30 minutes isn't enough time, keep going. Consider it spelunking into your soul. Find intimacy within yourself, get to know who you are, and ask yourself why you value what you do.

Using Authenticity in this way can also be a source of aspiration. It can encourage ENTJs to become gentle and kind, recognizing that each person has feelings and that they should matter. It allows the ENTJ to let go of fear of emotional pain and welcome a rich human experience. It helps them recognize that at the end of the day, we're all just people doing our best.

Reflection

The ways Authenticity can grip an ENTJ are:

_____

_____

_____

The ways I find myself being in the grip are (include behaviors and situations):

_____

_____

_____

I'm going to control the process by:

_____

_____

_____

My Authenticity 3-Year-Old inspires me/is my aspiration in these ways:

_____

_____

_____

CHAPTER 19

ENFJ Personality Type

ENFJs love human dynamics both in the practical and abstract sense. They have a natural talent for understanding how a group of people needs to feel in order to create change. When at their peak, ENFJs create and foster supportive culture across families, communities, and other groups of people. When they do focus on the individual, ENFJs are very attuned to the detailed and specific needs of the person.

Because of this intense focus on the details of other people's needs, ENFJs can sometimes become reactive and lose sight of the bigger picture. They pick up the energy and needs of the moment instead of focusing on a longer timeline and other players. If the ENFJ isn't careful, they can lose themselves to the service of others.

Letting others struggle instead of coming to the rescue can sometimes be the best way to meet needs of both the individual and the collective. If an ENFJ can remember the ebb and flow of human needs and interpersonal dynamics, and can take the position of a mentor rather than a rescuer, they can influence culture from a position of authority. When ENFJs are at their best, they become more responsible and less reactive, creating a deep, grounding energy that benefits everyone.

ENFJ CAR MODEL OVERVIEW

DRIVER — Harmony (Fe)	COPILOT — Perspectives (Ni)
• Prioritizes according to human need • Builds and communicates boundaries • Understands human dynamics	• Shifts into other people's perspectives • Has "a-ha" moments and insights • Forecasts
3-YEAR-OLD — Accuracy (Ti)	10-YEAR-OLD — Sensation (Se)
• Marginalizes facts that appear "antisocial" • Becomes critical or deceitful in stressful situations • Gives a sense of autonomy and self-confidence	• Enjoys sensory stimulation • Likes being realistic about the world, but struggles to be realistic about the self • Can get caught in image management and self-indulgence

The ENFJ Driver Is Harmony (Fe)

It's important to remember that the Driver process is a talent, but that doesn't mean every ENFJ will have the same skill level or use it in a healthy way. Developing Harmony as a healthy process is crucial to becoming an amazing ENFJ. Harmony can help an ENFJ identify the needs of all people, including the self, and meet those needs; build healthy boundaries; and deeply understand social dynamics and contracts.

Identify Needs

Fluctuating emotions are often the first sign that people have unmet needs. An ENFJ may be so tuned-in and sensitive to emotions that they find it easy to help people feel safe, loved, and stable. This can be as simple as hosting a party and making it look effortless, to being a shoulder for a grieving friend to cry on, to helping your friends with complicated relationship issues. People who have developed their Harmony process become so skilled at this, they often become the go-to person in a time of crisis. Learning to be available to help meet people's needs also helps you become extremely industrious and have lots of unexpected talents and skills in a variety of areas.

Making sure you're getting your needs met is equally important as—if not more important than—meeting the needs of others. You can't run on fumes all the time, and you can't be of help to others if you're perpetually exhausted. Express unmet needs out loud. Avoid behavior like walking away if you're unhappy, being silently disapproving, or only crying alone. When you are comfortable expressing your emotions, you become a role model for others to express themselves, and you are better able to help them get their needs met.

Exercise

Ask yourself, "What need is going unmet for me?" It could be alone time, better eating habits, more sleep, a conversation with a friend, a night out, or just some pampering. Once you identify it, ask yourself the easiest and fastest way to get that need met.

Reflection

Name your top three needs that frequently go unmet.

1. _____

2. _____

3. _____

Now, look at your schedule. What are you prioritizing that gets in the way of those needs being met? If it's people you care about, like your spouse, children, family, and friends, just remember that you can't get to their needs if you're running on fumes. Journal 3 to 5 ideas that you can begin implementing to fit those needs into your weekly schedule.

_____

_____

_____

_____

———————————————

Build Healthy Boundaries

Harmony is the process that is used to create and maintain unspoken social contracts. Contracts are designed for us to know each other's expectations and honor them (as long as they are agreed upon). If you, as an ENFJ, don't know your boundaries, Harmony will encourage you to spend time with people and experience both acceptable and unacceptable behavior. Once you know your boundaries, Harmony helps you create contracts around them.

That means you'll have to communicate them to the people in your life, making sure they fully understand and agree to your boundaries. In a moment where you feel taken advantage of or thrown under a bus, ask yourself which of your boundaries has been broken, and if it was you or the other person who broke it.

By setting up healthy boundaries, you will prevent misunderstandings and honor the limited resource that is your energy. When you give, you will give out of love and desire, not merely out of obligation.

Reflection

Follow the journal prompt below to become clearer about your boundaries. Feel free to repeat this journal prompt multiple times until you feel confident and authentic about the boundaries you've discovered and set. Once you've done so, share them with the three people who you feel closest to. If they are uncomfortable with your new boundaries, ask if it's because the boundaries are unreasonable, or because they will change the relationship. Be sensitive to resistance to change while staying firm with your requirements.

Remember: Boundary setting is a skill. It might be bumpy at first, but over time and with small successes, your boundaries will become a part of your identity.

Name three (or more) things you would like to see more of in your life:

1. _____

2. _____

3. _____

4. _____

5. _____

Name three (or more) behaviors you will never allow in your life again:

1. _____

2. _____

3. _____

4. _____

5. _____

I would like to strengthen the boundaries in these areas of my life:

_____

_____

_____

_____

_____

I can improve the boundaries in each area of my life by:

_____

_____

_____

_____

If someone crosses a boundary, my plan is to say:

_____

_____

_____

_____

Understand Social Contracts

Understanding unspoken social contracts means being able to know what's expected of yourself and others. This comes from a lifelong study of what offends other people versus what makes them feel comfortable.

This type of understanding is a major advantage in new circumstances and when first meeting people. You're very rarely going to say the wrong thing or alienate others. In fact, people of your type are often popular in group settings because you can help keep the conversation going without offending anyone or leaving anyone out.

Most importantly, tapping into the spectrum of social contracts reminds an ENFJ that people have different values and needs. This opens them up to a bigger, broader world. Creating relationships with a variety of people reminds the ENFJ that everyone has had a unique experience and may come with fresh ideas and relevant perspectives.

Make it your aim to meet many new people. The more people you meet, the more opportunities you have to understand the cultures they come from. What was their family's culture? What area of the country or world are they from? Do misunderstandings of culture get in the way of creating Harmony? How can your increased understanding of other people and their family or country help you to keep relationships between people in social settings congenial and happy?

— *Reflection* —

The way I feel about meeting new people is: _____

If I experience any hesitancy about meeting new people, what do I suspect is going on for me?

_____

_____

_____

I will meet one new person this week. Afterward, I will record the conversation and what I learned from it here:

_____

_____

_____

Setting Up the Right Conditions

The enemy of Harmony is a critical spirit. If you're judgmental of yourself or others, Harmony has difficulty doing what it does best: crafting a positive social climate and meeting other people's needs.

As your Driver, Harmony is your Flow state, and if you're not using this function enough, you'll eventually run out of juice and become depressed. Set up your conditions to access this mental process often. Keep in touch with loved ones and foster new relationships. Organize your space to be welcoming and warm.

Address conflict head-on. It will initially feel like you're feeding the problem, but discord doesn't go away by being neglected. All relationships face tension and clashes; it's part of human dynamics. If you're frustrated that people don't seem to be getting along, tap into the experience each person is having and discover their individual unmet needs. If you're involved in the conflict, remember what you know about each person and be as mindful of their situation as possible.

UNDEVELOPED HARMONY (Fe)	DEVELOPED HARMONY (Fe)
Avoid: • Ignoring your needs • Giving out of obligation • Conflict avoidance	Work Toward: • Getting your needs met • Communicating healthy boundaries • Resolving conflict

Reflection

The talents Harmony can give me are:

_____

_____

_____

The ways I usually use Harmony are:

_____

_____

_____

I'm going to develop Harmony more by:

_____

_____

_____

List three activities that put you into flow:

1. _____

2. _____

3. _____

The ENFJ Copilot Is Perspectives (Ni)

Without an introverted perceiving process, the ENFJ is not complete. Cultural expectations can be mistaken for personal identity. Without checking in to ensure that individual experiences, not just individual needs, are taken into consideration, the ENFJ may become judgmental and invasive.

An introverted perceiving process reminds the ENFJ to be patient, slow down, and think before acting. It also helps them connect to their subjective experience, remind them of which experiences have left the biggest impressions, and apply this understanding to the solutions they implement on behalf of other people.

It's important to remember that, like the Driver, the Copilot process is a talent. But that doesn't mean every ENFJ will have the same skill level or use it in a healthy way. Developing Perspectives as a healthy process is crucial to becoming an amazing ENFJ.

It can be difficult to actively develop an introverted function when one is an Extravert. It won't be as natural as working on Harmony, so discipline and an eye on the rich rewards Perspectives brings will be key.

Perspectives of Others

Since the Perspectives Copilot watches its own mind form patterns, it builds the skill of detaching from its own perspective. In this detached space, it is easy to jump into the perspective of others.

Being able to see things from another person's worldview helps the ENFJ explain why others do the things they do. Perspectives Copilots realize the simple truth that all actions, regardless of how confusing or distasteful they are to others, make sense to the person who committed them. It ceases to be a matter of explaining the behavior and becomes a matter of explaining how it made sense to the individual.

As an ENFJ, getting inside other people's minds means recognizing not only how their experiences have shaped them, but the conclusions they've come to about those experiences. This can include their beliefs, paradigms, and strategies of behavior.

Everyone has a bag of tricks life has taught them, and sometimes that includes strategies that are harmful to themselves and others. That is, "hurting people hurt others." ENFJs can recognize when people are in pain, and when they lash out because of it. The key for an ENFJ is not to get lost thinking about how trauma shapes the mind, but rather to focus on how it can be healed. Patterns of the mind are plastic, not static. As a natural seer into the mind and its relationship to self and others, the ENFJ has a talent for developing tools and strategies for shifting paradigms, especially as they relate to emotional and healing work.

This doesn't mean that all ENFJs must be therapists or counselors. However, there is a strong pull for ENFJs toward helping people find their path. And oftentimes, the ENFJ will find the healing they need for themselves from pointing others toward a better way.

Exercise

Think of a heinous action or controversial person that you can't see yourself ever condoning. Instead of jumping to condemn the action, take a moment to really get inside the head of the person who performed the action. How did their action make complete sense to them at the time? Can you understand it so well you could defend it to another person? Don't focus on the act itself, but on the mind of the person who committed it.

Now that you are in a Perspectives frame of mind, fill out the following journal prompt. If you cannot think of anything immediately, feel free to ruminate on the question. It may guide you to some uncomfortable places, and that's okay. Developing your Perspectives process means getting outside your comfort zone. It also means applying this same generosity of spirit to yourself.

— Reflection —

What patterns are inside of me (beliefs, perspectives, strategies of behavior) that I've been avoiding looking at?

_____

_____

_____

Being kind to myself, I'm going to address these patterns by:

_____

_____

_____

Deep Insight

This type of pattern recognition is best done unconsciously, allowing the mind to wander wherever it needs to go. ENFJs may find themselves getting their best ideas when they first wake up, or even while they dream. Attempting to direct these thoughts may actually interrupt the process. An insight in process can feel like a bloodhound on the scent, and it needs freedom to explore whatever is the next lead. The mind can offer up buried insights, if one is quiet enough to hear them.

Create a gentle, quiet space for one full hour. Turn off all sensory stimulation, turn off lights, and deaden any noise. Ensure no one will interrupt you during this time. Consider your favorite quote. (For example, Carl Sagan said, "We are a way for the universe to know itself." Rumi said, "The wound is the place where the Light enters you.") Set a timer. When one hour is up, immediately write down where your mind took you.

Reflection

My most recent insight from one hour of quiet time is:

_____

_____

_____

Conflict Management

Watching how one's own mind works can give clues as to how other people's minds are working. Take a word like *loyalty* or *love*. If we believe everyone defines *love* the same way, we're going to find ourselves in trouble when someone we're in a relationship with behaves in a way that doesn't match our own definition of *love*. These misunderstandings happen all the time. Because you have Perspectives as a strength, however, you catch these misunderstandings. It's not uncommon for people of your type to watch an argument between two people and say, "Wait a minute—you guys are using the same word to mean two totally different things." Or, "You guys are using two different words to mean the same thing. You actually agree."

Exercise

Listen to a conversation as a third-person observer. Using discretion, at certain points in the conversation—when one of the speakers uses a word with an ambiguous meaning—ask them to clarify what they mean by that word.

Ask the listener if that's the same meaning they took from it. Practice guessing the difference in meaning between the listener and the speaker.

Reflection

Name five ways people disagree on the definition of the word *love*.

1. _____

_____

2. _____

_____

3. _____

_____

4. _____

_____

5. _____

_____

Copilot Growth

Perspectives is the highest leverage point for growth in your personality. It helps you, as an ENFJ, make better decisions by reflecting on outcomes and personal meaning, as well as consider timelines and your impact on other people.

Here are some ways that an ENFJ can phrase questions using their Perspectives process:

- What are the long-term effects of this decision?

- What impact will this decision have on me? What about other people?

- Am I missing important details?

Perspectives encourages you to slow down, think through your plans, and have patience with the results. This process helps you to be thoughtful in actions, look at the big picture, and avoid completing tasks for their own sake. It also helps you determine which insights matter; Perspectives helps an ENFJ keep track of meaning.

It's easy for an ENFJ to get into action and cross things off their to-do list. But without slowing down enough to take their own intuition into consideration, ENFJs may find themselves dissatisfied, without meaning or meaningful relationships.

Growing your Perspectives can be a challenge for you as an ENFJ. It can feel like a threat to turn inward, facing painful scenarios and uncomfortable emotions. There's a fear that the further inward you go, the less control you will have. However, you should embrace this mental process because it gives you the opportunity to be inventive and imbue meaning into your daily flurry of activity. If you want to choose fulfillment over meaningless activity, you will need to get out of your comfort zone.

To develop your Perspectives function, start asking, "What bigger purpose am I working toward?" Then, take these actions as you go through life:

- Spend time alone with your thoughts. Run future simulations of probabilities.

- Before settling on a thought, check to see if you've already made a similar decision. Reflect on what you learned about human nature and how things played out.

- Ask your advisors and people you respect to spin you a narrative of what they see so you can learn from it.

- Be sensitive to anyone working under you. Get feedback on their experience and consider changes that could be made in everyone's best interest.

- Slow down, lean into your intuition, be honest about which actions actually make meaning, and be thoughtful toward all the people around you.

You will bring the best version of yourself to the world when you look inward and imbue humanity into your decisions.

Reflection

The talents Perspectives can give me are:

_____

_____

_____

The ways I usually use Perspectives are:

_____

_____

_____

I'm going to develop Perspectives more by:

_____

_____

_____

List three ways you can start growing your Perspectives process today:

1. _____

_____

2. _____

_____

3. _____

_____

The ENFJ 10-Year-Old Is Sensation (Se)

Sensation lives in the here and now. Its purpose is to be present, realistic, and to simplify challenges so they can be acted upon. Sensation asks questions like, "What are my senses telling me?", "How are people over-complicating this?", "What can I know to be empirically true?", and "What is other people's body language telling me?" Taking reality at face value is the name of Sensation's game. As it matures, it gets better at interpreting the information given to it and knowing how to respond quickly to situations.

There's an energy that ENFJs can tap into when using Sensation. Making meaning from personal experience means getting out and experiencing, and the Sensation function encourages the ENFJ to move through the world, finding stimuli to feed into their intuition. They become more practical in their speculations about how it all works. The meaning and impact the ENFJ wants to have is fueled by the Sensation function. It also means that not everything has to be taken seriously, as Sensation is the most playful function of the eight cognitive functions. However, as a 10-Year-Old process, Sensation may struggle with knowing how to respond to feedback from other people.

As an extraverted function, Sensation allows the ENFJ to access a perceiving process while staying focused on outer-world feedback. This can be okay at times, but if the ENFJ gets used to relying upon Sensation to support their conclusions, they can rationalize skipping development of their Perspectives Copilot. And that's when the trouble starts. For ENFJs, this usually manifests as getting a shallow read on a situation and/or acting thoughtlessly.

Sensation is, in a large part, about getting quick impressions and then taking an appropriate action. People who have Sensation as a strength are usually pretty good at it, and they use it to test limitations. But as an ENFJ, you're wired to be at your best when looking for deeper meaning, not just what's being presented.

If your 10-Year-Old acts without consulting the Copilot, it's going to sort intricate information at a 10-Year-Old level, and you'll find yourself justifying all sorts of bad decisions. If you're in a defensive place and feeling threatened by bad feedback, you'll end up seeing reality selectively.

Another way Sensation can manifest itself as a 10-Year-Old is by being self-indulgent with the senses. This can show up as a lack of self-discipline with food or substances, and sometimes laziness.

The Driver/10-Year-Old Loop

There are three ways an ENFJ experiences the loop, the echo chamber–like relationship between the Driver and 10-Year-Old functions. The way to get out of a loop is the same in all cases: focus on developing the Perspectives process.

Short-term loop. When stuck in an emotion and unable to get out, the ENFJ may get caught in a loop of aggressive behavior or "monkey mind" for a few moments up to a few days. In the first case, the ENFJ is reactive to the situation, upset, and unable to think things through. They may become violent and hostile, and even start to throw objects. Alternatively, when experiencing monkey mind, the ENFJ may become unsettled, restless, indecisive, and uncontrollable. They may feel an intense need to escape a situation.

Long-term loop. Compensating for insecurities they are unable to admit to themselves, the ENFJ will focus on their image. They will see superficial markers, such as how many friends they have or who they're in a romantic relationship with, as genuine examples of success. In this loop, the ENFJ will convince themselves they are deep and able to see things that others miss, but in reality, they avoid introspection out of the fear that they are not enough. A sense of superiority covers their fear of inadequacy, and the ENFJ may keep the people in their lives from meeting each other so no one has the full story.

Habitual loop. A less intense loop than the first, and far less offensive to others than the second, an ENFJ may stay in a loop of self-indulgence for an entire lifetime. Eating to mask emotions, binging on TV shows, following the path of least resistance…the ENFJ will fully embrace the monkey mind, chasing whatever is interesting to them in the moment, lacking any type of life plan, and drifting from one thing to the next. In this loop, the ENFJ hides from their real feelings and removes any meaning from their life.

The ways Harmony and Sensation can loop in an ENFJ are:

_____

_____

_____

The ways I find myself looping are (include behaviors and situations):

_____

_____

_____

I'm going to work on breaking my loop(s) by:

_____

_____

_____

How to Best Use Sensation

If you find yourself getting reactive, image-conscious, or self-indulgent, this is a bad use of the Sensation function. Tap into the Perspectives function and ask yourself, "What am I trying to accomplish here? Do these actions or judgments have the long-term consequences I want?"

That said, if you've considered personal meaning and long-range consequences, and your mind is eager for excitement, that would be the time to listen to Sensation. Its job isn't to keep you focused on the superficial; it's meant to give you energy and be lively. Just don't let it fool you into becoming impulsive or indulgent. And if you can't back up the answers to your questions with solid results, take some time to reevaluate your actions.

You can also engage your 10-Year-Old in times of play, love, and intimacy. People of your type often enjoy experiences with friends, hosting parties, being artistic, and dressing with flair. You can use Sensation for relaxation, self-care, and getting pampered. And you can use Sensation to be honest and humble about your limitations, inspiring others with your transparency.

The ENFJ 3-Year-Old Is Accuracy (Ti)

Accuracy helps us solve problems and build skills. The preferred function of many scientists and mechanics, Accuracy users prize data and systems thinking. Often communicating directly and with radical honesty, Accuracy helps people refine information by removing personal bias and social pressure.

As a 3-Year-Old function, Accuracy is the part of the ENFJ that whispers from the shadows. Normally capable of marginalizing information that appears antisocial, suddenly the ENFJ will feel an overwhelming need to analyze themselves and others, becoming coldly diagnostic.

There are three ways an ENFJ experiences the grip, the moments when the Driver process is stressed out, needs a break, and gives the 3-Year-Old function control of the car. This is most likely when an ENFJ avoids dealing with their thoughts or experiences, thus developing cognitive dissonance.

Short-term grip. When they are exhausted by social expectations, ENFJs will resort to extreme criticism. For some ENFJs, it will be self-criticism: They may beat themselves up for believing themselves to be failures, unable to explain their ideas, or unlovable or intellectually inferior. The negative self-talk can be relentless and crippling. For other ENFJs, the criticism will focus on others, turning the blast outward in an icy barrier between themselves and those that could hurt them.

Long-term grip. Some ENFJs will become deceitful. Acting uncharacteristically self-centered, the ENFJ will create a false front, allowing other people to believe wrong but flattering information about the ENFJ. If the situation requires, the ENFJ may directly lie to keep up their image. In this grip, ENFJs self-justify and overinflate their competence to both themselves and others.

Habitual grip. In the most subtle and difficult type of grip to disrupt, the ENFJ represses all negative emotions when facing the public. They fear others will see them for who they truly are—imperfect and unacceptable. By staying cheerful and showing high morale, they are above reproach and can put off the time of reckoning as long as possible. They may overanalyze relationships, project their inadequacies onto others, take credit for personal development they haven't done, and feel it is unjust that others don't have to work as hard to maintain their lives. Unfairness becomes a theme in their lives.

How to Best Use Accuracy

The best way to use Accuracy as a 3-Year-Old is to exercise it regularly, which will help prevent the grip from occurring. In this case, give yourself permission to check out of life for a while and do serious self-care. Remove yourself from relationship and emotion management. Find a quiet space for reflection and "me" time. Do a Sudoku puzzle or play Solitaire or video games.

The goal is to give yourself a break from caring about the needs of others. If 30 minutes isn't enough time, keep going. Consider giving yourself an entire day of independence and self-direction, answering to no one but yourself.

Accuracy can also be a source of aspiration, the voice that whispers in the back of your mind. It can encourage ENFJs to pursue their own interests, find autonomy, and be self-directed. It also encourages ENFJs to have confidence in their intelligence, accumulated knowledge, and ability to problem solve.

Reflection

The ways Accuracy can grip an ENFJ are:

_____

_____

_____

The ways I find myself being in the grip are (include behaviors and situations):

_____

_____

_____

I'm going to control the process by:

_____

_____

_____

My Accuracy 3-Year-Old inspires me/is my aspiration in these ways:

_____

_____

_____

———————————————

CHAPTER 20

ESTJ Personality Type

At their core, ESTJs are managers who want things to work with as little friction as possible. They are willing to try new things, diversify, and find creative solutions so they can get results at the end of the day.

The ESTJ superpower is the ability to simplify and organize timelines and logistics. As managers, they have a knack for creating schedules, strategies, workflows, and processes to streamline the lives of family and coworkers. They love to find the 20 percent of effort that will get 80 percent of the result.

While ESTJs are willing to think outside the box, they will only tolerate a high degree of creativity if it has an element of practical use. Because ESTJs tend to focus on the return on investment, they love to measure results in the outer world. They may perceive immeasurable efforts as unnecessary indulgences and they may become abrupt, judgmental, and unsympathetic.

ESTJs excel when they are open and acknowledge that they, too, can be quirky and creative. When they are at their best, they have a generous spirit.

DRIVER Effectiveness (Te)	COPILOT Memory (Si)
• Evaluates in terms of resource management (time, energy, currency) • Naturally thinks in and sets up streamlined systems • Has an instinct for leadership	• Reliable, careful, and honors tradition • Upholds old traditions and creates new ones • Resilience and acceptance of a difficult past
3-YEAR-OLD Authenticity (Fi)	10-YEAR-OLD Exploration (Ne)
• Resists need to be introspective • Can become emotionally overwhelmed and lost • Develops an artistic outlet, becomes kinder to self and others	• Solves problems creatively • Struggles with determining when to make changes and when to accept a situation • Can idealize the self and project weakness onto others

The ESTJ Driver Is Effectiveness (Te)

It's important to remember that the Driver process is a talent, but that doesn't mean every ESTJ will have the same skill level or use it in a healthy way. Developing Effectiveness as a healthy process is crucial to becoming an amazing ESTJ.

Effectiveness, when developed and sharpened, allows you to gain a natural understanding of resource management, set up streamlined systems, and build skills that may be uncomfortable, but are necessary for life.

Resource Management

Time, energy, money—everything that is built requires resources to build it. When it comes to determining which resources to use, the Effectiveness Driver has a natural interest in return on investment (ROI). Is a certain resource worth the effort? To answer that question, Effectiveness also pays special attention to stress tests, which help determine if something can hold up in the long run.

Ultimately, ESTJs use Effectiveness for sustainability. The least amount of effort for the most amount of return is great, but if it's going to break down quickly and require more effort in the long run, it's not truly worth it. Thinking on a large scale helps inform whether or not something will pass the test of time.

When an ESTJ is managing resources, they must consider their feelings and the feelings of others. This means they must learn to manage their emotional and psychological resources. Without allotting time for the personal things in life, unexpected emotions may creep in, shutting all production down. Scheduling time out for R&R and reconnecting with family is crucial for overall maintenance.

Exercise

Get good at determining the value of human or emotional factors. Time is often overlooked in ROI, as are things like emotional expense. When determining if something is worth effort, use monetary gain as only one consideration. Take into account enjoyment of process, learning, and quality of product. The standard ROI algorithm is ROI = (Gain − Cost) / Cost. Feel free to create your own algorithm to incorporate more factors.

Name three soft factors you tend to either waste (or overprotect) that may be interrupting your ROI:

_____

_____

_____

Journal one area of your life where you would like to improve your ROI. Using the algorithm above (or one you have created), state an actionable plan that will help you get more out of the resource than you're putting into it:

_____

_____

_____

_____

_____

————————

Streamlined Systems

If Effectiveness could be expressed in a single quote, it might be, "Freedom is defined as a system that runs so well, you no longer have to think about it."

Effectiveness, like Harmony, is about attempting to create an environment where people get their needs met. But unlike Harmony, the needs of Effectiveness aren't emotional, they're logistical. Systems help groups stay in a flow without participants getting in each other's way. Automobile freeway systems are a great example of how streamlining keeps us all moving forward without having to really think about it. Once these systems are in place, even bigger goals can be attained since accomplishments build upon themselves.

When ESTJs develop patience, they no longer feel the need to force things to happen too quickly. An efficient system should be set up according to the principle of water flowing downhill. In terms of money, it flows to the cheapest effective solution to a problem. This principle should be applied to all resources, not just money. It's tempting to jump on what is expedient, but if it's not a sustainable solution, it won't be effective overall. A good system recognizes a little acceptable loss while maintaining itself for the long term.

Exercise

The next time you perform a task, document the process with a goal of streamlining the task. Consider that there are two types of processes: critical and optional. Which steps are necessary to the task, and which can be cut? Which resources (time, money, energy) are necessary? Can you afford to pare the resources down for outcome? Once you have a step-by-step procedure, consult with others who have accomplished this same task and discover if there was anything you missed.

Reflection

Name three resources you need to improve your management of:

1. _____

2. _____

3. _____

Now, look at your schedule. What are you prioritizing that compromises the proper management of those resources? Record three to five ideas on how to recoup those resources into your weekly schedule.

_____

_____

_____

_____

_____

Building Necessary Skills

Effectiveness Drivers can shut off personal feelings in order to get things done. In fact, it may be argued that this is the core competency of Effectiveness. Daily tasks aren't always pleasant, nor is skill building outside one's area of expertise. While completing these tasks, ESTJs may struggle to show up authentically, or forget to manage people's emotional impressions, unintentionally coming across as having bad intent. Expanding their emotional and social intelligence can be a struggle, especially if the ESTJ has developed just enough to get what they want.

While it's easy to marginalize one's own weaknesses, eventually their effects can pile up. And at times, it's only obvious that these skills are underdeveloped when an opportunity for their use has already slipped by.

When an ESTJ builds a strong relationship with their Effectiveness Driver, they'll bite the bullet and focus on proficiency in areas that are necessary for life. Anything unnecessary can be delegated, as long as the resources have been built to hire them out or hand them off. But for anything that can't be delegated—cultivating friendships, finding love, maintaining physical health, performing household responsibilities—the ESTJ can lean on Effectiveness to help them put their head down, muscle through, and make it happen, all the while building a sustainable system to keep the benefits of the hard work going.

Exercise

Identify one area of your life where you care about improving but have been procrastinating. It could be getting into better physical shape, improving your diet, finding a spouse, doing public speaking, finding a better job, etc.… Make a list of why this is something you want, and identify what has been holding you back. Ask yourself how much more rewarding your life would be if you just started working toward it, even if it isn't optimal or ideal in the beginning. Paint a picture of what your life would look like if you were to succeed. Write this visualization out and put it on your refrigerator.

Reflection

Name one area of your life you would like to improve:

_____

_____

_____

Name three activities you can begin immediately that would address this improvement:

_____

_____

_____

At the beginning of each day, write down what you are going to do that day to improve this area of your life by 5 percent:

_____

_____

_____

At the end of each day, write down what you did to improve this area of your life by 5 percent:

_____

_____

_____

Setting Up the Right Conditions

The enemy of Effectiveness is emotional insecurity. If you're troubled, Effectiveness has difficulty doing what it does best: creating plans and making rational decisions to get the job done.

As your Driver, Effectiveness is your Flow state, and if you're not using this function enough you'll eventually run out of juice and become depressed. So, set up your conditions to access this mental process often. Keep life streamlined and manageable. And if life is throwing too many emotionally confusing things at you, make sure you schedule time to address them instead of letting them creep into all your activities.

Addressing your emotional state may feel self-indulgent, but it can also be seen as a task. Focus on actual effectiveness, not efficiency. While it may seem inefficient to give energy to introspection, if ignoring your feelings disrupts your life, then doing so robs you of your overall effectiveness. It can be as simple as reflecting on how far you've come, the lessons you've learned throughout your life, and how they influence your plans to move forward.

UNDEVELOPED EFFECTIVENESS (Te)	DEVELOPED EFFECTIVENESS (Te)
Avoid:	Work Toward:
• Emotional insecurity	• Scheduling time for the self
• Forcing outcomes	• Patiently building systems
• Marginalizing weaknesses	• Cultivating necessary skills

Reflection

The talents Effectiveness can give me are:

_____

_____

_____

The ways I usually use Effectiveness are:

_____

_____

_____

I'm going to develop Effectiveness more by:

_____

_____

_____

List three activities that put you into flow:

_____

_____

_____

———————

The ESTJ Copilot Is Memory (Si)

Without an introverted perceiving process, the ESTJ is not complete. They may demand that everyone contort themselves to serve the systems that have been put in place, forgetting that systems are there to serve people. Without checking in to ensure that individual experiences are taken into consideration, the ESTJ may become unsympathetic, rash, and presumptuous.

An introverted perceiving process reminds the ESTJ to be patient and recognize that longer timelines are always at play. It also helps them connect to their subjective experience, peer into future possibilities, speculate on outcomes, and apply this understanding to interactions with and on behalf of other people.

It's important to remember that, like the Driver, the Copilot process is a talent. But that doesn't mean every ESTJ will have the same skill level or use it in a healthy way. Developing Memory as a healthy process is crucial to becoming an amazing ESTJ.

It can be difficult to actively develop an introverted function when one is an Extravert. It won't be as natural as working on Effectiveness, so discipline and an eye on the rich rewards Memory brings will be key.

Reliable, Careful, and Honors Procedure

For people who use Memory as a Copilot, living in an unpredictable or unstable environment carries a huge penalty. To avoid this kind of environment, people of your type are amazing at maintaining procedures and processes to minimize instability. If no procedure exists, Memory is compelled to find one.

Memory users recognize the need for care and caution. There is no reason to make repeated mistakes if a process is established to track them. It can be a simple aphorism to pass helpful knowledge from one generation to the next, such as "Measure twice, cut once." There are important reasons we have standards. While it might sound fun to "reinvent the wheel," actual car wheels would be incredibly difficult to shop for if there weren't an established standard and series of regulations on their size and fit to most vehicles.

It's important for an ESTJ to develop patience and recognize long time-lines when making decisions. Without the Memory function, an ESTJ may unintentionally sabotage their efforts by only taking into account immediate returns and short-term statistics. Rewards come from playing the long game.

Exercise

Identify areas in your life that are unsafe or in violation of established standards, particularly things that (if left by themselves) could become a problem in the future. Look to a trusted organization, community, or family culture to gauge what the standard is and how you can correct it. If you're unsure, consult experts for guidance on how to correct the issue.

Reflection

What areas of my life am I letting turn into chaos? Is there a procedure I can implement to reestablish sanity?

_____

_____

_____

_____

Being kind to myself, I'm going to address this chaos by:

_____

_____

_____

_____

Holds Relationship with Tradition

Memory users recognize how much each individual is influenced by their experiences. They also understand the importance of ensuring that most of those memories are positive. It is a pleasure to create wonderful memories that can be replayed and enjoyed forever. For this reason, it's common for Memory users to enjoy holidays, family gatherings, and other times when loved ones get together for momentous occasions.

Traditions can also be used for healing. Trauma that is difficult to shake from the ESTJ's memory may require a healing tradition. For example, when a loved one dies, it may become an annual tradition to gather with others to talk about them, remember them, and pay tribute by living life fully in their honor.

The more sophisticated Memory gets, the more it's open to adopting new traditions. This is important to remember, as Memory in its infancy may be fearful of the unfamiliar. Changing one's traditions—including beliefs and paradigms—may feel disloyal to parents and other trusted authorities. But as it matures, Memory becomes a more adaptable function. It incorporates new experiences into its identity, learning to become whatever is appropriate to the context.

Exercise

Consider ways you can pass on the traditions of your family to the next generation. Is there a tradition you inherited that can be taught to your children, nieces, or nephews? Do they understand the importance of it, and will they contribute to passing it on after you're gone? How can you make the tradition more enjoyable in a way that will leave a lasting impression, help mold their experience, and help them want to carry the torch?

Reflection

The tradition that has had the biggest impact on me is:

_____

_____

_____

_____

_____

Resilience and Acceptance

It's not easy to accept things as they are, but Memory has the greatest natural talent for it, and therefore, Memory users demonstrate great resilience during trying situations. True acceptance includes letting go of judgment and blame (including of oneself) and instead addressing situations with tolerance and forgiveness. Memory meets unfair situations with fairness, and finds peace within.

An ESTJ will feel compelled to manage the situation, and without developing Memory, they may attempt to force an outcome or shoehorn a solution. To accept a situation may feel like defeat, like losing control over the situation. But acceptance is not passive, nor is it complacent. It's a recognition of what cannot be changed and coming to terms with its impact in one's life.

Memory users naturally understand the passage of time. They register change almost immediately and know how people are formed by their experiences. They get that we are who we are because of our past. Truly traumatic experiences can break people past their limits, but time can heal even brokenness. As it is said, "time heals all wounds," even if it takes decades, and we can be stronger people for it. In cases where an ESTJ is dealing with an abusive past, the Memory function can be used to mark growth and to see how far they have come.

It's important to remember that acceptance is not submitting to unhealthy situations. It's not needlessly putting up with physical pain, a bad relationship, or a toxic context. Predicaments that can be changed should be changed. Acceptance is not endurance; it's the opposite. It is ending the suffering that accompanies resisting reality, but it does not involve seeking out a painful reality.

Exercise

Practice self-acceptance. When you notice that you are judging or rating yourself, look for a time in your past that may have prompted the thought. Did this criticism originally come from a parent? Is this self-criticism from a time you believed you failed at something? If you are much older than you were at the origin of the thought, is there wisdom you have now that changes how you experience the inciting event? Did you do the best you could at the time? What connections do you see now that you missed then? Can you forgive your younger self? Does your younger self need forgiveness at all, or just a little understanding? Focus on letting go of the pain and the belief that caused the judgment.

Reflection

What's your biggest regret? What have you done to make amends with yourself or forgive yourself?

_____

_____

_____

_____

_____

_____

Copilot Growth

Memory is the highest leverage point for growth in your personality. It helps you, as an ESTJ, make better decisions based on solid information, and by considering timelines and the impact on other people.

Here are some ways that an ESTJ can phrase questions using their Memory process:

- What are the long-term effects of this decision?

- What impact will this decision have on myself as well as other people?

- Am I missing important details?

Memory encourages you to slow down, think through your plans, and have patience with the results. It recommends that you be moderate in habits, look at the details of a plan, and avoid jumping to conclusions. Without slowing down enough to consider the experiences of yourself and others, you may find yourself dissatisfied, without personal meaning or meaningful relationships.

Growing your Memory can be a challenge for you as an ESTJ. It can feel like a threat to look inward and face painful experiences and uncomfortable emotions. There's a fear that the further inward you go, the less control you will have. But if you embrace this mental process, you will have the opportunity to be reflective and imbue meaning into your flurry of activity.

Memory also encourages an ESTJ to know which details matter. Developing this process gives the ESTJ insight into what to focus on, and what is unnecessary minutiae.

To help develop this function, start asking yourself, "What am I actually trying to accomplish?" Spend time ruminating and thinking things through, especially if your desire is to jump to a conclusion.

- Consult experts in the field to see what has worked or failed.

- If you've already made similar decisions, reflect on how successful they were.

- Check in with family members before acting in a way that impacts them.

- Be sensitive to anyone under you in a project or work environment. Get feedback on their experiences and consider changes that could be made in everyone's best interest.

- Slow down, learn from past mistakes, be honest about which details actually matter, and be thoughtful toward all the people involved.

Reflection

The talents Memory can give me are:

_____

_____

_____

The ways I usually use Memory are:

_____

_____

_____

I'm going to develop Memory more by:

_____

_____

_____

List three ways you can start growing your Memory process today:

_____

_____

_____

The ESTJ 10-Year-Old Is Exploration (Ne)

Exploration users see patterns and make connections. They figure out what is possible, not simply what is probable. Exploration gets us to ask questions like, "If we put these two things together, what would that make?", "What's a creative solution to this problem?", "What am I seeing that everyone else seems to be missing?", and "What if...?"

Innovating and finding fresh, new solutions to old problems is the name of Exploration's game. As it matures, it gets better at knowing when it's seeing a pattern or forcing ideas together.

ESTJs can learn flexibility when using Exploration. While getting a solid plan in place and being patient with outcomes is preferred, you can't always know how things will pan out. It's easier to look at the big picture and have more fun in life if you're willing to diversify, come up with creative solutions, and foster open-mindedness to new people, places, and possibilities. ESTJs know that they don't have to have all the answers, and they don't always have to be right or in control. Bad habits should be acknowledged and changed, and uncertainty should accepted. However, Exploration may struggle with knowing when to trust itself. An ESTJ may be unaware that they are forming false patterns so they can see what they want to see.

As an extraverted function, Exploration allows the ESTJ to access a perceiving process while staying focused on external feedback. This can be okay at times, but if the ESTJ gets used to relying upon Exploration to support their conclusions, they can rationalize skipping development of their Memory Copilot. And that's when the trouble starts. For ESTJs, this usually manifests as getting a bad read on a situation and jumping to conclusions.

Exploration is, in a large part, about getting impressions beyond what can be immediately sensed or perceived. People who have it as a strength are usually pretty good at it, and they can usually spot creative solutions. But you're wired to be at your best when looking at the situation as it is, not as it could be.

If your 10-Year-Old Exploration function gets to influence your thought process, it's going to sort intricate information at a juvenile level—you'll find yourself justifying all sorts of bad decisions. Especially when you are feeling defensive and threatened by bad feedback, you'll end up inventing things that don't exist in order to avoid self-doubt. Another way Exploration can manifest itself as a 10-Year-Old is by looking for shortcuts, including ones that don't serve the ESTJ. An example would be chasing an unreliable opportunity, cheating, or otherwise rationalizing any ends to justify the means. You may tell yourself you don't have the time to vet everything, when really, you simply have not developed the characteristic of patience.

The Driver/10-Year-Old Loop

There are three ways an ESTJ experiences the loop, the echo chamber–like relationship between the Driver and 10-Year-Old functions. The way to get out of a loop is the same in all cases: focus on developing the Memory process.

Short-term loop. This impulsive, sometimes destructive, behavior may only last for a few moments up to a few days. Fleeing responsibility and feeling tied down, the ESTJ may become overindulgent with drinking, partying, or substance abuse. Shutting off the inner voice that recommends caution, they may make impetuous life decisions. If the voice is coming not from within but from another person, the fun stops, and the ESTJ can become angry, attempt to control the situation, or simply end a relationship (or quit a job) that feels too binding.

Long-term loop. Unable to take responsibility for their own life choices, the ESTJ will cast blame outward, harshly and critically projecting their discomfort onto other people, even those they do not personally know. They find clever reasons to blame people for their own uncomfortable feelings, and take the position that their troubles must be caused by others. Instead of taking the time to familiarize themselves with new people, places, and situations, ESTJs develop prejudices, cast judgments, and manipulate information to justify harsh conclusions.

Habitual loop. Possibly the most challenging loop to overcome, the ESTJ may take shortcuts in business by chasing one opportunity after another, over-diversifying interests, or by giving only cursory attention to important matters. They may take shortcuts in relationships by ignoring the people in their lives in favor of forming bonds with TV-show characters, shallow acquaintances, or even affairs and flings. Forgetting the anchor points of their past, the ESTJ won't seem to learn lessons and will repeat the same mistakes. They may get easily distracted by novelty and pursue extravagant new toys to feed a growing inner emptiness.

Reflection

The ways Effectiveness and Exploration can loop in an ESTJ are:

_____

_____

_____

The ways I find myself looping are (include behaviors and situations):

_____

_____

_____

I'm going to work on breaking my loop(s) by:

_____

_____

_____

How to Best Use Exploration

If you find yourself getting impulsive, casting blame, or taking shortcuts, that is a bad use of the Exploration function. Tap into the Memory function and ask yourself, "What am I trying to accomplish?" and "Do these actions or judgments provide the long-term consequences I want?"

That said, if you've carefully accepted responsibility and measured out consequences, and your mind is still telling you that a refreshing change is in order, that would be the time to listen Exploration. Its job isn't to project what you want to believe onto the world; it's meant to open you up to creative solutions and new ways of doing things. Just don't let it fool you into becoming impulsive or avoidant.

You can also engage your 10-Year-Old in times of play, love, and intimacy. People of your type often enjoy conversation with friends, hosting parties, and entertaining others with their bigger-than-life personalities. You can use Exploration to connect people with other people and opportunities you know they would love. And you can use Exploration to help open your mind to include other cultures, countries, and people.

The ESTJ 3-Year-Old Is Authenticity (Fi)

Authenticity helps us get in touch with our emotions and value systems. The preferred function of many artists and counselors, the Authenticity process helps us recognize that each person has their own subjective experience that should be honored. Authenticity users often share the kaleidoscope of emotional experience, which can be difficult to express, though nonverbal forms of expression, and try hard to stay true to themselves.

As a 3-Year-Old function, Authenticity for the ESTJ is a part of them that whispers from the shadows. Normally capable of ignoring their emotions in favor of productivity, suddenly the ESTJ will be overwhelmed by an intense emotional experience and a desire to be understood.

There are three ways an ESTJ experiences the grip, the moments when the Driver process is stressed out, needs a break, and gives the 3-Year-Old function control of the car. This is most likely when the ESTJ avoids dealing with their emotions or offends their sense of values.

Short-term grip. This grip surfaces when emotions become overwhelming. Typically preferring to ignore emotions, ESTJs can get hit with an emotional tsunami when situations become too intense. Rage, despair, terror, or even a panic attack will grip the ESTJ, who may not have developed the resources to navigate their way out of such an intense emotional experience.

Long-term grip. A less intense grip, insecurity can interrupt the ESTJ's ability to confidently make decisions. It may be accompanied by self-doubt, even helplessness. Generally uncomfortable with sharing their emotions, the gripped ESTJ may feel that no one understands them, or that people may lose faith in them if their lack of self-confidence were revealed. Unable to confide in others and process their emotions, they get trapped, leading to more anxiety. The ESTJ loses the clarity that usually accompanies their decision making. Despite their uncertainty, they may feel forced to take action, which may lead to bad consequences. This reinforces their fear of incompetence and perpetuates the cycle of insecurity.

Habitual grip. The third experience of being in the grip shows up as self-sabotage. Unable to communicate the pain within them and lacking the resources to address it, the ESTJ will project their feelings onto the outside world in a last, desperate attempt to understand their emotions. They may become passive aggressive, biting, and hurtful. This is to mirror their own feelings of being unappreciated, disrespected, and hurt. It's not uncommon for this grip to be accompanied with dysthymia, a persistent mild form of depression, though the ESTJ may not register it as depression. In this grip, the ESTJ has to monitor themselves for depression as they would a friend, by looking for the signs: low energy, trouble getting out of bed, an unhealthy relationship with food, and cheerlessness.

How to Best Use Authenticity

The best way to use Authenticity as a 3-Year-Old is to exercise it regularly, which will help prevent the grip from occurring. In this case, give yourself permission to be emotionally self-indulgent. Even though emotional expression seems time-consuming and impractical, do it anyway. Start an art project, write, make music, dance, or journal. Talk to a friend who is a good listener. Cry, laugh, emote, and express.

Give yourself a break from being productive and instead, be fully in your experience. If 30 minutes isn't enough time, keep going. Consider it spelunking into your soul. Find intimacy within yourself, get to know who you are, and ask yourself why you value what you do.

Using Authenticity in this way can also be a source of aspiration. It can encourage ESTJs to become gentle and kind, recognizing that each person has feelings and that they should matter. It allows them to let go of fear of emotional pain and welcome a rich human experience. It helps them recognize that at the end of the day, we're all just people doing our best.

Reflection

The ways Authenticity can grip an ESTJ are:

_____

_____

_____

The ways I find myself being in the grip are (include behaviors and situations):

_____

_____

_____

I'm going to control the process by:

_____

_____

_____

My Authenticity 3-Year-Old inspires me/is my aspiration in these ways:

_____

_____

_____

———————— ▬▬▬▬▬▬ ————————

CHAPTER 21

ESFJ Personality Type

ESFJs love to orchestrate shared positive experiences where everyone is getting along. They have a genuine energy and openness to new experiences that attracts people around them.

ESFJs gravitate toward situations where they can host, take care of, or otherwise meet the needs of others. If they become overwhelmed by the needs of people, they can actually become detached "need-meeting" worker bees, devoid of the deep connections they crave. However, honoring traditions and making space for others' unique quirks can be a stabilizing force for ESFJs that allows them to create deeper connections and shared experiences.

When unbalanced, ESFJs may appear wild or uncharacteristically erratic as they seek relief from their overwhelming need-meeting behaviors. This might look like impulsive shopping, frenetic or dispersed energy, last-minute travel choices, or at their worst, acting out of sync with their core values.

ESFJs shine when they are the social hub of friends and family. With maturity and balance, taking care of loved ones and clients are not obligations, but meaningful expressions of how they love.

ESFJ CAR MODEL OVERVIEW

DRIVER
Harmony (Fe)

- Prioritizes according to human need
- Builds and communicates boundaries
- Understands human dynamics

COPILOT
Memory (Si)

- Reliable, careful, and honors tradition
- Upholds old traditions and creates new ones
- Resilience and acceptance of a difficult past

3-YEAR-OLD
Accuracy (Ti)

- Marginalizes facts that appear antisocial
- Becomes critical or deceitful in stressful situations
- Gives a sense of autonomy and self-confidence

10-YEAR-OLD
Exploration (Ne)

- Solves problems creatively
- Struggles with determining when to make changes and when to accept a situation
- Can idealize the self and project weakness onto others

The ESFJ Driver Is Harmony (Fe)

It's important to remember that the Driver process is a talent, but that doesn't mean every ESFJ will have the same skill level or use it in a healthy way. Developing Harmony as a healthy process is crucial to becoming an amazing ESFJ. Harmony can help an ESFJ identify the needs of all people, including the self, and meet those needs; build healthy boundaries; and deeply understand social dynamics and contracts.

Identify Needs

Fluctuating emotions are often the first sign that people have unmet needs. An ESFJ may be so tuned-in and sensitive to emotions that they find it easy to help people feel safe, loved, and stable. This can be as simple as hosting a party and making it look effortless, to being a shoulder for a grieving friend to cry on, to helping your friends with complicated relationship issues. People who have developed their Harmony process become so skilled at this, they often become the go-to person in a time of crisis. Learning to be available to help meet people's needs also helps you become extremely industrious and have lots of unexpected talents and skills in a variety of areas.

Making sure you're getting your needs met is equally important as—if not more important than—meeting the needs of others. You can't run on fumes all the time, and you can't be of help to others if you're perpetually exhausted. Express unmet needs out loud. Avoid behavior like walking away if you're unhappy, being silently disapproving, or only crying alone. When you are comfortable expressing your emotions, you become a role model for others to express themselves, and you are better able to help them get their needs met.

Exercise

Ask yourself, "What need is going unmet for me?" It could be alone time, better eating habits, more sleep, a conversation with a friend, a night out, or just some pampering. Once you identify it, ask yourself the easiest and fastest way to get that need met.

Reflection

Name your top three needs that frequently go unmet.

1. _____

2. _____

3. _____

Now, look at your schedule. What are you prioritizing that gets in the way of those needs being met? If it's people you care about, like your spouse, children, family, and friends, just remember that you can't get to their needs if you're running on fumes. Journal 3 to 5 ideas that you can begin implementing to fit those needs into your weekly schedule.

_____

_____

_____

_____

_____

Build Healthy Boundaries

Harmony is the process that is used to create and maintain unspoken social contracts. Contracts are designed for us to know each other's expectations and honor them (as long as they are agreed upon). If you, as an ESFJ, don't know your boundaries, Harmony will encourage you to spend time with people and experience both acceptable and unacceptable behavior. Once you know your boundaries, Harmony helps you create contracts around them.

That means you'll have to communicate them to the people in your life, making sure they fully understand and agree to your boundaries. In a moment where you feel taken advantage of or thrown under a bus, ask yourself which of your boundaries has been broken, and if it was you or the other person that broke it.

By setting up healthy boundaries, you will prevent misunderstandings and honor the limited resource that is your energy. When you give, you will give out of love and desire, not merely out of obligation.

Reflection

Follow the journal prompt below to become clearer about your boundaries. Feel free to repeat this journal prompt multiple times until you feel confident and authentic about the boundaries you've discovered and set. Once you've done so, share them with the three people who you feel closest to. If they are uncomfortable with your new boundaries, ask if it's because the boundaries are unreasonable, or because they will change the relationship. Be sensitive to resistance to change while staying firm with your requirements.

Remember: Boundary setting is a skill. It might be bumpy at first, but over time and with small successes, your boundaries will become a part of your identity.

Name three (or more) things you would like to see more of in your life:

1. _____

2. _____

3. _____

Name three (or more) behaviors you will never allow in your life again:

1. _____

2. _____

3. _____

I would like to strengthen the boundaries in these areas of my life:

_____

_____

_____

_____

_____

I can improve the boundaries in each area of my life by:

_____

_____

_____

_____

_____

If someone crosses a boundary, my plan is to say:

_____

_____

_____

_____

Understand Social Contracts

Understanding unspoken social contracts means being able to know what's expected of yourself and others. This comes from a lifelong study of what offends other people versus what makes them feel comfortable.

This type of understanding is a major advantage in new circumstances and when first meeting people. You're very rarely going to say the wrong thing or alienate others. In fact, people of your type are often popular in group settings because you can help keep the conversation going without offending anyone or leaving anyone out.

Most importantly, tapping into the spectrum of social contracts reminds an ESFJ that people have different values and needs. This opens them up to a bigger, broader world. Creating relationships with a variety of people reminds the ESFJ that everyone has had a unique experience and may come with fresh ideas and relevant perspectives.

Exercise

Make it your aim to meet many new people. The more people you meet, the more opportunities you have to understand the cultures they come from. What was their family's culture? What area of the country or world are they from? Do misunderstandings of culture get in the way of creating Harmony? How can your increased understanding of other people and their family or country help you to keep relationships between people in social settings congenial and happy?

The way I feel about meeting new people is:

_____

If I experience any hesitancy about meeting new people, what do I suspect is going on for me?

_____

_____

_____

I will meet one new person this week. Afterward, I will record the conversation and what I learned from it here:

_____

_____

_____

Setting Up the Right Conditions

The enemy of Harmony is a critical spirit. If you're judgmental of yourself or others, Harmony has difficulty doing what it does best: crafting a positive social climate and meeting other people's needs.

As your Driver, Harmony is your Flow state, and if you're not using this function enough, you'll eventually run out of juice and become depressed. Set up your conditions to access this mental process often. Keep in touch with loved ones and foster new relationships. Organize your space to be welcoming and warm.

Address conflict head-on. It will initially feel like you're feeding the problem, but discord doesn't go away by being neglected. All relationships face tension and clashes; it's part of human dynamics. If you're frustrated that people don't seem to be getting along, tap into the experience each person is having and discover their individual unmet needs. If you're involved in the conflict, remember what you know about each person and be as mindful of their situation as possible.

UNDEVELOPED HARMONY (Fe)	DEVELOPED HARMONY (Fe)
Avoid:	Work Toward:
• Ignoring your needs	• Getting your needs met
• Giving out of obligation	• Communicating healthy boundaries
• Conflict avoidance	• Resolving conflict

Reflection

The talents Harmony can give me are:

_____

_____

_____

The ways I usually use Harmony are:

_____

_____

_____

I'm going to develop Harmony more by:

_____

_____

_____

List three activities that put you into flow:

_____

_____

_____

The ESFJ Copilot Is Memory (Si)

Without an introverted perceiving process, the ESFJ is not complete. Cultural expectations can be mistaken for a personal identity, and without checking in to ensure that individuals are taken into consideration, the ESFJ may become judgmental and invasive.

An introverted perceiving process reminds the ESFJ to be patient and recognize that longer timelines are always at play. It also helps them connect to their subjective experience, peer into future possibilities, speculate on outcomes, and apply this understanding to interactions with and on behalf of other people.

It's important to remember that, like the Driver, the Copilot process is a talent. But that doesn't mean every ESFJ will have the same skill level or use it in a healthy way. Developing Memory as a healthy process is crucial to becoming an amazing ESFJ.

It can be difficult to actively develop an introverted function when one is an Extravert. It won't be as natural as working on Harmony, so discipline and an eye on the rich rewards Memory will be key.

Reliable, Careful, and Honors Procedure

For people who use Memory as a Copilot, living in an unpredictable or unstable environment carries a huge penalty. To avoid this kind of environment, people of your type are amazing at maintaining procedures and processes to minimize instability. If no procedure exists, Memory is compelled to find one.

Memory users recognize the need for care and caution. There is no reason to make repeated mistakes if a process is established to track them. It can be a simple aphorism to pass helpful knowledge from one generation to the next, such as "Measure twice, cut once."

It's important for an ESFJ to develop patience and recognize long timelines when making decisions. Without the Memory function, an ESFJ may unintentionally create chaos in their life by missing important details or becoming unsettled and restless.

— Exercise —

Identify areas in your life that are unsafe or in violation of established standards, particularly things that (if left by themselves) could become a problem in the future. Look to a trusted organization, community, or family culture to gauge what the standard is and how you can correct it. If you're unsure, consult experts for guidance on how to correct the issue.

— Reflection —

What areas of my life am I letting turn into chaos? Is there a procedure I can implement to reestablish sanity?

_____

_____

_____

_____

Being kind to myself, I'm going to address this chaos by:

_____

_____

_____

_____

Holds Relationship with Tradition

Memory users recognize how much each individual is influenced by their experiences. They also understand the importance of ensuring that most of those memories are positive. It is a pleasure to create wonderful memories that can be replayed and enjoyed forever. For this reason, it's common for

Memory users to enjoy holidays, family gatherings, and other times when loved ones get together for momentous occasions.

Traditions can also be used for healing. Trauma that is difficult to shake from the ESFJ's memory may require a healing tradition. For example, when a loved one dies, it may become an annual tradition to gather with others to talk about them, remember them, and pay tribute by living life fully in their honor.

The more sophisticated Memory gets, the more it's open to adopting new traditions. This is important to remember, as Memory in its infancy may be fearful of the unfamiliar. Changing one's traditions—including beliefs and paradigms—may feel disloyal to parents and other trusted authorities. But as it matures, Memory becomes a more adaptable function. It incorporates new experiences into its identity, learning to become whatever is appropriate to the context.

Exercise

Consider ways you can pass on the traditions of your family to the next generation. Is there a tradition you inherited that can be taught to your children, nieces, or nephews? Do they understand the importance of it, and will they contribute to passing it on after you're gone? How can you make the tradition more enjoyable in a way that will leave a lasting impression, help mold their experience, and help them want to carry the torch?

Reflection

The tradition that has had the biggest impact on me is:

_____

_____

_____

_____

Resilience and Acceptance

It's not easy to accept things as they are, but Memory has the greatest natural talent for it, and therefore, Memory users demonstrate great resilience during trying situations. True acceptance includes letting go of judgment and blame (including of oneself) and instead addressing situations with tolerance and forgiveness. Memory meets unfair situations with fairness, and finds peace within.

An ESFJ will feel compelled to manage a situation, and without developing Memory, they may attempt to force an outcome or shoehorn a solution. To accept a situation may feel like defeat, like losing control over the situation. But acceptance is not passive, nor is it complacent. It's a recognition of what cannot be changed and coming to terms with its impact in one's life.

Memory users naturally understand the passage of time. They register change almost immediately and know how people are formed by their experiences. They get that we are who we are because of our past. Truly traumatic experiences can break people past their limits, but time can heal even brokenness. As it is said, "time heals all wounds," even if it takes decades, and we can be stronger people for it. In cases where an ESFJ is dealing with an abusive past, the Memory function can be used to mark growth and to see how far they have come.

It's important to remember that acceptance is not submitting to unhealthy situations. It's not needlessly putting up with physical pain, a bad relationship, or a toxic context. Predicaments that can be changed should be changed. Developing the Memory function helps an ESFJ gauge when to stay with a situation and when it's time to graduate to something else.

Exercise

Practice self-acceptance. When you notice that you are judging or rating yourself, look for a time in your past that may have prompted the thought. Did this criticism originally come from a parent? Is this self-criticism from a time you believed you failed at something? If you are much older than you were at the origin of the thought, is there wisdom you have now that changes how you experience the inciting event? Did you do the best you could at the time? What connections do you now see that you missed then? Can you forgive your younger self? Does your younger self need forgiveness at all, or just a little understanding? Focus on letting go of the pain and the belief that caused the judgment.

Reflection

What's your biggest regret? What have you done to make amends with yourself or forgive yourself?

_____

_____

_____

_____

_____

_____

Copilot Growth

Memory is the highest leverage point for growth in your personality. It helps you, as an ESFJ, make better decisions based on solid information, and by considering timelines and the impact on other people.

Here are some ways that an ESFJ can phrase questions using their Memory process:

• What are the long-term effects of this decision?

• What impact will this decision have on myself as well as other people?

• Am I missing important details?

Memory encourages ESFJs to slow down, think through your plans, and have patience with the results. It recommends that you be moderate in habits, look at the details of a plan, and avoid jumping to conclusions. Without slowing down enough to consider the experiences of yourself and others, you may find yourself dissatisfied, without personal meaning or meaningful relationships.

Growing your Memory can be a challenge for you as an ESFJ. It can feel like a threat to look inward and face painful experiences and uncomfortable emotions. There's a fear that the further inward you go, the less control you will have. But if you embrace this mental process, you will have the opportunity to be reflective and imbue meaning into your flurry of activity.

Memory also encourages an ESFJ to know which details matter. Developing this process gives the ESFJ insight into what to focus on, and what is unnecessary minutiae.

To help develop this function, start asking yourself, "What am I actually trying to accomplish?" Spend time ruminating and thinking things through, especially if your desire is to jump to a conclusion.

- Consult experts in the field to see what has worked or failed.

- If you've already made similar decisions, reflect on how successful they were.

- Check in with family members before acting in a way that impacts them.

- Be sensitive to anyone under you in a project or work environment. Get feedback on their experiences and consider changes that could be made in everyone's best interest.

- Slow down, learn from past mistakes, be honest about which details actually matter, and be thoughtful toward all the people involved.

Reflection

The talents Memory can give me are:

_____

_____

_____

The ways I usually use Memory are:

_____

_____

_____

I'm going to develop Memory more by:

_____

_____

_____

List three ways you can start growing your Memory process today:

_____

_____

_____

The ESFJ 10-Year-Old Is Exploration (Ne)

Exploration users see patterns and make connections. They figure out what is possible, not simply what is probable. Exploration gets us to ask questions like, "If we put these two things together, what would that make?", "What's a creative solution to this problem?", "What am I seeing that everyone else seems to be missing?", and "What if…?"

Innovating and finding fresh, new solutions to old problems is the name of Exploration's game. As it matures, it gets better at knowing when it's seeing a pattern or forcing ideas together.

As a 10-Year-Old process, Exploration may struggle with knowing when to trust itself. An ESFJ may be unaware that they are forming false patterns to see what they want to see, though they are generally better at using this function than people who do not have it represented in their Car.

ESFJs can learn flexibility when using Exploration. While getting a solid plan in place and being patient with outcomes is preferred, you can't always know how things will pan out. It's easier to look at the big picture and have more fun in life if you're willing to diversify, come up with creative solutions, and foster open-mindedness to new people, places, and possibilities. ESFJs know they don't have to have all the answers, and they don't always have to be right or in control. Bad habits should be acknowledged and changed, and uncertainty should be accepted. However, Exploration may struggle with knowing when to trust itself. An ESFJ may be unaware that they are forming false patterns so they can see what they want to see.

As an extraverted function, Exploration allows the ESFJ to access a perceiving process while staying focused on external feedback. This can be okay at times, but if the ESFJ gets used to relying upon Exploration to support their conclusions, they can rationalize skipping development of their Memory Copilot. And that's when the trouble starts. For ESFJs, this usually manifests as getting a bad read on a situation and jumping to conclusions.

Exploration is, in a large part, about getting impressions beyond what can be immediately sensed or perceived. People who have it as a strength are usually pretty good at it, and they can usually spot creative solutions. But you're wired to be at your best when looking at the situation as it is, not as it could be.

If your 10-Year-Old Exploration function gets to influence your thought process, it's going to sort intricate information at a juvenile level—you'll find yourself justifying all sorts of bad decisions. Especially when you are feeling defensive and threatened by bad feedback, you'll end up inventing things that don't exist in order to avoid self-doubt. Another way Exploration can manifest itself as a 10-Year-Old is by looking for shortcuts, including ones that don't serve the ESFJ. An example would be chasing an unreliable opportunity, cheating, or otherwise rationalizing any ends to justify the means. You may tell yourself you don't have the time to vet everything, when really, you simply have not developed the characteristic of patience.

The Driver/10-Year-Old Loop

There are three ways an ESFJ experiences the loop, the echo chamber–like relationship between the Driver and 10-Year-Old functions. The way to get out of a loop is the same in all cases: focus on developing the Memory process.

Short-term loop. This impulsive, sometimes destructive, behavior may only last for a few moments up to a few days. Fleeing responsibility and feeling tied down, the ESFJ may become overindulgent with drinking, partying, or substance abuse. Shutting off the inner voice that recommends caution, they may make impetuous life decisions. If the voice is coming not from within but from another person, the fun stops, and the ESFJ can become angry, attempt to control the situation, create drama, or simply end a relationship (or quit a job) that feels too binding.

Long-term loop. Unable to take responsibility for their own life choices, the ESFJ will cast blame outward, harshly and critically projecting their discomfort onto other people, even those they do not personally know. They find clever reasons to blame people for their own uncomfortable feelings, and take the position that their troubles must be caused by others. Instead of taking the time to familiarize themselves with new people, places, and situations, ESFJs develop prejudices, cast judgments, and manipulate information to justify harsh conclusions.

Habitual loop. Possibly the most challenging loop to overcome, the ESFJ may become addicted to novelty through compulsive shopping, overspending on restaurants and other indulgences, chasing one opportunity after another, or by giving only cursory attention to important matters. They may take shortcuts in relationships by ignoring the people in their lives in favor of forming bonds with TV show characters, shallow acquaintances, or even affairs and flings. Forgetting the anchor points of their past, the ESFJ won't seem to learn lessons and will repeat the same mistakes. Unable to sate the growing emptiness inside, they inadvertently damage or destroy important relationships in favor of temporal pleasures.

Reflection

The ways Harmony and Exploration can loop in an ESFJ are:

_____

_____

_____

The ways I find myself looping are (include behaviors and situations):

_____

_____

_____

I'm going to work on breaking my loop(s) by:

_____

_____

_____

How to Best Use Exploration

If you find yourself getting impulsive, casting blame, or taking shortcuts, that is a bad use of the Exploration function. Tap into the Memory function and ask yourself, "What am I trying to accomplish?" and "Do these actions or judgments provide the long-term consequences I want?"

That said, if you've carefully accepted responsibility and measured out consequences, and your mind is still telling you that a refreshing change is in order, that would be the time to listen Exploration. Its job isn't to project what you want to believe onto the world; it's meant to open you up to creative solutions and new ways of doing things. Just don't let it fool you into becoming impulsive or avoidant.

You can also engage your 10-Year-Old in times of play, love, and intimacy. People of your type often enjoy conversation with friends, hosting parties, and entertaining others with their bigger-than-life personalities. You can use Exploration to connect people with other people and opportunities you know they would love. And you can use Exploration to help open your mind to include other cultures, countries, and people.

The ESFJ 3-Year-Old Is Accuracy (Ti)

Accuracy helps us solve problems and build skills. The preferred function of many scientists and mechanics, Accuracy users prize data and systems thinking. Often communicating directly and with radical honesty, Accuracy helps people refine information by removing personal bias and social pressure.

As a 3-Year-Old function, Accuracy is the part of the ESFJ that whispers from the shadows. Normally capable of marginalizing information that appears antisocial, suddenly the ESFJ will feel an overwhelming need to analyze themselves and others, becoming coldly diagnostic.

There are three ways an ESFJ experiences the grip, the moments when the Driver process is stressed out, needs a break, and gives the 3-Year-Old function control of the car. This is most likely when an ESFJ avoids dealing with their thoughts or experiences, thus developing cognitive dissonance.

Short-term grip. When they are exhausted by social expectations, ESFJs will resort to extreme criticism. For some ESFJs, it will be self-criticism: They may beat themselves up for believing themselves to be failures, unable to explain their ideas, or unlovable or intellectually inferior. The negative self-talk can be relentless and crippling. For other ESFJs, the criticism will focus on others, turning the blast outward in an icy barrier between themselves and those that could hurt them.

Long-term grip. Some ESFJs will become deceitful. Acting uncharacteristically self-centered, the ESFJ will create a false front, allowing other people to believe wrong but flattering information about them. If the situation requires, the ESFJ may directly lie to keep up their image. In this grip, ESFJs self-justify and overinflate their competence to both themselves and others.

Habitual grip. In the most subtle and difficult type of grip to disrupt, the ESFJ represses all negative emotions when facing the public. They fear others will see them for who they truly are—imperfect and unacceptable. By staying cheerful and showing high morale, they are above reproach and can put off the time of reckoning as long as possible. They may overanalyze relationships, project their inadequacies onto others, take credit for personal development they haven't done, and feel it is unjust that others don't have to work as hard to maintain their lives. Unfairness becomes a theme in their lives.

How to Best Use Accuracy

The best way to use Accuracy as a 3-Year-Old is to exercise it regularly, which will help prevent the grip from occurring. In this case, give yourself permission to check out of life for a while and do serious self-care. Remove yourself from relationship and emotion management. Find a quiet space for reflection and "me" time. Do a Sudoku puzzle or play Solitaire or video games.

The goal is to give yourself a break from caring about the needs of others. If 30 minutes isn't enough time, keep going. Consider giving yourself an entire day of independence and self-direction, answering to no one but yourself.

Accuracy can also be a source of aspiration, the voice that whispers in the back of your mind. It can encourage ESFJs to pursue their own interests, find autonomy, and be self-directed. It also encourages ESFJs to have confidence in their intelligence, accumulated knowledge, and ability to problem solve.

Reflection

The ways Accuracy can grip an ESFJ are:

_____

_____

_____

The ways I find myself being in the grip are (include behaviors and situations):

_____

_____

_____

I'm going to control the process by:

_____

_____

_____

My Accuracy 3-Year-Old inspires me/is my aspiration in these ways:

_____

_____

_____

———————————

CHAPTER 22

The FIRM Model

What you resist not only persists, but will grow in size.
—Carl Jung

As we've established, your personality type pinpoints what you are intrinsically wired to focus on and what you're wired to ignore. It's the cost of specialization: No one has enough time in their life to be excellent at everything.

Life is made up of attempts to be balanced. Giving yourself permission to *not* be all things to all people is a great first step. But on the flipside, you can also fall into the trap of fixating on a single thing. This tendency generally comes from attempting to meet a hardwired need, and each of the cognitive functions has a different need or desire that they may fixate upon. Though the influence of a fixation is subtle and not generally conscious, a fixation can overwhelm you and derail your life. You can end up destroying relationships, sabotaging careers, and even compromising your health to feed the deeper need of the fixation.

A person's specific fixation is usually determined by the Driver cognitive function. When the needs of the Driver process are perpetually left unmet, it can become insatiable. Like a once-starving child that becomes obese when food is no longer scarce, the Driver can feel perpetually malnourished and build defense strategies to compensate, causing it to become hyperinflated later on.

The further down the rabbit hole of fixation an individual goes, the more likely they are to experience the Driver/10-Year-Old loop. Sometimes the identification with their 10-Year-Old process is so strong they mistakenly experience it as their Driver process and end up with a confusing mistype.

FIRM stands for Freedom, Invulnerability, Rightness, and Management, the four things we're all fundamentally trying to create in our lives in a healthy or unhealthy way. Depending upon your Driver and your personality type, you can become fixated on any of those four components. These trends are established by the dichotomies of Extraversion/Introversion and Judging/Perceiving.

If you don't come to terms with the control your specific fixation has over you, you can become an increasingly worse version of yourself, crawling deeper into a rut of unmet desire. This is why understanding your FIRM fixation helps bridge the gap between how you're wired and why you take the actions you do.

Of course, out of our greatest challenges come our greatest strengths. When you have mastery over your FIRM orientation, it no longer controls you; you control it. You can separate the behaviors from the fixation and utilize any skills you've developed in more healthy, appropriate ways.

Find Your Fixation

The first and last functions in your cognitive function stack can help you determine your fixation.

FIXATION	DICHOTOMY	TYPES
Freedom	EP (Extraverted Perceivers)	ESFP, ENFP, ESTP, ENTP
Invulnerability	IJ (Introverted Judgers)	ISFJ, INFJ, ISTJ, INTJ
Rightness	IP (Introverted Perceivers)	ISFP, INFP, ISTP, INTP
Management	EJ (Extraverted Judgers)	ESFJ, ENFJ, ESTJ, ENTJ

Depending upon your type, you will have an unconscious fixation on a specific desire. Most of the time, you can quiet this fixation by saying to yourself "It's going to be okay, I've got this." But if for some reason you can't—circumstances, poor function development, poor health, or anxiety—the desires will become more insistent. You may become relentless about getting this desire met.

Freedom

Extraverted Perceivers may become fixated on Freedom, and in its less healthy state, unfettered freedom. This is the idea that you can do whatever you want, whenever you want. Unfettered freedom is unrealistic, but EPs may act out in self-destructive ways to try to obtain it. The more self-destructive and cavalier the path, the less freedom they ultimately experience, as they are chained to the consequences of their own actions.

Invulnerability

Introverted Judgers may become fixated on Invulnerability, and in its least healthy state, impenetrable invulnerability. They aim to always be safe, in a state where nothing could possibly touch them. This is an idealistic fantasy, but it points to their actual fear of being fundamentally vulnerable.

Rightness

Introverted Perceivers may become fixated on Rightness, and in its less healthy state, inarguable rightness. Their ideal is for their decisions, feelings, and logic to never be questioned. No matter what, they want to be right. This, too, is an unrealistic goal that points to their ultimate fear of self-doubt.

Management

Extraverted Judgers may become fixated on gaining Management (control), and in its less healthy state, total management of a situation. They seek a role where they can be totally in charge. The underlying fear that impels this behavior has two sides. First, they fear that without their involvement everything would collapse, putting great burden upon them; and second, they fear that they're not actually needed at all, and so they must reinforce their value by creating a system that cannot run without them.

Personality Fixations

Each cognitive function has limitations. That's why you need more than one to be a complete person. When you over-identify with your Driver process, however, these limitations make themselves known. The life you build to frequently engage your Driver function can turn self-indulgent if you're not also giving attention to the other functions in your Car. When this happens, the Driver becomes sensitive about what it perceives as "attacks," which are usually just expressions of the Driver's inherent limitations.

Learning Point Pause

Name the core fears and fixations for each dichotomy.

EP's core fear: _____

EP's core fixation: _____

IJ's core fear: _____

IJ's core fixation: _____

IP's core fear: _____

IP's core fixation:_____

EJ's core fear: _____

EJ's core fixation: _____

EPs and Freedom

Extraverted Sensing (Sensation) and Extraverted Intuition (Exploration) are both extraverted perceiving functions. People with these traits want to learn, experience, and engage. If circumstances limit an EP's ability to utilize their Driver process, it can feel like being handcuffed or imprisoned. While each EP experiences this a little differently depending on which Driver they're using and which Copilot they're paired with, there is always a feeling that others may limit the EP from doing what they want to do.

EPs are usually highly energetic children, but when they grow up, they may be told to settle down and be quiet on a regular basis. Training to be more socially acceptable to the world of adults can feel like torture, and the EP starts to create strategies to feed their curiosity and adrenaline-seeking behaviors. As they age, they find that the easiest way to be free is to simply avoid people and circumstances that try to limit them.

Each EP becomes fixated on a slightly different variation of Freedom, though if you're an EP, you will most likely identify with all four versions.

- ESTPs want freedom of movement, or full physical sovereignty.

- ESFPs want the freedom to play and pursue pleasure.

- ENTPs want freedom of thought, without social pressure to conform.

- ENFPs desire the freedom to perform and express themselves without constraint.

In all cases, the fixation and resulting strategies are there to protect the interests of the Driver process. If the EP senses that their Driver function is becoming obstructed, they become protective, and their freedom-seeking strategies may actually trap them in their own form of prison. For example, ESFPs may harm their bodies by eating or drinking whatever they want, resulting in a prison of poor health. Or an ESTP may make cavalier, consequence-bearing decisions in the name of sovereignty. An ENTP may loudly spout personal positions without proper vetting or respect for others' opinions, affecting their relationships. And an ENFP may jump from one situation to another, undermining their ability to create a life of expression by sabotaging their own stability.

IJs and Invulnerability

Introverted Sensing (Memory) and Introverted Intuition (Perspectives) are both introverted perceiving functions. That means information is taken in and post-processed. If an IJ wasn't taught in childhood how to filter information, they will indiscriminately absorb what they hear and experience. Things that are extremely painful will be brought inside to be contemplated and figured out later, and the exercise of post-processing can be agonizing. Some experiences feel like a bull in the china shop of the IJ's inner terrain, and the IJ will create a narrative that they are vulnerable to anything and everything.

Instead of creating strategies for managing and working through pain, they will develop strategies for never feeling pain. And in the place of thoughtful boundaries, barriers are created with uncompromising gatekeepers.

Each IJ has a slightly different variation of Invulnerability upon which they become fixated, though if you're an IJ, you will, to some extent, identify with all four versions.

- ISFJs want invulnerability from conflict.

- ISTJs want invulnerability from feelings.

- INTJs want invulnerability from being controlled.

- INFJs desire invulnerability from other people's emotional pain.

In all cases, the fixation and resulting strategies are there to protect the interests of the Driver process. If the IJ senses that their Driver function is being aggravated, the protective strategies they implement may actually do the opposite and make them more vulnerable. For example, an ISFJ may keep their personal expression so bottled up that their lack of transparency leads to the very conflict they wanted to avoid. Or an ISTJ may find themselves at the mercy of emotions long suppressed and hidden, metastasizing from within. An INTJ can find themselves dealing with loneliness, unwilling to meet others halfway in a relationship, for fear of being controlled by their own deep-down sympathetic nature. And an INFJ may feel completely exposed if the protective wall they've constructed is breached through illness, stress, or emotional overload.

IPs and Rightness

Introverted Thinking (Accuracy) and Introverted Feeling (Authenticity) are both introverted judging functions. Their purpose is to evaluate the worth or merit of information, but they do so subjectively, with internal metrics. It's sometimes difficult for them to explain why something makes sense or is felt strongly, especially if there's nothing in the outside world to point to as evidence. And there's no reason another person should be persuaded by the IP's conclusions if there isn't some form of proof.

This is a conundrum for IPs throughout their entire lives. If they don't develop the ability to "show their work," so to speak, they may find themselves perpetually feeling defensive about their conclusions. This can become not only fatiguing, but crushing. When people question them, it marginalizes not only their Driver process, but their very identity. In an effort to stave off this feeling, the simplest strategy is to claim that they are right and everyone else is wrong.

Each IP has a slightly different variation of Rightness upon which they become fixated, though if you're an IP, you will to some extent identify with all four versions. Think of Rightness as moral or intellectual high ground, unable to be questioned.

- ISFPs want blamelessness.
- ISTPs want competence.
- INTPs want rightness of logic.
- INFPs want rightness in their ethical position.

In all cases, the fixation and resulting strategies are there to protect the interests of the Driver process. If the IP senses that their Driver function is being questioned, they become protective, and their inability to receive feedback from others can result in their being wrong. For example, an ISFP who cannot take responsibility for their own actions may never be able to get their life together. An ISTP without constructive criticism will become incompetent. An INTP who is certain that their logic outclasses all others may miss an imperative piece of information just outside their framework, and an INFP may lose the ethical high ground when their conviction causes them to justify bad behavior.

EJs and Management

Extraverted Thinking (Effectiveness) and Extraverted Feeling (Harmony) are both extraverted judging functions. Their purpose is to evaluate the worth or merit of information based on what they see play out in the world. While the criteria of Effectiveness (*what works*) and Harmony (*what meets the needs of others*) are different, they share the sentiment that how people should be performing is obvious, whether that is following societal structure or adopted roles. If an EJ is raised in a context that affords them little to no control over their environment, and worse, causes them pain, the EJ may start to think other people aren't qualified to govern their surroundings. The more fear an EJ has of the general incompetence of others, the more they'll become fixated on Management to ensure they're not on the receiving end of other people's ineptitude.

EJs know there are things to do, and they think that they are the most qualified to get them done. They often seek leadership, and the compulsion to be in charge can grow organically. But if the EJ has had to compensate for people who were meant to take care of them, like parents, they can get the sense that without them, everything would collapse. They become increasingly overbearing.

Each EJ has a slightly different variation of Management upon which they become fixated, though if you're an EJ, you will to some extent identify with all four versions. Think of Management as the need to dictate the outcome, either by control or manipulation.

- ESFJs want to manage people's relationships.

- ESTJs want management of the schedule.

- ENTJs want management of resources.

- ENFJs want management of people's emotional experience.

In all cases, the fixation and resulting strategies are there to protect the interests of the Driver process. If the EJ senses that their Driver function is becoming obstructed, they become protective, and their need for control may actually cause them to lose influence over a situation. For example, an ESFJ who is certain that two people need to be nice to each other at a family reunion may unintentionally cause a greater rift. An ESTJ who always insists on their timeline may lose the attention of others who need more wiggle room. An ENTJ unable to see people as more than resources may lose them altogether. And an ENFJ orchestrating everyone's emotional experience may appear judgmental, further adding fire to a hostile situation.

Reflection

Which fixation do you identify with most?

_____

_____

What fear do you identify with most?

_____

_____

⎯⎯⎯⎯ ▬▬ ⎯⎯⎯⎯

What If You Don't Identify with Your Type's Fixation?

Becoming fixated on an element of the FIRM model is usually the result of trauma from which you have not healed. Trauma is generally experienced through your primary lens for understanding the world—the Driver process—and a FIRM fixation is an early strategy you may have developed to protect that function. You may not have trauma that still needs healing, or alternatively, you may be fully in your fixation but blind to its grip on you.

It's important to remember that this isn't a diagnostic tool, meaning your FIRM fixation doesn't dictate your type, and your type doesn't dictate your FIRM fixation. That said, there are trends in how FIRM shows up based upon each cognitive function's natural tendencies and patterns in how they like to be protected. For example, the desire to be inarguably right is an understandable result of constant questioning, but not all IPs develop that desire. That said, it's a *common* desire for them to develop, so be aware this may be happening without your realizing it.

What If You Identify with a FIRM Fixation of a Different Type?

This actually happens quite often. A FIRM fixation is primarily based on our relationship with our cognitive functions. As mentioned earlier, you may be caught in a loop where you become hyper-focused on the relationship between your Driver and 10-Year-Old processes. In such cases, it's common to identify with the FIRM fixation that would appeal to the 10-Year-Old. For example, an ISTJ who can't stand being wrong is most likely in a low-grade loop and protecting the 10-Year-Old Authenticity in addition to the Driver, Memory. An ENFJ who avoids making commitments may be protecting their 10-Year-Old Sensation.

You can also identify with the FIRM fixation of your 3-Year-Old process. When we're in the grip of our 3-Year-Old process, it can indicate significant trauma, which can lead to a FIRM fixation. The most fragile parts of us are, unfortunately, the most likely to harbor pain and trauma, because they are the easiest to ignore for great lengths of time. We don't call upon them for our adult functions, or put them through many stress tests. They become the unwitting harbor masters of our deepest pain, despite being the least qualified parts of us to handle it.

If your FIRM fixation matches the types that have your 3-Year-Old cognitive function as their Driver, that can spell real trouble. An ESTJ who is unable to be wrong about anything may need to comb their past for when their 3-Year-Old Authenticity process was threatened, hurt, or abused. For example, if they were repeatedly told they were a bad person or had a bad motive, they may be shutting off any outer-world feedback that would question their identity. An ISFP who needs to have control over how everything is done may be in the same position, but with their 3-Year-Old Effectiveness process. If they were sexually abused as a child and felt completely out of control in the situation, their unconscious may be driven by the thought of "that will never be allowed to happen again."

When we're fixated on the 10-Year-Old or 3-Year-Old functions, we're still trying to protect the Driver. In the example of the abused ISFP, for example, the need to control all situations is an attempt to prevent a situation that was too much for their Authenticity Driver function to process.

Do we ever become fixated on the Copilot? This is less likely to happen, as focus on the Copilot is generally the path to growth. But we can master a single element of the Copilot to get by in life and turn it into a one-trick pony. An INFJ who is fixated on managing the emotional experience of others has discovered a method of avoiding icky emotions they would otherwise absorb, as opposed to developing healthy conflict resolution or building appropriate boundaries. An INTP fixated on Freedom may simply be avoiding situations where they'll be questioned, learning that if you don't stay in one place too long, you never have to face your logical fallacies. The universe doesn't have time to mirror them back to you.

Of course, because there are many different experiences of trauma, pain, or abuse, there are many styles of strategies. And not all of them are type-related. But if you are experiencing any of these fixations, it's good to know their etymology, and to have language for how they manifest.

And even if you're not fully fixated, there's still going to be a little bit of each of these inside of you. There's a spectrum represented in the FIRM model. It can be something that completely controls your behavior and outlook on life, or something that pops up in your mental real estate from time to time. Simply being aware of where you tend to fall in the FIRM model and watching your behavior can help you overcome the power of fixation.

Reflection

Think of a story about when you were immersed in a fixation or fear that you identified early:

_____

_____

_____

_____

How did your fixation help you?

_____

_____

_____

_____

What would happen if you didn't rely on your fixation strategy in the story above?

_____

_____

_____

_____

Brainstorm five ways you could approach the same situation without accessing your fixation.

_____

_____

_____

_____

_____

Conclusion: The Path Forward

To truly know who we are and become the best version of ourselves, it is vital that we learn to understand our own sovereignty and take control of ourselves and our growth. To do this, there are three essential steps: awareness, permission, and development.

Think of Yourself as a Sovereign Person

Personal sovereignty is the authority an individual has to govern their own ideas, values, beliefs, and actions.

While we are not always able to choose our circumstances, we can choose our relationship with those circumstances. We can alter how we feel and think about them, and notice when opportunities for change present themselves. Sometimes we wait for those opportunities; other times, we take action to express our desires. And still other times, we recognize that we don't really want change, as in the case of a sullen teenager who wishes she had different parents, only to grow up and determine that they were the best parents for her.

As humans, we are meaning makers. There are many stories humans tell each other to represent reality. It's easy to adopt the worldview of our parents, teachers, influencers, and societies, as their narratives are frequently reinforced in our lives. But we are most empowered when we take control of the stories we tell about ourselves and how the world works.

The Italian film *Life is Beautiful* is a story of a Jewish Italian bookshop owner who taps into the sovereignty of his imagination to shield his son from the horrors of internment in a Nazi concentration camp. Though their outer world is being dictated to them by an authoritarian and oppressive system, the father decides to take control of the narrative and reinterpret it as a game for his young son. In this way, he is exhibiting sovereignty over his interpretation of a terrible reality.

You, too, have more sovereignty over the self than you may acknowledge. As children, we look to systems outside ourselves to change so that we can have more agency. But as we grow into maturity, we realize change starts with the self. It is from within that the outer world can be adjusted.

There is no board of directors or council of wise elders planning and orchestrating your life for you. You can claim sovereignty and the responsibility that comes along with it. You get to define your life's meaning for yourself.

Find Access Points to Become Who You Were Meant to Be

There are many access points to finding ourselves. We recommend exploring yourself beyond typology to incorporate ego transcendence work, skill building, expression, experiences, self-reflection, community, meditation, relationships, your parenting style, and overcoming challenges. However, we find typology and personality types to be excellent tools for personal development. They allow us to map out how we think. A map allows us to chart a course of growth. It gives us a place to start.

As you've seen in the pages of this book, there is a lot to understanding how our minds are wired. While some elements of personality are hardwired and cannot be changed, the one thing that remains plastic is our ability to grow and strive for excellence.

Obviously, you can't be distilled down to one out of sixteen types of humans. That's ridiculous; there are about seven billion unique personalities on the planet. And, of course, your experience as the personality type that resonates the strongest with you is unique. You have your own stories of what that type means, and of what relationship you will form with your personality type. Using typology is helpful if it empowers you and adds to your sense of sovereignty.

Change the World by Loving and Developing Yourself

Of course, action is required to change the world. Loving yourself and taking action impacts the world around you. And when you are secure in who you are, magic can happen. You are at ease in life. You begin to live the life you desire. It's almost as if that ideal life was right beneath the surface the whole time. Before, you were living in its photo negative, its shadow.

We see three basic steps on the path to the ideal self: awareness of difference, permission for authenticity, and self-development.

Step 1: Awareness of Difference

We have a human tendency to overvalue our individual experiences. We assume our strengths are everyone's strengths, and that our blind spots are shared. This is why it is important for you to be aware that you are wired differently than others are.

It's an awakening experience to realize why you think, feel, and act the way you do. Most people feel a deep sense of relief when their view of the world is validated. Some enjoy learning typology to hone the skill of interacting with their fellow humans. No matter the reason, feeling validated in your perspective allows you to access the next stage of personality development.

Step 2: Permission for Authenticity

When you fully accept yourself as you are, the next step is to give yourself permission to be your authentic self. This permission is powerful, and no one can grant it but you. Once you give yourself permission to be authentic, you will have the energy and resolve to make important and positive changes in your life. These changes can affect all areas of your life: career, family, relationships, and health.

When you accept yourself and act authentically, you unconsciously give that gift to others as well. If you cannot allow others to be themselves without their having to change something, then you have not fully given this gift to yourself.

This is why typology is so incredibly helpful for personal development. It creates clear distinctions between strengths and weaknesses. We have language for how we're different from others, and we can acknowledge that we are neither holistically superior nor inferior to others. We can just *be*, without having to perpetually prove our worth or hide our weaknesses.

And when another person points out a deficiency in our thinking, we can spot the difference between objective feedback and that other person's subjective experience. Eventually, we can even get to a place where we realize that all feedback has both objective and subjective components. When our egos aren't rushing to our defense, we can slow down and really think about other people's perspectives. We become smarter for it.

Step 3: Self-Development

You are the only one who can develop yourself. Focusing on building skills and growing your Copilot process is the best action we can recommend for your personal growth journey. Both of us, as well as many of our clients and students, have benefited from intentionally growing our Copilot functions.

Be warned, it takes work. Sometimes it takes hard, grueling work. You will have to face things about yourself that will challenge who you are, how you think, and what you do. You may be faced with big choices that could change the direction of your life forever. Consciously choosing a challenging growth path forges you into the person you were meant to be.

Be careful not to confuse understanding with growth. It's easy to get caught up in the fascination of how the "system of you" works. Typologies are models that can be understood at their base level and at the same time can be endlessly expanded upon. But the attention people apply to typology models like Myers-Briggs can simulate actual personal growth, seducing you to think, "If I just understand every nook and cranny of who I am, that's personal growth!" This is not true. First, you will not live long enough to understand every nook and cranny of who you are. Second, awareness is the first step, but it must be coupled with thoughtful goals, the discipline to reach those goals, and a sense of personal responsibility.

It's okay to dive deep into typology systems, as long as you use what you learn for real advancement. The work happens when you change your behaviors and strategies, rather than simply learning endlessly about how you're wired. And the real work manifests when you let go of your defense mechanisms and your ego attachment.

So get to know yourself. Find your personality map. Be honest about your authentic desires and dreams. Get to know your true identity. Find the growth path forward. If you're unsure of what to do, trust your gut and try something new.

If all people on the planet were able to accept themselves, accept others, and transcend their egos, we could graduate from the conflicts that waste enormous amounts of resources to the real enjoyment of evolving and connecting as humanity. We might even be able to catch up to our own technological creations. If we can continue to calibrate the trajectory of humanity by being personal examples, maybe in the future, we'll reach that point.

Let's go change the world together and create the amazing lives and world we dream about.

Appendix

Discovering your Myers-Briggs Type

Use the analysis tool on the following pages to discover your Myers-Briggs type, which will help you fill out your Car Model and use the information in this book. Here are a couple tips to help you answer the questions:

- The assessment is all about preference, so there are NO right or wrong answers.

- The assessment is designed to find your natural talents, so choose the answers that come closest to how you are naturally.

- With some questions, you may feel that neither answer is accurate for you. That's OK; just choose the answer that comes closest.

- With some questions, you may feel that both answers apply to you. That's ok too. Just choose the answer that applies MORE, even if it's only slightly more.

- Test likes these are guides and starting places. If you read a type description earlier in the book that fits you better, that may be your best-fit type.

It should take less than 20 minutes to complete the assessment. Have fun!

1. My friends say that I am...

❏ **A.** Easy to read and get to know

❏ **B.** Somewhat private, and difficult to read

2. I value...

❏ **A.** Realism and common sense

❏ **B.** Innovation and imagination

3. I enjoy receiving...

❏ **A.** Respect more than appreciation

❏ **B.** Appreciation more than respect

4. I am most comfortable when I can be...

❏ **A.** Prepared

❏ **B.** Spontaneous

5. When I meet someone new, I usually...

❏ **A.** Do most of the talking

❏ **B.** Do most of the listening

6. While knowing that everyone is a unique individual, deep down I feel...

❏ **A.** Like I am basically the same as most people

❏ **B.** Like there is something different about me, compared to most people

7. An argument with feeling...

❏ **A.** Has more effect on me than a cold, rational one

❏ **B.** Has the same or less effect on me than a cold, rational one

8. I get a lot of satisfaction from...

❏ **A.** Finishing projects

❏ **B.** Starting projects

9. People would describe me as...

❏ **A.** Outgoing

❏ **B.** Reserved

10. It is better to be...

❏ A. Practical   ❏ B. Inventive

11. I have stronger...

❏ A. Social skills   ❏ B. Analytical skills

12. I am more of a...

❏ A. Planner   ❏ B. Improviser

13. I think best when I can...

❏ A. Bounce my ideas off of someone else   ❏ B. Work out my ideas internally before I share them with others

14. I like to...

❏ A. Use and refine existing skills   ❏ B. Pick up new skills—I can get bored once a skill is mastered

15. For me, it is more interesting to know...

❏ A. How people feel   ❏ B. How people think

16. At work I would rather...

❏ A. Follow a plan   ❏ B. Go with the flow

17. I usually...

❏ A. Act first, and think while I am acting   ❏ B. Think first, before acting

18. I am drawn to...

❏ A. The realistic   ❏ B. The surrealistic

19. It is more important to be...

❏ A. Tactful   ❏ B. Truthful

20. I am most comfortable when...

❏ A. Things are settled and decided   ❏ B. My options are open

21. Ask me a question, and I will usually...

❏ **A.** Start talking to come up with an answer

❏ **B.** Take the time to form an answer in my head before I respond

22. I am usually more absorbed in...

❏ **A.** Things I can see, hear, feel, taste, or touch

❏ **B.** My daydreams, thoughts, and imagination

23. I tend to value...

❏ **A.** Compassion more than competence

❏ **B.** Competence more than compassion

24. I am sometimes accused of being too...

❏ **A.** Rigid

❏ **B.** Wishy-washy

25. It is more difficult for me to be...

❏ **A.** Quiet

❏ **B.** Loud

26. I solve problems by...

❏ **A.** Grounding myself in the facts until I understand the problem

❏ **B.** Jumping between different ideas, possibilities, and perspectives

27. When interacting with others...

❏ **A.** I am friendly and have difficulty remaining businesslike

❏ **B.** I am usually brief and businesslike

28. I try things...

❏ **A.** That I am reasonably sure will work

❏ **B.** Just to see what will happen

29. I talk about the things most important to me...

❏ **A.** Whenever the subject comes up

❏ **B.** Only with those I trust

30. I think rules and regulations are...

❑ **B.** Necessary for other people

31. I make most decisions...

    ❑ **A.** Guided by my feelings ❑ **B.** Based on logic and facts

32. I usually prefer to work...

    ❑ **A.** At a steady pace ❑ **B.** In bursts

33. If I have to spend a lot of time alone, I will feel...

    ❑ **A.** Bored or depressed ❑ **B.** Relaxed and refreshed

34. Regardless of what other people say, deep down I feel that I am...

    ❑ **A.** Pretty normal ❑ **B.** Kind of weird

35. I value...

    ❑ **A.** Harmony and authenticity ❑ **B.** Accuracy and effectiveness

36. I think best when...

    ❑ **A.** My surroundings are clean and uncluttered ❑ **B.** I do not have to follow a procedure

37. I prefer to...

    ❑ **A.** Engage ❑ **B.** Observe

38. I am usually more entertained by...

    ❑ **A.** The reality of what is going on around me ❑ **B.** My interpretation of what is going on around me

39. I usually obey...

    ❑ **A.** My heart more than my mind ❑ **B.** My mind more than my heart

40. I like...

    ❑ **A.** To know what I am getting into ❑ **B.** Adapting to new situations

41. When I am problem solving, I tend to...

❑ **A.** Think out loud

❑ **B.** Close my eyes to shut out distractions

42. A conversation about purely abstract ideas and theories is usually...

❑ **A.** Kind of annoying

❑ **B.** Totally energizing

43. I believe feelings are...

❑ **A.** Always valid, whether they make sense or not

❑ **B.** Valid, as long as they make sense

44. I take pride in being...

❑ **A.** Dependable

❑ **B.** Free-spirited

45. If I go to the gym or library...

❑ **A.** I take the opportunity to interact with people

❑ **B.** I find a place by myself and focus on my work

46. Under most circumstances, I naturally pay more attention to...

❑ **A.** What is happening

❑ **B.** What could be happening

47. I trust...

❑ **A.** What my heart tells me

❑ **B.** What my head tells me

48. I am naturally more...

❑ **A.** Organized

❑ **B.** Disorganized

49. I prefer to discuss things with...

❑ **A.** A group of people

❑ **B.** One person at a time

50. When I need to do my best work, the feeling of inspiration is...

❑ **A.** Great, but if I do not feel inspired, it does not affect my ability to get things done right

❑ **B.** Vital, and if I do not feel inspired, it is very difficult for me to produce something I am happy with

51. I tend to pay more attention to my...

❏ **A.** Emotions   ❏ **B.** Thoughts

52. I am more...

❏ **A.** Orderly   ❏ **B.** Random

53. When working, I love to...

❏ **A.** Be in the middle of the action   ❏ **B.** Close my door and enjoy the quiet

54. Sometimes...

❏ **A.** I pay so much attention to the facts, either past or present, that I miss new possibilities   ❏ **B.** I think so much about new possibilities that I do not look at how to make them a reality

55. It is worse to be...

❏ **A.** Unsympathetic   ❏ **B.** Biased

56. In general, I think people would benefit from more...

❏ **A.** Responsibility   ❏ **B.** Spontaneity

57. Whenever possible...

❏ **A.** I connect with people   ❏ **B.** I avoid unnecessary interaction

58. In everyday life...

❏ **A.** I often meet people who seem to see things the way I do   ❏ **B.** It is rare to meet someone who really seems to be on the same "wavelength" as me

59. It is more important to be...

❏ **A.** Kind   ❏ **B.** Fair

60. For appointments, I am usually...

❏ **A.** On time or early   ❏ **B.** On time or a little late

To score:

1. Use the chart on the next page to tally your A and B answers. Add the total number of A answers in the box at the bottom of each column. Do the same for the B answers you have checked. Each of the 8 boxes in the Totals column should have a number in it.

2. Now you have four pairs of numbers. Circle the letter below the larger total for each pair. If the two numbers of any pair are equal, circle both. Read the corresponding type description for both options. For example, if your score is ESxJ, having circled both T and F, read the type descriptions for both ESTJ and ESFJ and choose the description that is your best-fit type.

When you discover your best-fit type, it often fits like a glove. Look for the principles within each type description, and try not to get caught up in too many details. Every person manifests their type uniquely without disrupting the overall pattern.

Scoring Mechanism

	A	B		A	B		A	B		A	B
1			2			3			4		
5			6			7			8		
9			10			11			12		
13			14			15			16		
17			18			19			20		
21			22			23			24		
25			26			27			28		
29			30			31			32		
33			34			35			36		
37			38			39			40		
41			42			43			44		
45			46			47			48		
49			50			51			52		
53			54			55			56		
57			58			59			60		
Totals											
	E	I		S	N		F	T		J	P

My Car Model

Using your Myers-Briggs four-letter code, create your Car Model here. Reference Part 1: Systems and Theory for information on cognitive functions, dichotomies, Myers-Briggs types, and the Car Model. Use the space below to take notes if needed.

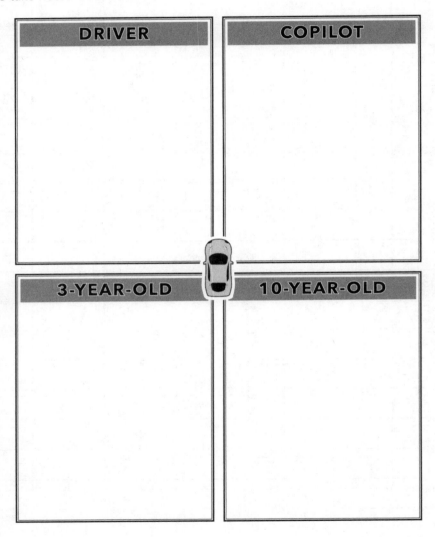

DRIVER	COPILOT

3-YEAR-OLD	10-YEAR-OLD

Car Model Notes

Acknowledgments

The world is a better place thanks to people who want to develop themselves and help lead others to do the same. This book was possible because of the people like this in our lives.

We would love to thank all the mentors, friends, and family members who have influenced us. It would be impossible to name everyone here, but we would like to name a few people who were part of the creation of this book.

Thanks to the amazing Charis Branson who helped keep our company running smoothly while we were taking long writing absences. Your attention to detail and help in editing portions of the material was our secret weapon for accomplishing this project.

Thanks to the rest of our team during the writing of the book: Nii Codjoe, Ryan Park, Holly McIntosh, and Kimberly Ruffner. You all demonstrated leadership, patience, and support while we were away writing.

To our children Gunnar, Sawyer, and Piper… sorry for the long days of writing. We are done now and can hopefully return to normal life. Thank you for being great kids and for all your patience.

To Joel's parents, Mark and Debbi, for watching grandkids for long stretches of time so we could focus on writing.

Thank you to the Personality Hacker community, the Intuitive Awakening Facebook group, and particularly to the moderators in IA for holding down the fort, reading over sections of the book, and giving feedback.

And thanks to you. This book is nothing without you as a reader. We are grateful that you've decided to read our little book on personality types and we hope you take these ideas and create the most epic and passionate life you can.

About the Authors

Joel Mark Witt and **Antonia Dodge** are podcasters, entrepreneurs, personal development coaches, and personality typology experts who have consulted with companies like Zappos, Oracle, American Express, CNN, and many others. Through their Profiler Training Course, they have taught hundreds of students, including CEOs, coaches, investors, and law enforcement agents, to use their  unique conversational typing method and help others uncover their best-fit Myers-Briggs personality. Joel and Antonia also host the popular Personality Hacker podcast. Each episode is a conversation that helps you create awareness around how you are wired, gives you permission to be who you truly are, and design a custom personal growth path for your life.

They live in Pennsylvania with their daughter Piper, Joel's sons Gunnar and Sawyer, and a golden retriever named Duncan.